The Moment of Explosion

William Blake. *The Descent of Peace.* (*Nativity Ode* 1).

University of Nebraska Press: Lincoln and London

THE
MOMENT
OF
EXPLOSION

*Blake
and the Illustration
of Milton*

Stephen C. Behrendt

Publication of this book was aided by a grant from
the National Endowment for the Humanities.

The paper in this book meets the guidelines for
permanence and durability of the Committee on
Production Guidelines for Book Longevity of
the Council on Library Resources.

Library of Congress Cataloging in Publication Data

Behrendt, Stephen C., 1947-
The moment of explosion.
Bibliography: p.
Includes index.
1. Milton, John, 1608-1674. Paradise lost.
2. Milton, John, 1608-1674. Paradise lost –
Illustrations.   3. Blake, William, 1757-1827.
I. Title.
PR3562.B38 1983   821'.4   82-13561
ISBN 0-8032-1169-4

For Pat

William Blake. *The Shepherds and the Choir of Angels.* (Nativity Ode 2).

Contents

William Blake. *The Overthrow of Apollo and the Pagan Deities*. (*Nativity Ode* 3).

Figures

Plates

William Blake. *The Flight of Moloch.* (*Nativity Ode* 4).

Acknowledgments

This book has grown out of my fascination with the complexity of William Blake's genius. A masterful poet and painter, as the twentieth century has come to acknowledge, Blake proves also an acute literary critic, a penetrating commentator in both the verbal and the visual media. As our insight into the nature of Blake's art increases, we can only stand in ever greater awe of this remarkable artist and thinker, whose works in both media can be at once troubling and serene, torturously complex and disarmingly simple.

I am indebted as well to remarkable colleagues and friends whose own work has contributed so importantly not just to this book but to the whole of modern Blake scholarship. To my friend and colleague Joseph Anthony Wittreich, Jr., with whom I began serious study of Blake and whose careful reading, comments, and suggestions on the manuscript as it developed have proven invaluable, go my deepest thanks and my continuing admiration. My appreciation extends as well to Stuart Curran, Leslie Tannenbaum, Anne Kostelanetz Mellor, and John E. Grant, who have read and commented on various portions of the manuscript. I am likewise grateful to Martin Butlin for sharing his expertise and for allowing me to consult portions of his catalogue of Blake's art before its publication. I thank as well the editors of *Blake Studies*, *Philological Quarterly*, and *Milton and the Romantics* (now *Romanticism Past and Present*) for allowing me to draw on articles published in their pages, and to the University of Pittsburgh Press for permission to draw from my "Bright Pilgrimage: William Blake's Designs for *L'Allegro* and *Il Penseroso*," in *Milton Studies*, vol. 8, edited by James D. Simmonds (Pittsburgh: University of Pittsburgh Press, 1975). I wish to express gratitude also to the University of Nebraska–Lincoln Office of Research and Graduate Studies, who supported my collection of materials. My thanks to Roma Rector for her swift and accurate typing of the manuscript.

My greatest debt is to my wife, Patricia Flanagan Behrendt, whose patience, support, and encouragement have been unfailing and whose incisive comments and suggestions on my subject and on the manuscript itself in its various stages have so often enabled me to sharpen my perceptions and to probe with greater sensitivity the nuances of Blake's art. Like Blake himself, I am blessed with an extraordinary wife and colleague, and while this book has been a labor of love in many ways, its dedication can reflect but a small return on the investment of love that brightens my days.

William Blake. *The Descent of the Gods into Hell.* (*Nativity Ode* 5).

Abbreviations

Annot. Reynolds. William Blake, Annotations to *The Works of Sir Joshua Reynolds*

B Martin Butlin, *The Paintings and Drawings of William Blake*, 2 vols. (New Haven, Conn., and London, 1981)

BM Museum of Fine Arts, Boston

C John Milton, *Comus*, illustrated by William Blake

E William Blake, *The Poetry and Prose of William Blake*, ed. David V. Erdman, 4th ed., rev. (Garden City, N.Y.: Doubleday and Co., 1970)

FZ William Blake, *The Four Zoas*

H John Milton, *John Milton: Complete Poems and Major Prose*, ed. Merritt Y. Hughes (New York: Odyssey Press, 1957)

HH Henry E. Huntington Library and Art Gallery

IB William Blake, *The Illuminated Blake*, annot. David V. Erdman (Garden City, N.Y.: Doubleday and Co., 1974)

J William Blake, *Jerusalem*; references to plate and line numbers

K William Blake, *The Letters of William Blake*, ed. Geoffrey Keynes (Cambridge, Mass.: Harvard University Press)

M William Blake, *Milton*; references to plate and line numbers unless otherwise specified

MHH William Blake, *The Marriage of Heaven and Hell*; references to plate and line numbers unless otherwise specified

P Marcia R. Pointon, *Milton and English Art* (Toronto: University of Toronto Press, 1970)

PL John Milton, *Paradise Lost*, illustrated by William Blake

PR John Milton, *Paradise Regained*, illustrated by William Blake

VLJ William Blake, *A Vision of the Last Judgment*

William Blake. *The Night of Peace.* (*Nativity Ode* 6).

Introduction

The poet, in *his* treatment of a story, is enabled to bespeak the reader's favour by a graceful introduction, describing his characters, relating what has already happened, and showing their present situation, and thus, preparing him for what is to come, to lead him on, step by step, with increasing delight, to the full climax of passion and interest; whilst the painter, on the contrary, deprived of all such auxiliary aid, is obligated to depend on the effect of a single moment. That, indeed, is a critical moment, in which all the most striking and beautiful circumstances that can be imagined are concentrated,—big with suspense, interest, passion, terror, and action; in short, the moment of explosion, which illuminates and brings at once into view the *past, present,* and *future,* and which, when well rendered, is often more than equivalent to all the successive energies of the poet.

JOHN OPIE, R.A.

Lecture on Invention (1807)

On one of his visits to William Blake, Henry Crabb Robinson pressed the poet for details of his relationship with his seventeenth-century predecessor, John Milton. The response Robinson recorded in his *Reminiscences* provides a striking indication of Blake's strong views on that relationship. Milton, said Blake, had appeared to him many times and on one occasion had delivered a unique request: "He said he had committed an error in his Paradise Lost which he wanted me to correct, in a poem or picture; but I declined."[1] Though he may have declined Milton's request on this occasion, he responded to it amply in word and picture throughout the course of his career.

There existed in the eighteenth century a clear tradition of corrective criticism. In addition to "process" criticism based upon notes, drafts, and other working materials of an author, and "product" criticism in the form of formal analytical and interpretive essays, Ralph Cohen has distinguished a third type: "by-product" criticism, which consists of "explanations, interpretations, or evaluations incidental to other artistic activities" and takes the form of parodies, illustrations, and poems modeled upon the precursor's original. While the nonverbal criticism of Blake's illustrations may strike our modern word-oriented sensibilities as unconventional, such criticism was both generally recognized and widely employed in the eighteenth and nineteenth centuries. As Cohen insightfully observes, illustrations frequently "implied solutions to such literary problems as emotive unity, often before such unity was articulated and . . . pointed to a range of meaning which criticism for social or literary reasons often ignored."[2]

Blake's Milton illustrations are both interpretive and corrective.[3] They form a cumulative critical statement that undertakes to correct not only Milton but also the presumed faults of his eighteenth- and early nineteenth-century critics. Blake focuses not merely upon the primary source—Milton's poems—but upon secondary sources as well: a tradition, more than a century old, of verbal and visual commentary. We need not be surprised to discover in Blake's criticism a radical revision of both original text and accumulated critical response, for Blake sets out in all his Milton illustrations to rescue Milton's vision from the conventional misreadings *imposed upon it* (though, in fairness to Blake, readings he felt the poetry inherently *invited*) by impercipient critics. His illustrations break with interpretive traditions, often dramatically so, and yet he deviates always in the direction of presenting more accurately the fundamental vision he perceived in Milton's poetry. Hence the visionary iconoclasm informing Blake's criticism is necessarily destructive of the comfortable tradition of safe, orthodox Milton commentary.[4]

In his history of criticism, George Saintsbury called Dryden the first major English critic consistently to practice "true criticism," citing him as an example of the critic "who tries, without prepossession or convention, to get a general grasp of the book or author, and then to set forth that grasp in luminous language, and with a fair display of supporting analysis and argument."[5] Saintsbury's remark offers a useful guide for evaluating Blake's critical accomplishment. Blake likewise set forth, both verbally *and* visually a "general grasp" of Milton's poetry, based upon his own extraordinarily perceptive reading. Blake's designs for other authors' writings have often been neglected out of an unwillingness to acknowledge that criticism articulated in a visual language is just as surely criticism—though perhaps more difficult to read than the *words* to which we are accustomed—as criticism presented in the conventional verbal essay. Saintsbury gave Blake some credit as a critic, however, as did Yeats in his essays and in his edition of Blake's poetry. But as the twentieth century progressed, Blake's contributions as a critic were customarily minimized. Even so acute a Blake scholar as Sir Geoffrey Keynes early on declined comment on some of the Milton illustrations (such as those to the *Nativity Ode*), mistakenly regarding them as mere visualizations of the text.[6] Only recently has come the widespread realization that Blake's designs establish him as a major Milton critic.

The Romantic poet frequently views his poetry as a sort of criticism that looks back at its poetic antecedent as text.[7] Blake's designs—and much of his poetry—function in just such relation to Milton's work. As a true critic in the line in which Saintsbury places Dryden, Blake is primarily concerned with discovering the essence of Milton's vision and presenting it in "luminous" visual terms. This Blake seeks to accomplish, finally, by inducing in his reader-viewer the same visionary insight into the poetry that informs the designs themselves.[8] In so doing Blake daringly corrects the errors he felt had hindered that visionary perception—errors both implicit in Milton's text and imposed upon it by years of misguided verbal and visual criticism. This study considers Blake's Milton illustrations from several perspectives: in light of Blake's direct comments on Milton as man and thinker, in light of his vision and revision of Milton's ideas and works, and in light of the rich tradition of Milton illustration with which Blake, as a commercial artist, was particularly conversant and upon whose iconography he drew significantly. It further examines the large interpretive significance of differences between versions of both particular scenes and entire series in those instances in which Blake made multiple sets of designs for individual works. It proposes a unified view of these remarkable illustrations, a collective body of criticism that forms one of the major statements on Milton's intellectual and artistic achievement, not just of the Romantic period but of all time.

Chapter 1: Blake's Estimate of Milton as Man and Artist

The concept of illustration as criticism relates directly to the practice of copying from the accepted masters which the eighteenth century typically accounted a routine part of any young artist's training. To Sir Joshua Reynolds, whose deprecation of copying in the second of his *Discourses on Art* contains the note, "Much copying discountenanced—the Artist at all times and in all places should be employed in laying up materials for the exercise of his art," Blake responded in a marginal note, "To learn the Language of Art Copy for Ever. is My Rule" (E, p. 626).

Blake distinguished between "the Language of Art" and art itself, however. Language, whether verbal or visual, is merely the vehicle for communication and does not in itself constitute communication. As Blake recognized, what the artist gains by copying forever is indeed a language—the language of tradition. Its vocabulary is manifested in associative allusion; its grammar, in artistic tradition or convention.[1] This language is the outward form, the container, in which the artist delivers his abstract content to his audience. It is a referential language, operating on the simplest level by association of word and object or abstract concept; on a more sophisticated level it operates by associating the artistic symbol (the verbal or visual counter) with both its denotation and the connotations it has accumulated through its traditional use in the medium. The language of tradition is an accumulative language whose symbols constantly acquire new connotations—connotations that tend less to eliminate or replace than to *add to* previous connotations. Hence this language is constantly modified as each day's artistic production is cemented on to the near end of tradition.

This language may be a blessing or a curse, depending on the nature of the particular artist who works with it. The conservative traditionalist tends to allow his artistic production to be shaped significantly by the tradition he inherits. Hence his progress is frequently impeded by his own roots, tangled inextricably in his heritage. The revolutionary artist, on the other hand, finds in tradition, not a prison (however lovely it may seem to the artist slaving therein), but a rich vein to be mined. Consequently, he typically selects what advances his own needs and dispenses with all else. In effect, he reshapes tradition to suit himself, often infusing dynamic new meaning into its vocabulary in the process, rather than allowing tradition to dictate the form to which he must accommodate his vision.

In pointing out that "The difference between a bad Artist & a Good One Is the Bad Artist Seems to Copy a Great Deal: The Good one Really Does Copy a Great Deal" (E, p. 634), Blake implies that the bad artist makes his language both the form *and* the content—the means *and* the end—of his work. His is a reactionary, narcissistic aesthetic that retards progressive change by blindly perpetuating the past without discriminating between the relevant and the outdated. Such an artist sacrifices his individuality to the demand for conformity imposed by tradition and the generally conservative public taste. The good artist, on the other hand, perceives his language to be merely the form, the vehicle for accomplishing his real end: communicating his unique vision. The good artist acknowledges and employs tradition but refuses to be bound by it. He copies a great deal from his predecessors, to be sure, but his copying stems from his drive toward the clearest communication of truth, not from a desire to recapitulate what is accepted and popular. Blake calls this artist good because he recognizes that such an artist operates by reasserting in his unique terms the essential vision—the universal truths—glimpsed by his predecessor. Often, as in Blake's case, this reassertion involves a major corrective statement. In short, Blake's view is that the bad artist is bound by convention whereas the good artist is bound only by truth.

By the close of the eighteenth century the definition of *to read* had been extended to visual as well as verbal expression: references to "the language of art" occur regularly in critical and aesthetic discussion regarding works in various media. Contemporary Blake criticism employs the same term, as students of Blake's work come increasingly to recognize that his visual work involves "a highly sophisticated pictorial *language*" that reflects his careful and deliberate manipulation of personal and traditional iconography. But while Blake asserts the importance of visual language acquisition, saying, "Copying Correctly . . . is the only School to the Language of Art" (Annot. Reynolds; E, p. 628), his assertion that "Imitation is Criticism" (E, p. 632) is an important one, indicating the degree to which Blake subscribed to a critical tradition that regarded the imitative work as both interpretation and elucidation of the original work it assumed as context.[2] Blake's commitment to this latter ideal governs his practice in both his verbal and his visual responses to Milton's poetry.

In imitating any given work, the artist necessarily learns a lesson in language. Still, the act of imitation itself implies critical assessment: it begins with an act of selection based upon evaluation of originals. A work worthy of imitation, in whatever fashion, the reasoning goes, must have some intrinsic value; otherwise the imitation is a pointless exercise. "But to copy the best author is a kind of praise," Dryden said. Imitative works like the parody, the illustration, and even the literal copy represent critical assessments and often function as elucidation. Such critical imitation is not to be confused with plagiarism, a point made by Bishop Hurd, who asserted that the merit of an imitation by a genuine poet may even be greater than that of the original. Imitation does not exclude invention, in Hurd's eyes; the poet should always try to "improve the *expression*, where it is defective, or barely passable: he must throw fresh lights of fancy on a common *image*: he must strike out new hints from a vulgar *sentiment*." This incremental movement toward the perfection of a work by means of successive applications of imitative criticism as artful correctives is specifically cited by Coleridge as a revolutionary process: "Great good . . . of such revolution as alters, not by exclusion, but by an enlargement that includes the former, though it places it in a new point of view."[3]

The idea of critical imitation is already implicit in the term *illustration*, whose original meaning was "explanation" or "spiritual enlightenment." By 1676 *to illustrate* had come to mean "to make famous, or noble, to unfold or explain." *Illustration, illustrious*, and *lustre* were all applied by Henry Felton in 1713 to spiritual illumination in literature or life. Finally, by the end of the eighteenth century the term had been applied to engravings and its meaning extended to include both "embellishment" and "explanation,"[4] reflecting the duality in the intentions of eighteenth-century illustrators.

A general overview of eighteenth- and nineteenth-century Milton illustrations bears out the suggestion that the imitator of any work of art tends to crystallize the interpretation *and taste* of the period in which he is working.[5] Illustrations both before and after Blake's were, for the most part, more faithful to the taste and preconceptions of their times than to the poetry they accompanied. The most obvious exceptions to this trend toward infidelity are the illustrations of Medina and Blake.

Milton's first major illustrator, John Baptist Medina, and his finest, William Blake, succeed where others fail because their illustrations concentrate upon the enduring vision implicit in Milton's poetry regardless of—and sometimes in Blake's case in spite of—the time and place in which that poetry was being read and discussed. Their commitment is to artistic vision, to elucidating the text, rather than patronizing the questionable taste of polite society. Blake frequently mocks the English taste: "The Enquiry in England is not whether a Man has Talents. & Genius? But whether he is Passive & Polite & a Virtuous Ass: & obedient to Noblemens Opinions in Art & Science. If he is; he is a Good Man: If Not he must be Starved" (Annot. Reynolds; E, p. 632). In June of 1806, defending Henry Fuseli's work to the publisher of the *Monthly Magazine*, Blake blasted what he considered the insidious, cultivated public malice against "true art," declaring that "under pretence of fair criticism and candour, the most wretched taste ever produced has been upheld for many, very many years; but now, I say, now its end is come. Such an artist as Fuseli is invulnerable, he needs not my defence" (K, p. 122). It is altogether consistent, though, that Blake should have rallied to Fuseli's side, faced as both men were with the disapprobation of the conservative public taste.

We can safely say of virtually all of Blake's visual art that his details are selected, not for mere decoration, but rather for clear iconographical purposes. His works, though their details may trace the shadows of their predecessors, are never simply derivative; however numerous the allusions to the traditions of his visual language, Blake continually strives to create his own system, metamorphosing old forms into new. Like Los, Blake might assert,

> I must Create a System, or be enslav'd by another Mans
> I will not Reason & Compare: my business is to Create.
> [*Jerusalem* 10.20–21; E, p. 151]

Blake is far too meticulous a craftsman to be accused of randomness. He says of his own work, for instance, that "not a line is drawn without intention & that most discriminate & particular as Poetry admits not a Letter that is Insignificant so Painting admits not a Grain of Sand or a Blade of Grass Insignificant much less an Insignificant Blur or Mark" (E, p. 550). Further, he remarks, "I hope that none of my Designs will be destitute of Infinite Particulars which will present themselves to the Contemplator" (K, p. 28), for "General Knowledge is Remote Knowledge it is in Particulars that Wisdom consists & Happiness too" (E, p. 550). Hence we are admonished to "Labour well the Minute Particulars" (*Jerusalem* 55.51; E, p. 203). We do especially well to heed Blake's advice when we come to his Milton designs.

We have to remember that those designs are the work of an illustrator who conceived of his work as criticism and whose illustrations to other authors (like Edward Young and Thomas Gray) are replete with penetrating critical statements. Illustration was for Blake a vigorous critical activity, "an encounter—in Eternity . . . —of one visionary experience with another, the dramatic confrontation of two images of the truth."[6] Coleridge's observation that the revolutionary process enlarges upon an original in such a way as to place it in a new light is singularly appropriate to Blake's illustrations, which demonstrate "no pale reflection of another's conceptions, but a passionate concentration of original thinking on the subject prescribed, resulting in the development of an unsuspected point of view, a new aspect."[7]

Blake himself provides the key. Annotating his copy of Johann Kaspar Lavater's *Aphorisms on Man*, the poet identifies precisely the motive that informs his Milton illustrations: "I write from the warmth of my heart. & cannot resist the impulse I feel to rectify what I think false in a book I love so much. & approve so generally" (E, p. 589). Obviously, any act of criticism involves the meeting of two sensibilities: author's and commentator's. Hence the process of interpretation involves filtering both the form and the content of the original work through the personality, sensibilities, and artistic abilities of the critic. This process Harold Bloom calls "an act of creative correction." But while Bloom contends that this act is the inevitable result of a deliberate misreading of the original artist by his critic, Blake's consideration of Milton produced, not a misreading, but rather a true reading, a penetration of the essential nature of Milton's poem.[8] Blake's designs represent the most concentrated effort by any of Milton's illustrators to explain the poetry.

They attempt visually to liberate the poetry from the very intellectual encumbrances that had obscured it. Blake abstracts the spiritual or symbolic essence of the poetry, rediscovering and realigning Milton's mythical and metaphorical structures in order to induce in the reader a visionary perception comparable to the artist's. Blake deliberately places referential details from the texts within the larger context of the unfettered conception of Milton's vision his pictures provide. He is less interested in merely visualizing Milton's text than in symbolically recreating the *ideas* embodied therein, thus transforming the original. Blake wishes to provide a corrective not just to the vision he considers Milton himself sometimes to have misrepresented in his poetry but also to the uninformed critical visions of illustrators who had, out of their own inability to recognize or respond to his imaginative vision, misrepresented Milton in their own visual medium.[9] Blake is, in fact, taking on virtually everyone in this struggle, but he is doing so in the same spirit in which he penned his objections to Lavater's aphorisms, for as we are told in *The Marriage of Heaven and Hell*, "Opposition is true Friendship" (*MHH*, pl. 20; E, p. 41).

Criticism is for Blake a complex imaginative act involving at once both creation and destruction. The process of critical analysis is one of dissection in which the artifact is destroyed by being pulled apart for examination while it is at the same time recreated or reanimated by the critic in his effort to make that artifact more accessible to the reader.[10] The process involves both the original artist and his critic and, particularly in the case of imitative criticism, encourages a qualitative comparison of the two versions by the perceptive reader. Blake's manipulation of the language of his medium in the Milton illustrations is particularly complex, since his designs respond at once to Milton's verbal language, to the language of his eighteenth-century commentators, both verbal and visual, and to a rich tradition of Genesis illustration.

Blake has neither deviated from nor added to Milton's text in his designs to nearly the extent he was once routinely assumed to have done. Unlike many of his predecessors, Blake tends, not to add new material to Milton's originals, but rather to reveal what had been there all along, though he may place it in a new, unexpected context: a vision that had been obscured both by Milton's narrative and doctrinal details and by the impercipience of his critics. Blake's choice of detail is never without method; he scrupulously includes textual details to suggest the precise contexts within which he wishes us to view the designs, contexts which contain the keys to our comprehension of the abstract critical statements made visually about the vision encoded within the language of the texts. The very language Milton employs to communicate his vision, Blake implies, loses its power to communicate when it tames that vision, reducing its essential dynamism to the cliche-ridden language of artistic or doctrinal orthodoxy. The inherent audacity of such linguistic diminution finds its parallel in that of the presumptuous "immortal hand or eye" that dares attempt to frame—to form into the empirical, vegetative objectivity that characterizes "single vision & Newton's sleep"—Blake's tiger. Like the tiger, Milton's vision is for Blake a dynamic force—however destructive its artistic and intellectual failings tend to make it—burning in the darkened English forests of error. Hence Blake wishes to liberate Milton's vision, not by changing it radically, but by expressing it in its original, unfettered state, free of its encumbrances, revealing it in its original glory. Such a liberation is necessarily revolutionary.[11]

While Milton's poetic reputation varied among his eighteenth-century critics, there is much truth in the remark that for most of eighteenth-century critical opinion "it was [the] poetic platform of Milton, made concrete and irresistible in *Paradise Lost*, that read itself into the secret heart of the English people, and, more than anything else, stimulated the revolt in literature, and transformed the national taste so much that the conventional, the commonplace, and the couplet, were all alike intolerable."[12] The three central planks of that platform were generally accounted to be (1) a prophetic consecration of the creative imagination, (2) the conviction of a fundamental religious inspiration in poetry, and (3) a moral purpose in poetry.

By the Romantic period, however, the values for which Milton was most revered had changed dramatically. Still regarded as a model of creative imagination, Milton was now accounted a master in his use of myth and genre, an important questioner of political, religious, and moral institutions, and a heroic exponent of political radicalism. Artists and critics of the Romantic period, though their views of Milton were necessarily colored by their own emotional responses, probably stood nearer him in imaginative sympathy than had their predecessors and were consequently better able to apprehend the real nature of Milton's poetic quality and symbolic significance.[13] Since any act of interpretation directly involves both critic and original artist, we can see how, in irresponsible criticism, Milton tended to become what his critics wished him to be. Such irresponsible criticism is not confined to any single period, of course, but may arise at any time. Still, it is interesting to review the various eighteenth-century criticisms of Milton's poetry (particularly those of *Paradise Lost*, whose great popularity with both illustrators and readers has been documented).[14] We find that the criticisms leveled at Milton generally reflect the particular poetic practices and prejudices of the individual critics more than the merits or faults of the poetry. The critical evaluations of Milton—or of any artist—that arise at any given period tend to reveal much about that particular age and about the intellectual and aesthetic environment of its critical spokesmen. What many a critic sees in Milton's poetry depends, finally, upon much that concerns Milton only obliquely, if at all.

Despite Blake's warning that "General Knowledges are those Knowledges that Idiots possess" (E, p. 630), we should make some general observations about the Blake-Milton relationship before delving into its minute particulars.[15] Blake's verbal discussions of Milton are scattered, fragmentary, and constantly evolving; often seemingly straightforward remarks prove ironic. *Milton* (1804–18) is the most obvious place to look, but we must also consider plates 5 and 6 of *The Marriage of Heaven and Hell* (1790–93), as well as the various notes and asides scattered through Blake's letters, marginalia, poetry, and recorded conversations. In addition to the verbal comments, we must look with particular care at Blake's *visual* discussions of Milton, a body of material whose importance is underscored by the significant number of years in Blake's career it actually spans. These visual works fall into two classes: (1) those that delineate Blake's conception of Milton as man, poet, and thinker (such as the representations in *Milton* and the portrait for William Hayley's library) and (2) those that constitute interpretive or corrective criticism of the poetry itself (such as the designs in series for the *Nativity Ode, Comus, Paradise Lost,* and *Paradise Regained,* as well as those separate designs dealing with Milton's poems). The designs for *L'Allegro* and *Il Penseroso* belong to both classes, involving both evaluative depictions of the poet and critical assessments of the poetry. Further to complicate matters, multiple sets of designs, dating from different periods, exist for the *Nativity Ode, Comus,* and *Paradise Lost.* To discuss any of these properly it is necessary first to deal with Blake's other Miltonic references.

The first Romantic life of Milton was written by William Hayley shortly before he became Blake's patron. Hayley's biography reflects the distinctively Romantic concern with the discovery of John Milton—the man within the poet. "Even among those who love and revere him," writes Hayley, "the splendor of the poet has in some measure eclipsed the merit of the man." Blake's own attentive investigation of the man Milton mirrors the period's growing concern with discovering the real Milton. Hayley commissioned Blake in 1800 to execute a series of "heads of the poets" for a frieze in his library at Felpham. However much Hayley may have influenced Blake's finished portrait of Milton, its style and its masterful manipulation of iconography are distinctively Blakean. The very fact that it is distinguished from the other portraits by being, as William Michael Rossetti observed, "more than usually worked up," indicates Blake's considerable concern with its execution—no great surprise when we remember that Milton had "shown his face" to Blake early in the artist's life (K, p. 38) and had remained a strong influence upon him ever since.[16]

Blake's portrait is based upon William Faithorne's original, though Blake executes the likeness as though he were copying a sculpted bust. Following a convention of portraiture well established by 1800, Blake surrounds the portrait itself with iconographical emblems of Milton's work, imbuing them, however, with additional personal connotations.[17] The harp suspended on the trees, for instance, visually invokes the succession of bard figures illustrating Blake's own poetry (for example, "The Voice of the Ancient Bard," from *Songs of Experience,* and the bard of *America*) and that of others (most notably Gray's "Bard").

Blake depicts Milton himself with a stringed instrument in his design for Gray's "Ode for Music." Furthermore, such harps continue to figure in Blake's visual work after the portrait, introduced always in a context of prophecy or insight. Milton himself, of course, refers repeatedly in his epics to both his inspiration and his poetry in terms of song.[18]

We should recall also Blake's 1805 painting, *By the Waters of Babylon*, (B, pl. 541) illustrating Ps. 136:1–3 and depicting a scene of the Babylonian captivity, with harps and horn of the manacled Israelites hung upon the branches of a willow tree. The context of the psalm relates the harp to prophecy through its part in both the lost prosperity of the past and, more important, the prosperity that is to return. This dual temporal connection indicates something of the prophet's special nature as Blake conceived it. The prophet's insight into both past and future liberates him from the confines of ordinary chronological time, placing him in an imaginative state in which past and future are fused in an eternal present and thus affording him the visionary perspective that makes him a fit guide for his fellow men. This same point applies to both *The Hymn of Christ and His Apostles* (B, pl. 546) and *Job*, plate 21, where the prophetic figures of Christ and Job are linked with other figures bearing musical instruments. In each depiction a bard's harp and a small harp like that in the Milton portrait are visible. The harp on the tree in the Milton portrait, then, links Milton visually both in nature and in function with the traditional national bards of England and with the biblical prophets. Milton's harp in the Gray illustration implies that Blake considers him a prophet, but, if Newton's presence in the design is any indication, a prophet in captivity.

The nature of Milton's captivity is further explained by the wreath surrounding the bust in the portrait. The bay leaves attribute the conventional praise of Milton's achievement, but the oak leaves intertwined in the garland carry a special significance in light of their association elsewhere in Blake's work with "stubborn, rooted Error."[19] Here the very wreath symbolizing Milton's achievement is infiltrated and subverted by symbols of the error inextricably entangled with his art. Blake hints still further at Milton's error by depicting him, like Homer and Demosthenes in the portrait series, with blind eyes, violating the precedent of William Faithorne's portrait but following that of Jonathan Richardson, Sr., from which Blake may have borrowed both the motif of the serpent with the fruit in its mouth and the wide collar. This apparent blindness may find an analogy in the curious animal with which Blake illuminated "The Tyger," both providing visual devices that warn us by their very inconsistency that Blake's meaning goes deeper than the conventional, superficial explanation. Milton's blindness, we recall, was not externally apparent. In Blake's pictures external conditions frequently reflect the internal, and such is presumably at least partly the case here, Milton's blindness being equated with artistic and doctrinal matters with which Blake elsewhere takes specific issue. Taken together, Blake's various iconographic hints to this effect constitute a

Figure 1. William Blake. Portrait of Milton. About 1800–1803. 40.1 cm by 90.9 cm. *City of Manchester Art Galleries*

strong case, a case further advanced by the critical attitude Blake expresses toward his predecessor in the years before 1800.

Milton (1804–1808) presents a portrait in Blake's unique medium of illuminated poetry. Though it offers a remarkable view of the intellectual kinship of the two poets, *Milton* is less concerned with that kinship than with the imaginative resurrection of John Milton as performed and recorded by William Blake. Blake's purpose here is not to demonstrate how much he is like Milton, or Milton like him, either as man or as poet. It is rather to illustrate the process and consequences of imaginative awakening as perceived by one already awakened. Blake undertakes in the poem a discussion of Milton's failure during his lifetime to cast off entirely the restrictive garments of Puritan orthodoxy, a failure whose correction requires of Milton a journey in eternity that culminates in his triumph over his error and his embrace of truth in the person of his emanation.

Blake speaks of "Milton the Awakener" (*M* 21.33; E, p. 115) coming to awaken sleeping humanity (Albion) from its lethargy.[20] But Blake conceives of himself as already awakened. This conception of his own imaginative state enables Blake, as omniscient prophetic narrator, to present and interpret the material relating to Milton's journey and to place it in its proper context within eternity. Thus *Milton* represents and commemorates Blake's rediscovery and reassertion of the essential truth of Milton's vision, a vision that, despite its errors, places Milton squarely in the succession of true bardic poet-prophets. It is an indication of Milton's genuine greatness that he is "unhappy tho in heav'n" (*M* 2.18; E, p. 95), bothered by a sense of the imperfections in his work and thus in himself. Though marred by error, Blake's Milton is great enough to overcome that error by rooting it out at its source as the poem describes.

The central mythic theme in *Milton* has been described by Northrop Frye as a struggle with Satan in which Milton occupies the place Jesus occupies in *Paradise Regained*. That is, Milton's journey is ultimately psychic: like Christ, Milton "into himself descended" (*PR* 2.111). The renunciation of his spectre and the annihilation of his selfhood coincide with Milton's discovery of his real, imaginatively pure self and his consequent redemption of his emanation, leading Frye to sum up the Miltonic dimension of the poem as "Paradise Regained by John Milton," with no comma. *Milton* has actually two heroes, though. While Milton is the titular hero of the narrative, in terms of the poem as an aesthetic whole Blake is himself the ultimate hero. John Beer has observed of *Paradise Lost* that "the hero of the poem was not Adam, or Satan, or the Son of God, or even God the Father, but Milton himself. An epic poem devoted to the Fall can have no hero: the only possible hero is the poet who creates the Fall and shows it to the world. He is humanity's hero, the inspired Bard who tames Chaos."[21] The same is necessarily true of Blake in *Milton*. He is the controlling creator, the inspired bard who delineates the nature of mental Chaos and details Milton's triumph over it, who sets all things in order in the poem and who orchestrates truth in all its aspects to make it comprehensible to his audience.

The evolution of the epic form owes much to the desire among its practitioners to teach their audiences—their peoples or nations—some aspect of their cultural heritages. The epic is uniquely suited to the vicarious participation by both poet and audience in the particular worth of the poem's heroes; indeed, the epic customarily emphasizes this empathetic identification overtly. The epic poet, of course, traditionally apprehends his role as prophet, but for a Christian poet like Milton this function takes on added significance. The Christian epic poet's function becomes analogous to that of a prophet of God, a faithful—though frequently solitary, misunderstood, and unpopular—defender of ideals that know no compromise with evil.[22] That Blake's conception of the poet is much like this underscores the significance of his adoption of the epic mode in *Milton*.

Blake understood his prophetic role clearly, even when his well-intentioned friends and contemporaries did not. He writes of himself in *Jerusalem:*

> Trembling I sit day and night, my friends are astonish'd at me.
> Yet they forgive my wanderings, I rest not from my great task!
> To open the Eternal Worlds, to open the immortal Eyes
> Of Man inwards into the Worlds of Thought: into Eternity
> Ever expanding in the Bosom of God. the Human Imagination[.]
> [*J* 5.16–20; E, p. 146]

In *What Is Literature?* Jean-Paul Sartre writes that "reading is directed creation," that "the writer appeals to the reader to collaborate in the production of his work," for "the work is never limited to the painted, sculpted, or narrated object. . . . through the various objects which it produces or reproduces, the creative act aims at a total renewal of the world."[23] Blake wishes to engage his reader or viewer in just such a dynamic act of renewal, an act both regenerative and apocalyptic that involves a rejection of error and an embrace of truth (*VLJ*; E, p. 555) that propels that reader-viewer into what Blake would regard as the correct view of Milton's poetry. Like his own poetry, Blake's Milton illustrations function as "the end of a golden string" we are to "wind . . . into a ball" by means of the sort of "directed creation" of which Sartre speaks. The reader-viewer must become emotionally and intellectually engaged in discovering the work of art he perceives, *giving* (or perhaps more properly *lending*) it meaning even as he extracts meaning from it. He must surrender his sense of self, of separateness, and enter into the internal unity of the images he contemplates. When this happens, reader-viewer and artist suddenly meet—almost telepathically—on a higher imaginative plane in the realm of pure idea and joyously "meet the Lord in the Air" (*VLJ*; E, p. 550). Blake included as epigraph to *Milton* Moses' admonition to Joshua (Num. 11:29): "Would to God that all the Lords people were Prophets" (*M* 1.17; E, p. 95). Like Milton before him, as the inspired prophet and apostle of liberty in a restrictive age, Blake regarded his work as doctrinal to his nation, declaring that "The times require that every one should speak out boldly; England expects that every man should do his duty, in Arts, as well as in Arms, or in the Senate" (E, p. 539). Both artists saw themselves as critical instruments in the raising up of a nation of prophets.

Blake's reference to Numbers suggests that for him the highest duty of the poet-prophet is not merely to present his own vision but to teach his audience to see as he sees, to perceive the truth for itself, a point Blake makes repeatedly in another context in works like the *Public Address*, the *Descriptive Catalogue*, and *A Vision of the Last Judgment*. The sentiment itself recalls the note struck by Milton in the *Areopagitica*:

What could a man require more from a nation so pliant and so prone to seek after knowledge? What wants there to such a towardly and pregnant soul but wise and faithful laborers to make a knowing people, a nation of prophets, of sages, and of worthies. . . . For now the time seems come, wherein Moses, the great prophet, may sit in heaven rejoicing to see that memorable and glorious wish of his fulfilled, when not only our seventy elders, but all the Lord's people, are become prophets. [H, pp. 743–44]

Like Milton's assertion, Blake's epigraph points to the role of Moses, not as lawgiver, but as prophet, a role that *encourages* creative individual activity rather than sacrificing it to the demands of strict, unquestioning acceptance of another's dictates. Blake intends to suggest that while his own dynamic vision is the exception to the prevailing manner of seeing in the polite world, it provides a viable paradigm for correct vision. The apocalyptic vision of which the inspired poet is capable is equally within the reach of all men, if only they will see.

The poet-prophet has to take the lead, however; he must be the shaper of men's minds and destinies, a sculptor of the imagination who effectively counters the stifling, deadening influence of a social and cultural environment dominated by restrictive reason. He must be "of the

Devil's party," aligned with Satan on the side of desire, of energy and rebellion against the comfortably conventional, and must ever strive to free the creative impulse in all men in order that they may effect their own imaginative liberation. In Blake's view, the true poet's obligations permit him no relaxation of energy and vigilance, no compromising of the essential truth of his vision. Joseph Chiari's observations on the priorities of the great artist are particularly relevant to Blake's attitude toward Milton:

A truly great artist . . . never allows the motif or the functional aspect of his work to dominate him. . . . His primary aim is to bring into existence the unique marriage between his individuality and that of his sitter or the theme he is dealing with. The artist may be a very religious and devout man, but art cannot be a substitute for religion. The only way for the artist to remain both true to himself and to his religious beliefs is by remaining faithful to the necessity of his art. He cannot submit the inner necessity of his artistic creations to the rules of religious dogma without leading himself into plain functionalism and contrivance. . . . It is neither the subject nor the end to which the work is destined that makes or unmakes a work of art. It is the artist's intensity of genius and his capacity to remain faithful to the inner necessity of the imaginative entity which he is creating.[24]

Blake saw in Milton a proclivity toward the submission to dogma of which Chiari speaks, one that fettered Milton's genius and clouded his vision. This is the tendency that characterizes Milton's spectre and that Blake has Milton undertake in *Milton* to renounce: the prophet must be purified, the awakener awakened.

The formal narrative in *Milton* centers upon Milton's purgatorial journey of redemption and regeneration, a torturous passage of self-discovery in which, like the Jesus of *Paradise Regained*, he discovers within himself the divine impulse toward integrative humanity. Like Jesus' return to his mother's house following the expansion of insight by which he discovers his divinity and thus renders Satan and his temptations irrelevant, Milton's redemption of his sixfold emanation is a gesture of humanistic integration based on a newly discovered sense of physical and psychic wholeness. It is a gesture of assurance, of self-sufficiency: Milton is no longer threatened by the female principle that, in her separateness, has embodied Milton's own seeming latent anti-feminism, his Puritan views on chastity and the subordination of woman. The process of growth recorded in *Milton* enables Milton to enter into the androgynous fourfold state of "imaginative Man," rendering the whole matter of separation of the sexes as irrelevant as Satan becomes to Jesus in *Paradise Regained*. In fact, the flight of Ololon's virginal female will (M 42:2–6; E, p. 142) is reminiscent of Satan's astonished fall (PR 4.562–81). As Bloom notes, Milton and Ololon learn that their relationship in Eden will henceforth be one of dynamic interaction of contraries, for having repudiated "Female Love, the sexual conventions of society and religion," they may now discover that "Opposition is true Friendship" (MHH, pl. 20; E, p. 41). Milton's is a journey from self-conscious separatism to selfless integration of personality and a mutualism both intellectual and imaginative. By its very nature that journey constitutes also a renunciation of the poet's doctrines of sexual repression, for in casting off his electness Milton reunites with his emanation, first "unveiling the Whore and the Virgin to disclose the true Bride," with whom integration is then possible. Blake would doubtless have agreed with Bloom's perception that Milton's emanation is not just his physical family—his wives and daughters—but a larger world he created or helped to create, a world that also includes his poems and their vision as well as the generations of readers whose attitudes had been molded by those works.[25]

Blake's visual portrayals of Milton in *Milton*, like his verbal descriptions, endeavor to depict the poet's spiritual—or imaginative—form, much as the artist portrayed those of Lord Nelson and William Pitt within the apotheosis tradition in separate paintings (B, pls. 876, 877).[26] Blake deliberately explodes the tradition that had developed in Milton portraiture of depicting the poet "clothed in black, severe & silent" (M 38.8; E, p. 137), the straitlaced Puritan. Blake is not interested in this outwardly dour and passive Milton, except to be rid of the misleading conception once and for all. Blake removes Milton's sombre garb—indeed *all* his clothing—already on the poem's title page. In the latest version of *Milton* (Copy D, printed on paper bearing an 1815 watermark), the title page (fig. 2) presents the naked Milton—his spiritual or imaginative form—stepping boldly forward into the fires of purgation, hand thrust palm outward as if to part the flames. If we accept

Figure 2. William Blake. Title page, *Milton*, Copy D. About 1815. 15.8 cm by 11.2 cm. *Lessing J. Rosenwald Collection, Library of Congress, Washington, D.C.*

the argument that for Blake *Paradise Lost* constituted the record of Milton's submission to error,[27] then it is altogether appropriate to consider *Milton* the record of Milton's self-redemption, a process already in progress on the title page.

The title page for Copy D represents a later stage in Milton's imaginative purification than do the other title pages. The great dark, smoky cloud of Copies A and B and the similar cloud with tongues of flame at its base in Copy C give way in Copy D to the burst of flame that appears to spring from the front of Milton's body as he moves forward. This latter depiction dramatically increases Blake's emphasis both on the dynamic energy involved in Milton's purgation and on the chronologically later moment. In Copy D Milton is no longer merely confronting the brooding cloud of his own error spread over Europe but has moved forward and has actually begun to penetrate it, signaling his descent into the fires of purgation. Likewise, the crosshatching of lines covering Milton's body in the earlier versions is removed from Copy D, a fact suggesting a later moment, the net having been thrown—or purged—off.[28]

To consider differences in chronological sequence in even a single design and its variants necessarily brings us face to face with Blake's handling of time in both his verbal and his visual works. We know that *Milton*, for instance, describes a single visionary action—Milton's journey—that is both instantaneous and eternal. Blake would have us understand that the whole six-thousand year cycle of the world is contained, as are "all the Great Events of Time," "Within a Moment: a Pulsation of the Artery" (*M* 29.1–3; E, p. 126). For Blake as prophet chronological time does not exist. For him "the core of reality is mental and present, not physical and Past," a principle that governs Blake's ordering of events in his poetry and its illustrations, his separate paintings, and his illustrations to other authors.[29] Thus in Blake's work, as we see most clearly in *Jerusalem*, events from all historical periods tend to become contemporaneous. This conception of the nature of visionary time allows Blake to take a momentary event and fragment it, revealing in successive representations a variety of perspectives upon both the whole and its fragments. These he invites the reader-viewer to reintegrate through an act of creative imagination on his own part whereby he actively creates an aesthetic whole that is essentially greater than the sum of its parts.[30] This point becomes most significant when we study Blake's designs to *Paradise Lost* and *Paradise Regained*, all of which, like *Milton*, examine various aspects of single instants of visionary insight.

This time displacement also has its effect upon the narrative organization of *Milton*. As an awakened visionary prophet, Blake comprehends the nature of Milton's fallenness and exposes for us the error of selfhood Milton himself finally recognizes and rejects. But Blake is also involved in a process of development, for he is apparently unable to enter fully into eternity himself until the moment at which Milton enters his foot as a star and, again, the moment at which Milton's innate visionary capacity is strapped to Blake's foot as a golden sandal (*M* 21.3–14; E, p. 114). Besides his representational portraits of him, Blake depicts Milton symbolically as a star already on plate 2. In this form he enters Blake's left foot (*M* 15.47–50; E, p. 109) on two occasions in the illuminations, on plates 17 and 32, and is once shown entering the foot of Blake's dead brother Robert, on plate 37. These plates forcefully illustrate the idea that Blake speaks and draws in *Milton* as the inspired and self-acknowledged heir to the Miltonic legacy, the recipient of a prophetic vision that he in turn recasts and presents to his audience. This transferal of the prophetic mantle is accomplished verbally as Blake accepts his obligation:

> And all this Vegetable World appear on my left Foot,
> As a bright sandal formd immortal of precious stones & gold:
> I stooped down & bound it on to walk forward thro' Eternity.
> [*M* 21.12–14; E, p. 114]

His acceptance is sanctified moments later as Los descends and also binds on Blake's sandals—an act that, by its implicit reference to John the Baptist's comment regarding his unworthiness to bind the sandals of Christ, links Blake with the public ministry of Christ as teacher and redeemer—and in effect binds to Blake's vision the entire tradition of visionary prophecy:

> While Los heard indistinct in fear, what time I bound my sandals
> On; to walk forward thro' Eternity, Los descended to me:
> And Los behind me stood; a terrible flaming Sun: just close
> Behind my back; I turned round in terror, and behold.
> Los stood in that fierce glowing fire; & he also stoop'd down
> And bound my sandals on in Udan-Adan; trembling I stood
> Exceedingly with fear & terror, standing in the Vale
> Of Lambeth: but he kissed me, and wishd me health.
> And I became One Man with him arising in my strength:
> Twas too late now to recede. Los had enterd into my soul:
> His terrors now posses'd me whole! I arose in fury & strength.
> [*M* 22.4–14; E, p. 116]

But the poem's verb tenses indicate that even as Blake writes he is actually recalling the entire visionary experience from his awakened state, recreating it by the act of recollection. And since all time is instantaneous to the visionary, Blake is simultaneously *already* awakened, *newly* awakened, and *still* awakening.

Another important aspect of the time displacement is made clear with plate 16 of *Milton*. In response to the inspiration of the bard's narrative, Milton undertakes his journey. The illustration would seem to refer to the act of disrobing described on plate 14:

> Then Milton rose up from the heavens of Albion ardorous!
> The whole Assembly wept prophetic, seeing in Miltons face
> And in his lineaments divine the shades of Death & Ulro
> He took off the robe of the promise, & ungirded himself from the
>   oath of God
> And Milton said, I go to Eternal Death!
> [*M* 14.10–14; E, p. 107]

Figure 3. William Blake. *The Dance of Albion*. About 1794. 27.5 cm by 20.2 cm. *Reproduced by permission of the British Library, London*

But the illustration also completes visually, approximately a third of the way through the poem, the psychic process concluded verbally only much later. Like *Tristram Shandy*, *Milton* demonstrates that a linear work that must be perceived chronologically in reading is an inadequate vehicle for the communication of truth.[31] The structure of time is not the structure of truth; truth is a totality into which one earns admission by bits and pieces. All Blake's prophecies make the same point: we constantly receive important bits of information that only later—in the long view of reflection on the work as a whole—assume their full weight. The reception, perception, and evaluation of this incoming material engages the reader in the "Mental Fight" to which Blake commits himself in the opening hymn of *Milton* (M 1.14; E, p. 95). Blake typically shifts the sequence of his poems' plates in order to suggest alternative contexts and structures as well as simply to frustrate our rationalistic expectations of chronology and sequence. Thus the full-page plate illustrating Blake turning from binding his sandal to see Los occurs in Copies A and B as plate 21, near the verbal description of the moment (plate 22), but Blake makes it plate 43 in Copy C and plate 47 in Copy D, moving it ever further from its immediate verbal context. Blake's point here, as in plate 16, is that visionary time is instantaneous and eternal—and hence irrelevant—unlike chronological, narrative time. Milton's entire journey into himself is completed at the moment it is undertaken: the end is coincident with the beginning.

Plate 16, in fact, involves several contextual images outside the poem itself. Milton's posture is reminiscent of the *Dance of Albion* (or *Glad Day*, as it is sometimes miscalled) figure (fig. 3), a pose that in Blake's visual language typically represents a joyful unleashing of energy and a participation in visionary delight. The garment and girdle Milton holds in the design for Copy D (fig. 4) relate him also to the Christ image of Rev. 1:13, where "one like unto the Son of man, clothed with a garment down to the foot, and girt about the paps with a golden girdle" descends in the vision of the candlesticks. Milton's nearly cruciform posture recalls Blake's view that the Crucifixion represented Christ's triumph over the cross, the symbol of vengeance for sin.[32] Its inclusion here likewise signifies a stage in the process of Milton's repudiation of his error, linking him with the self-realizing Christ (and the Albion of *Jerusalem*, plate 76) at the moment of his own transformation. The conflation of the garments and posture with the rising sun (whose rays, like Milton's nimbus, are blood red in Copy D) associates Blake's picture still further with the traditional iconography of Christ's transfiguration.

The corresponding plates in Copies A, B (fig. 5), and C show Milton in the act of removing his old, dark-colored clothing, the "Sexual Garments, the Abomination of Desolation / Hiding the Human Lineaments" (M 41.25–26; E, p. 141). These are the garments of restrictive orthodoxy and sexual repression Milton began to remove earlier, when "he took off the robe of the promise, & ungirded himself from the oath of God" (M 14.14; E, p. 107), and began his journey to "Eternal

Figure 4. William Blake. *Milton*, plate 16, Copy D. *Lessing J. Rosenwald Collection, Library of Congress, Washington, D.C.*

Figure 5. William Blake. *Milton*, plate 16, Copy B. *Reproduced by permission of the Huntington Library, San Marino, California*

Death" (*M* 14.14; E, p. 107), which journey is about to begin on the title page of Copies A, B, and C and which is already under way on the title page of Copy D.

Blake had, of course, associated two types of garments with Milton. The first, the "rotten rags," the "filthy garments" of memory and rationalistic thinking (*M* 41.4–6; E, p. 141) are a "false Body," an "Incrustation" over the immortal spirit (*M* 40.35–36; E, p. 141) which Milton must shed if he is to undergo his imaginative purification. The second, the garments of redemption,[33] like the garments of the lamb at his marriage (Rev. 19:13), to which Blake clearly alludes, are donned as Milton emerges from his epic journey into the mental underworld:

> Round his limbs
> The Clouds of Ololon folded as a Garment dipped in blood
> Written within & without in woven letters: & the Writing
> Is the Divine Revelation in the Litteral expression[.]
> [*M* 42.11–14; E, p. 142]

Copy D, the latest Blake produced, should probably be considered the definitive statement of the artist's intentions in plate 16. In this case we should regard the figure of the purified and triumphant Milton of plate 16 in light of the line Blake inscribed on the back of a preliminary drawing for plate 42: "Father & Mother I return from the flames of fire tried & pure & white" (E, p. 730). For in Copy D we see, as early as the title page, Milton's active involvement (as opposed to his more preparatory consideration in Copies A, B, and C) in his trial by fire. In this copy, likewise, we see already at plate 16 the end result (rather than another stage of *preparation*) of his journey into eternal death. In thus anticipating visually what happens verbally only much later in the poem, Blake further upsets our preconceptions about chronological sequence, underscoring the visionary simultaneity of the events documented in the poem.

Further, plate 16 is illuminated equally by the radiance of Milton and by that of the rising sun, a visual technique Blake also employs in the *L'Allegro* and *Il Penseroso* designs for much the same purpose. This double illumination suggests that the radiance of the imaginatively resurrected and purified Milton (Copy D), and even that of the Milton who is only just casting off the old garments (Copies A, B, and C), at the very least equals that of the natural sun. Traditional Christian iconography suggests Milton's nimbus as a type of halo visually reflected in the sunrise and Milton himself as a type of the resurrected Christ as the sun. The natural new day is paralleled by a spiritual new day, the rebirth of Milton the man into his spiritual, imaginative form. Blake had already conflated much the same imagery in the rebirth image at the bottom of *America*, plate 2. In 1 Corinthians Paul admonishes that at his entry into eternity man will put off his mortal, corruptible part and put on immortality (15:50–54). *Milton* describes this process in terms of that poet's spiritual form. Milton puts off the old—his spectre—and puts on the new. Interestingly, though, Blake makes no attempt to portray Milton actually wearing the white garment, clearly implying that it is unnecessary for Milton to don it. Once the old is removed, there is really nothing new to put on. Rather, the old is put off to reveal the new that is *already there* and that has been implicit, though hidden, in the old all along.[34] Thus

> To cast off the rotten rags of Memory by Inspiration
> To cast off Bacon, Locke & Newton from Albions covering
> To take off his filthy garments

is inherently to "clothe him with Imagination" (M 41.4–6; E, p. 141), the two acts being one and the same. Further, in not actually clothing Milton here with the bloody garment, and in having him in Copy D in fact stepping on it, Blake is subtly voicing his criticism of the stern doctrine of the Atonement. His emphasis, as we shall see in the *Paradise Lost* designs, is on Redemption not as bloody sacrifice—itself a seeming concession to and validation of Satan's powers[35]—but as paradigmatic act of integrative self-discovery and imaginative example.

Blake's new Milton is a type both of the Christ of the Apocalypse, the "human form divine," and of the prophetic potential of every man, the poetic genius that, once liberated, shines forth in its full glory. Personal apocalypse comes in the form of self-discovery—the process accomplished by Jesus in *Paradise Regained* and carefully elucidated in Blake's

Figure 6. William Blake. *Milton*, plate 42, Copy D. *Lessing J. Rosenwald Collection, Library of Congress, Washington, D.C.*

illustrations to that poem. *Milton*, in fact, illustrates the process Blake describes in *A Vision of the Last Judgment* (1808–10): "Whenever any Individual Rejects Error & Embraces Truth a Last Judgment passes upon that Individual" (E, p. 551). Blake views both Fall and Apocalypse as individual mental events, the second of which can only be accomplished through recognition and repudiation of the first. To reject error, the individual must necessarily confront it; to rise from fallenness, he must first experience the fallen condition. There are no shortcuts. The process of recognition and rejection—even for the most perfect individual—is a continual dialectical struggle involving repeated choices, both intellectual and imaginative: it cannot be accomplished in a state devoid of dynamic conflict. This is why Blake speaks of a "marriage" of contraries rather than a simplistic annihilation of one or the other; the conflict of contraries forms the basis of the "Mental Fight" that leads to the building of Jerusalem. But since man frequently fails to recognize error, much less reject it, he requires guidance in the form of both exhortation and examples, a point Blake addresses in *Milton*.

In *Milton* the visionary poet-prophets, the bard and Blake himself, have already attained an apocalyptic state of vision. But as Blake reminds us immediately at the outset, the goal is to make "all the Lords people" prophets. Northrop Frye has observed of Romantic art in general: "The most comprehensive and central of all Romantic themes . . . is a romance with the poet for hero. The theme of this romance is *the attaining of an expanded consciousness*, the sense of identity with God and nature which is the total human heritage, so far as the limited perspective of the human situation can grasp it."[36] The point is still more apropos of prophecy, a genre that long antedates the romance. *Milton* involves such a quest, with the added feature that not only does the central character (Milton) attain his heroism as he attains his expanded consciousness, but the poet-hero narrator (Blake) is both *already in* and constantly *awakening into* that state himself, inviting us as empathetic participants in the epic to join him there.

Yet another conflation of references defines a particular imaginative state for us, this time on plate 42 (fig. 6), which presents an emblem of the separationist, or isolationist, selfhood, from which Milton is rising, from which Albion is awakening (as Albion does in a similar image in *Jerusalem*, pls. 94–95). Among the more recent interpretations of this plate is Joseph Anthony Wittreich, Jr.'s fusion of the two figures: he equates the eagle with Milton as the spirit of genius, "poised to awaken Albion, to prepare England for apocalypse."[37] We need to go still further, however, and see the eagle as an emblem also for Blake himself. In this capacity he hovers over both Milton (his prophetic predecessor) and Albion (his nation), both of whom he perceives to be engaged in doubtful struggle for liberation from their own errors. As presiding spirit, Blake both *exhorts* them to increase their "Mental Fight" and *chastizes* their lethargy. Hence the eagle, traditional emblem of John (the author of another book of revelation) and symbol of prophetic inspiration, simultaneously awakens, inspires, and torments the male figure who appears to look at it. In Copy D Blake places a glimmer of reflected sunlight on the eagle's head and wings, perhaps alluding to traditional mythic suggestions of the eagle's power to renew itself in the sun. This reflecting sunlight, however, is added only in Copy D. In fact, despite the ferocity seemingly suggested by its open beak and exposed talons, the eagle of Copy D is somehow less ominous than its predecessors, a point that further underscores the ambivalence of this plate. The multiplicity of the eagle's implied functions—awakener, inspirer, tormentor—makes him an apt representation of poetic inspiration, a sort of muse figure operating upon the slumbering figure below.

If plate 42 shows a postcoital moment, as David V. Erdman suggests, (*IB*, p. 258),[38] the eagle may well be emblematic of the positive value of sexual—and psychological—unification, a return to Edenic integration and "the lineaments of Gratified Desire" (E, p. 466), a value that Milton is here perhaps only just beginning to appreciate. (Note, for instance, the man's hand sensually placed across the woman's thigh, complementing her hand across his chest.) Blake's comment that Milton wished him to correct the misconception regarding the connection between sexual activity and the Fall makes greater sense when we recognize that it is, not sexual activity, but rather the concepts of separation and subordination underlying the repressive orthodox moral views of sexuality that constitute for him the real matter of the Fall. The Fall is for Blake a mental act of dis-integration: the divisive separation of male and female principles into warring entities, a rupture Milton repairs in his own case in *Milton*.

It is useful to compare Milton, plate 42, with Blake's penultimate design for *Il Penseroso*, *Mysterious Dream* (fig. 10), where the sleeping Milton is visited by the figure of "Sleep descending with a Strange Mysterious Dream upon his Wings of Scrolls & Nets & Webs" (E, p. 666). Milton is physically asleep but *imaginatively* alert to the pure, unorganized inspiration furnished directly by Sleep. It is a scene of poetic inspiration followed immediately, in the final design (*Milton, Old Age*—fig. 11), by a scene of prophetic rapture on Milton's part. These final two designs mark crucial stages in Milton's progress toward attaining his poetic-prophetic maturity. The sort of achievement Blake credits Milton with in the *Il Penseroso* designs stems from an awakened condition subsequent to that represented in both *Mysterious Dream* and *Milton*, plate 42. But since Milton has not yet completed the annihilation of his selfhood and the redemption of his emanation, it is only natural that the eagle-muse of plate 42 should be both menacing and heraldic to the unawakened poet.

Blake does hint that the figure on the couch in plate 42 is Albion. His posture is reminiscent of Blake's description in *The Four Zoas*:

> Of Man who lays upon the shores leaning his faded head
> Upon the Oozy rock inwrapped with the weeds of death
> . . . .

And the Strong Eagle now with num[b]ing cold blighted of feathers
Once like the pride of the sun now flagging in cold night
Hovers with blasted wings aloft watching with Eager Eye
Till Man shall leave a corruptible body[.]
[FZ 108.29–30, 109.1–4; E, p. 369]

But it is more accurate to recognize within the context of *Milton* the figure of whom Albion is himself a type: Milton. Blake says of Milton that

when he enterd into his Shadow: Himself:
His real and immortal Self: was as appeard to those
Who dwell in immortality, as One sleeping on a couch
Of gold. [M 15.10–13; E, p. 108]

Though the rock upon which the figures recline is colored a greenish hue in the early copies of *Milton*, in Copy D it is clearly colored gold. Only Milton is specifically mentioned as lying upon a golden couch. Hence we ought to see in plate 42 a fusion of Albion and Milton in the male figure, a representation of the state of intellectual and imaginative decline and slumber that is most pertinent to Milton within the context of the poem. Here that deathly state stands as the outward manifestation of the terrible effects of Milton's selfhood. Like plate 16, plate 42 depicts an instant that is isolated from the narrative sequence of the lines preceding and following it. That the scene depicted on plate 42 actually occurs *before* that shown on plate 16 again upsets chronology and underscores the simultaneity of all aspects of Milton's awakening within the context of visionary time.

Plate 45 (fig. 7) shows Milton embracing the collapsing Ololon in an integrative, encompassing gesture of forgiveness. He is not *supporting* her, nor is there sufficient force in his hand gestures for him to be holding or forcing her down. Erdman's suggestion that the collapsing figure is Urizen (*IB*, p. 261) is surely invalid, as a glance at Urizen on plate 18 reveals. The color of this figure's garment and its cinched waist suggest another figure, almost certainly female. The picture's sexuality is in keeping with the awakened Milton's redemption of his emanation and his rejection of sexual asceticism. Further, the symbolic juxtaposition of head and genitals—emblematic of reason and desire—suggests Blake's interpretation of the fundamental truth about sexuality Milton has successfully discovered. Finally, the iconography of the picture—Milton's striking nimbus which is the sole illumination, his nakedness, and the setting beside the water—recalls that of the baptism of Christ, particularly as represented frequently in eighteenth-century frontispieces to *Paradise Regained* (figs. 17, 18), which poem Blake regarded as testimony to Milton's ultimate embrace of truth.

In its view of the apocalyptic instant, however, plate 16 remains the visual epitome of the entire poem. The other depictions of Milton in the poem illustrate particular aspects of the precept from *A Vision of the Last Judgment:* "Whenever any Individual Rejects Error [*VLJ*, pls.

Figure 7. William Blake. *Milton*, plate 45, Copy D. *Lessing J. Rosenwald Collection, Library of Congress, Washington, D.C.*

1, 16, 18, 19, 43, 46] & Embraces Truth [pls. 16, 42, 45] a Last Judgment passes upon that Individual [pl. 16]."

Blake had grappled with the nature of Milton's error as early as *The Marriage of Heaven and Hell* (1790–93). Though we shall look more closely at *The Marriage* later, we should consider here Blake's claim that "Milton wrote in fetters when he wrote of Angels & God, and at liberty when of Devils & Hell . . . because he was a true Poet and of the Devils party without knowing it" (*MHH*, pl. 6; E, p. 35). The statement reflects Blake's conviction that those weak minds who restrain desire become passive slaves to repressive reason, unlike the active radicals who rebel against rationalistic oppression, espousing the principles of energy and exuberance. Blake saw the value of Milton's rebellious politics and vision, but he clearly felt Milton had not gone far enough in his revolt against orthodox religious and moral opinion by the time he composed *Paradise Lost*. As a result, Blake contended, the orthodox dogma in which Milton clothed his vision often obscured that vision, subverting (or, more accurately, "perverting") it and placing him on the side of the repressive forces, the "restrainers of Desire."[39] Milton's fetters prove, on closer inspection, to be his own "mind-forged manacles."

In assigning Milton to "the Devils party" Blake advances his perception that the *real* Milton (the true poet—not his spectre) implicitly resembled what the *original* Satan was.[40] Blake saw in both the Orcian resistance to the tyranny of received order. The original Satan resisted the narcissistic self-aggrandizement of the Old Testament God, the tyrannical patriarch, which is manifested in his demand for total obeisance; Milton at first subscribed to the related conservative ethic, but ultimately rebelled against it, turning it against itself. Blake consistently condemns the dead-end nature of narcissistic behavior: Thel is a serious example, the designs for Gray's cat ode a lighter one. True, it is an inward-turning; but it is a movement of self-deception, not of self-discovery, for it involves reflections of the surface, not of the interior. The original Satan discerned symptoms of this narcissism in the Father and rebelled. But Satan's own degeneration occurred as he established within himself a similar narcissism, becoming, not an antithesis, but merely a demonic parody of the Father. Satan's activities against God and man are ultimately aimed at self-delusion and the perpetuation of a perverse system, and so, it seemed at first to Blake, were Milton's poems. Properly speaking, then, for Blake Milton wrote "at liberty" when of the party of Satan-rebel, not Satan-Narcissus. This is an important distinction, for as John Beer remarks, "the very existence of Blake's heaven involves the maintenance of a dialectic"[41] or "Mental Fight" between contraries. The idea of the dialectic is, of course, central to Blake. Thus in becoming a mere parody of (Satan) or apologist for (Milton) the Father, Satan and Milton share a self-isolating error that short-circuits the dynamism of the dialectic. Milton's awakening in *Milton* constitutes a declaration of independence from received orthodoxy that results in a revision of his opinions and a reentry into the dialectic through the embrace of truth symbolically epitomized on plate 45. Satan, on the other hand, degenerates from the righteous indignation of Orc to the narcissistic obduracy of the very Urizen figure against whom he had rebelled, aping in demonic parody all the oppressions of the Father.

Frye asserts that Milton's Satan is Orc, "the power of human desire which gradually and inevitably declines into passive acceptance of impersonal law and external reason."[42] But this claim minimizes a more insidious situation: Satan remains active, not passive. Frye's point about Orc's critical limitation—his tendency to evolve into Urizen—links Orc to Satan and suggests why Blake's great exemplar of self-realization and independence is Jesus, not Orc. In *The Marriage* Milton's Jesus is not Blake's Jesus, but is, like the Satan of *Job*, merely another dispenser of unmerited afflictions. Blake's Jesus is a rebel against orthodoxy, as *The Everlasting Gospel* most clearly indicates. But he is a sublime rebel, free of narcissistic taint. He includes none of the degenerative tendencies Blake originally associated with the Son portrayed in *Paradise Lost*, manifesting instead the alternative, heroic inward-turning epitomized by the hero of *Paradise Regained*.

It has been suggested that Blake perceived in Milton a split between the moral philosopher or theologian and the poet (between the priest and the bard, Blake might say), a disjunction that accounts in *Paradise Lost* for what Blake considered "a falsification *in the poem* of the relation between human desire and the idea of holiness,"[43] a blurring of the fact that human desire *is* holy. In *Milton*, Milton must recognize his Urizenic spectre (the erroneous pronouncements informed by his Puritanism—M, pl. 18), reject it by accepting his responsibility for those portions of his poetry written under its domination, and then repudiate that pernicious influence. He must redeem his emanation (his sixfold female principle) by effecting a liberation by which Ololon can free her passionate self ("Desire") from the bondage of a severe ethical code. Thus in *Milton* the removal of the garments and the celebration of nakedness (epitomized in *M*, pl. 16) corresponds to the shedding of the Puritan moral ethic—a garment that had served to hide the natural (naked) state implicit beneath—in a personal "Last Judgment."

Blake's most revealing *visual* discussion of Milton as poet and thinker occurs in his illustrations to *L'Allegro* and *Il Penseroso*,[44] which elucidate the considerable difference between the youthful poet of polite society (and his productions) and the ultimately superlative poet-prophet Milton (and *his* works). The *L'Allegro* designs document the development of the former, with whom Milton is for a time associated, as Blake's note to the third design suggests. Presided over by the open, active figure of Mirth (*L'Allegro*, pl. 1—fig. 8), this youthful poet's lovely world is one in which the poet's vision somehow never develops beyond the limits established by convention, perhaps because the poet is seduced from the more strenuous pursuit of truth by the more immediate successes he can achieve by sticking to the popular. *The Youthful*

Figure 8. William Blake. *L'Allegro*, plate 1: *Mirth*. About 1816. 16.1 cm. by 12.1 cm. *The Pierpont Morgan Library, New York*

Figure 9. *William Blake. L'Allegro, plate 6: The Youthful Poet's Dream. About 1816. 16.1 cm by 12 cm. The Pierpont Morgan Library, New York*

Poet's Dream (*L'Allegro*, pl. 6—fig. 9) is crucial to this point. While Pamela Dunbar reads this design as overwhelmingly positive, the picture pointedly exposes the young poet's greatest weakness: the vision contained in the poet's dream-sphere, we are told, "is being mediated to him by the spirits of Jonson and Shakespeare, who hover in mid-air on either side of it." Therein lies the problem. Flanking that vision like a pair of parentheses, they control its shape, restrict its bounds, retard its development. While it may seem at first "to glorify the splendour of the poet's vision,"[45] the picture reveals the pressure exerted by convention and tradition upon even a great young artist by his famous, accepted predecessors. The youthful poet is still in service to the past here, still unemancipated into the fullness of his unique vision, still taking dictation. That the dream-sphere illuminates the scene as much as the natural sun, visible at the lower left, is, of course, a positive sign that suggests even this sun of derivative poetic vision outshines what Wordsworth called "the light of common day." There is other positive evidence here as well: the mystic marriage presided over by Hymen, for instance.

The youthful poet's world is lovely, to be sure, full of potential for the artist who knows how to see with his own eyes and not those of his predecessors. But Blake demands more from a true poet—a Milton— than the youthful poet delivers here: he demands progress beyond what is already accepted, what has already been done. Blake's prophet is no follower in other men's tracks, but a visionary who forges ahead and away, risking the misunderstanding and the ostracism Blake knew all too well.

The young poet's world is, in fact, that of generation, of experience, a material world from which the poet seemingly finds temporary escape through his dream. But that dream is infiltrated by the ritualistic figures, motifs, and iconography of convention even as it still manages to exclude from the picture what cannot conveniently be fitted in, like the small figures beneath the sphere who move through individualistic worlds of their own. In allowing his own artistic or intellectual desire—his natural creative impulse toward independent vision and imaginative freedom—to be framed by the taste and standards of the common material world much in the way his dream-sphere is limited by the distinct outline encircling it, the young artist becomes entrapped. In his waking hours and in his conscious productions he is bound by the imperatives of this world, imperatives so strong they even shape his dreams. He is on the verge of becoming the bad artist we met earlier in this chapter, in danger of settling into comfortable, wasteful copying forever in the language of his art and saying nothing original. That the *L'Allegro* series ends on this note suggests that in Blake's view the young poet's imaginative progress is at the moment mistakenly being sacrificed to the unimaginative strictures of poetic orthodoxy.

Progress, however, is vital to the whole Blakean scheme of liberation and personal apocalypse, even as it is to Milton's own system. And that progress involves the dialectical conflict of contraries, for "Without Contraries is no progression" (*MHH*, pl. 3; E, p. 34). The failures of Thel and Tiriel in Blake's early poems stem from their inability to choose the difficult but necessary forward step in crises that demand choices among conflicting alternatives of imagination or experience. On the other hand, Urizen's ultimate correct choice in the final night of *The Four Zoas* is marked by his immediate transformation (or transfiguration) into a radiant youth, a miracle further attesting to the appropriateness of his choice. In Blake's work, as in Milton's, correct choices are frequently followed by miracles of some sort, as we shall see. In Blake's world there can be no permanent rest from "Mental Fight," the continual struggle toward apocalypse: Beulah can never be also Eden or Eternity, but only an inferior resting place, a place to catch one's imaginative breath. Only through a continuing cycle of trial, informed choosing, and retrial can progress be made, the bardic fullness of vision attained. Importantly, though, that bardic state ultimately subsumes all former states. Blake—and Milton, for that matter—would have us recognize that the prophet is both piper and bard, just as that superior state beyond Innocence and Experience involves a marriage of the contraries, not a divorce. Thus, for instance, the chimney sweeper of the *Songs of Experience* preserves the joy of Innocence and the world-knowledge of Experience but reconciles them in a healthy perspective that is neither illusory nor jaundiced, but healthy and insightful.

Blake's comparative assessment of the youthful poet's and Milton's progress in the twelve designs is suggested in the several conspicuously paired pictures. The youthful poet's history provides the yardstick by which we are to measure Milton's achievement. Significantly, it proves too short. Whereas the youthful poet's dream constitutes the final design for *L'Allegro*, the corresponding dream in *Il Penseroso, Mysterious Dream* (*Il Penseroso*, pl. 5—fig. 10), is only the penultimate. This is a particularly important point, especially when we recall that in his notes to the *L'Allegro* designs Blake never says specifically that the youthful poet *is* Milton, though he does so identify Milton in all the *Il Penseroso* designs except *Melancholy* (*Il Penseroso*, pl. 1).[46] Blake's point here is that Milton gets beyond the sort of automatic dictation-taking of the youthful poet (note, for instance, that unlike the youthful poet, Milton makes no attempt to write during his dream), achieving and articulating an independent, prophetic song of vision that enables him to transcend his physical and intellectual blindness by means of his internal illumination (*Milton, Old Age; Il Penseroso*, pl. 6—fig. 11). Milton's dream itself is enormously different from the young poet's, a wild, "direct" inspiration that spills from Sleep's magnificent wings, totally free of the restraints of convention.[47] Rather than *transcribing* his vision, Milton *absorbs* it, giving free rein to the inspiration. As Don Cameron Allen has noted in another context, "the dream of 'L'Allegro' is slighter in substance, common in poetic experience," while "the dream of 'Il Penseroso' is of a far higher order, a 'strange mysterious dream.'"[48] Given over entirely to the experience of his dream, Milton here nears the attainment of his true greatness; withdrawn from the material world, not to a conventionalized dream, but to a dynamic, unrestricted and imaginatively free one, Milton is in contact with the visionary sublime.

The consequences of Milton's superior achievement are visible in the final design, *Milton, Old Age*, a design that quite naturally has no counterpart in the *L'Allegro* series and that is in fact the apotheosis of both sets of designs. Transcending the various physical, intellectual, and imaginative limitations the first eleven designs suggest—the "weary age" (1.167) of mortal, vegetable body and mind—Milton bursts forth in timeless prophetic *song*, like the bards of Blake's own prophecies, illuminating the design with the visionary radiance of his own person. Not at all the sort of figure Edward J. Rose suggests in locating him in a "living grave," comforted only by "memories and the past,"[49] Milton is rather at the joyful moment of imaginative regeneration—of rebirth into eternity. His progress is completed; having overcome the debilitating influence of convention through repeated correct intellectual and aesthetic choices, Milton has arrived at the prophetic vision of the bard. We need to recall that while Blake copied lines 167–74, including "Till old Experience do attain / To somewhat like Prophetic strain," he removed all possible ambiguity regarding his intentions with the descriptive lines that follow, writing that Milton "bursts forth into a rapturous Prophetic Strain" (E, p. 666). There is no question that for Blake the

Figure 10. William Blake. *Il Penseroso*, plate 5: *Mysterious Dream*. About 1816. 16.3 cm by 12.4 cm. *The Pierpont Morgan Library, New York*

Figure 11. William Blake. *Il Penseroso*, plate 6: *Milton, Old Age*. About 1816. 15.9 cm by 12.5 cm. *The Pierpont Morgan Library, New York*

Milton of *Il Penseroso*, plate 6 is the awakened Milton of *Milton* who composed *Paradise Regained*. While the *L'Allegro* designs begin and end with their poet firmly in the grip of the materialistic world of generation and convention, the *Il Penseroso* designs delineate their poet's progress from that state into a superior imaginative state in which he may be not just a *poet* but a *Milton*. The imaginative superiority of a poet-prophet like Milton or Blake enables him to transcend the material universe of generation by projecting his own inner consciousness, participating in the "Human Imagination Divine" that is the perfect artist, Jesus Christ. Blake's observation, "As a man is, So he Sees" (K, p. 30), proves a shrewd psychological insight, and the unintentional trope on Milton's physical and intellectual blindness is not inappropriate.

In a sense, the *Il Penseroso* designs present us with a corollary view of the events related in *Milton*, with the difference that here we lack the specific mythological context of Milton's struggle for victory and self-liberation. The selfhood Milton renounces in the *Il Penseroso* designs is that same selfhood of conservative doctrine and convention with which he grapples throughout *Milton* (here visually abbreviated in icons like the academic garb of *Il Penseroso*, pl. 2, the troublesome Platonic vision of *Il Penseroso*, pl. 3, and even the external guidance of Melancholy), where the struggle is epitomized in the design for plate 18. The final *Il Penseroso* design, *Milton, Old Age*, is closely related to *Milton*, plate 16, in which we have observed Milton's apocalyptic self-discovery. In both designs Blake presents the triumph of the internal vision, the liberation of the poetic genius from the strictures of conservatism. As additional proof of this apocalyptic moment's miraculous import, Blake illuminates both designs with the radiance of the transfigured Milton. Both designs announce the completion of apocalyptic awakenings, the culmination of long and difficult processes of conscious intellectual and imaginative choice.

If, as we have assumed, Milton is the awakener, he is also, finally, the awakened as well. To report Milton's transfiguration properly, Blake must necessarily also be already awakened. Having already recognized and renounced his own spectre and embraced truth—a process at once both past and present in the simultaneous vision of *Milton*—Blake can accurately delineate the nature of Milton's original error, as he had intimated to Crabb Robinson. Blake places Milton at the near end of a tradition of poet-prophets—"awakened seers"—and then sets himself up as Milton's successor in an imaginatively superior state, already purged of his error and awakened in his natural lifetime on earth, a poet for whom "This World is all One continued Vision of Fancy or Imagination" (K, p. 30). From this superior, informed perspective, Blake sets about presenting us in his designs with a unified critical reading of Milton's poetry, a reading calculated to break once and for all the perverse hold of previous criticism that seemed to him obstinately determined to misread his prophetic predecessor.

Chapter 2: The Theme of Choice

The theme of choice is central to all Blake's Milton illustrations. Every set of designs explores the nature and consequences of some critical choice made in response to temptations more psychological than physical. Blake suggests everywhere that the psychological testing, self-definition, and completion we observe in *Milton* pertains to every man's experience. This process of choosing has particular ethical and aesthetic relevance for the artist. Leslie Brisman reminds us that any artist's function is to recapture the past and recast it so as to recreate the sense of available alternatives, thereby recapturing the possibility for renewed choosing; to recapture the past in this manner is to redeem it.[1] Hence it is particularly appropriate that Blake should have Milton set out in *Milton* to redeem himself by repudiating his incorrect ethical and artistic choices, in effect choosing again—this time correctly and from an enlightened perspective—and thereby redeeming the past.

The process of trial is inherently psychological: though every individual likes to believe himself master of his responses, society's rewards or punishments for his behavior reinforce his personal conviction of right or wrong even as they shape it. Not surprisingly, Blake regards such conditioning with great suspicion. More often than not that shaping force, exerted as it is externally and arbitrarily, is detrimental, manifesting the conservative, repressive tendencies of the institutionalized status quo that Blake frequently exposes in *Songs of Experience*.

The visionary—the spiritual man—regards this external reinforcement of man's behavioral patterns as a rationalistic perversion of the correct order by the forces of the natural man, the material, vegetative world.[2] The taste and vision of the multitude too often fall victim to the manipulations of those cultural spokesmen who would dictate taste by choking off any creative conflict with tradition, who denounce change as corruption of a pure line. The unwary artist and his audience ultimately stand in danger of becoming involved in an incestuous and mutually destructive stagnating relation that produces deadly progeny, "reptiles of the mind" (*MHH*, pl. 19; E, p. 41), a situation to which Satan, Sin, and Death provide a not inappropriate analogy. It seems to Blake that the true visionary artists are invariably denied their rightful status:

While Sr Joshua was rolling in Riches Barry was Poor & Unemployd except by his own Energy   Mortimer was calld a Madman & only Portrait Painting applauded & rewarded by the Rich & Great. . . . Fuseli Indignant almost hid himself—I am hid.

Who will Dare to Say that Polite Art is Encouraged, or Either Wished or Tolerated in a Nation where The Society for the Encouragement of Art. Sufferd Barry to Give them, his Labour for Nothing A Society Composed of the Flower of the English Nobility & Gentry Suffering an Artist to Starve while he Supported Really what They under pretence of Encouraging were Endeavouring to Depress.

The Neglect of Fuselis Milton in a Country pretending to the Encouragement of Art is a Sufficient Apology for My Vigorous Indignation if indeed the Neglect of My own Powers had not been. [Annot. Reynolds; E, pp. 625–26, 631]

That Blake regarded this oppressive artistic climate as the prevailing one in England during much of his lifetime helps to explain the artist's frequently misunderstood violent reaction to Joshua Reynolds's *Discourses on Art*. Blake attacks Sir Joshua with such vehemence less because of what he considers that artist's innate wrongheadedness than because of Reynolds's public reputation as a principal spokesman in the shaping of a national taste, a position of authority that enables him to disseminate and promote his opinions from a broad base of influence. Blake would undoubtedly have agreed wholeheartedly with Northrop Frye's comment that "there is no way of preventing the critic from being, for better or for worse, the pioneer of education and the shaper of cultural tradition." Those who object to the shrillness of Blake's remarks forget that they are passing judgment on immediate and private impressions of the text he had before him. Blake's annotations are a compressed and highly personal set of *marginal notes*, not an elaborately reasoned and meticulously rhetoricized treatise, and it is unwise to attempt to make the one into the other.[3] Likewise, though, to shrink from Blake's heat is to run the risk of missing his light, as well. For the marginalia in which Blake responds so passionately to what he regards as pernicious errors can help us better to understand his Milton criticism.

The relationship of Reynolds and Milton as objects of Blake's criticism becomes most enlightening when we view the two as artistic and—particularly in the case of Milton—intellectual spokesmen. The differences of greatest import to Blake are several. First, Milton had already withstood the test of time. His work had been the object of a great volume of verbal and visual criticism, both friendly and hostile, so that new critical statements on his work were routinely tested rigorously. In a very real sense, Milton criticism had become a popular intellectual pastime. This critical sifting process had at last generated a reevaluation of Milton's genius that was to typify Romantic opinion of the poet and of which Blake's criticism was an early and radical instance. But Milton's poetic vision had flowered alone, in virtual isolation; his major poetry was published late in his life and only gradually gained distinction. Hence the poet had little opportunity in his lifetime to use a public reputation as an artist to mold public taste along his own lines or to correct misconceptions of his work. Reynolds, on the other hand, had such an opportunity for influence and, to Blake's dismay, appeared bent on exercising it to the fullest. As president of the Royal

Academy, for instance, he exerted an enormous formative influence not only over the emerging English artists but over their critics as well. Nor did Sir Joshua have denigrators of the stature and influence of such Milton critics as Dr. Johnson. Thus it is perhaps inevitable that Blake should have seen fit to play devil's advocate both in his private remarks and in his public practice, attempting to provide in his own works the contrary and corrective to Reynolds's influence.

Blake discerned in both artists a submission to error that corrupted their visions and compromised their integrity. Hence, especially during the years of his earlier reading of Milton—the same period in which Reynolds's *Discourses* were published together[4]—Blake saw in both the dangerous tendency to mislead their audiences by engaging in rationalistic dogmatism. With Reynolds, the intellectual error lay in his seeming rejection of the dynamic world of internal vision and imagination. While Reynolds's *artistic* achievement is generally progressive, moving away from the academic studio painting of classicism and pointing toward the liberating achievements of Constable and Turner, and while Blake's own artistic preferences are actually reactionary, it is the *intellectual* underpinnings of that art—the Lockean conviction that the imaginative fabric of mind "has at most a limited authority as truth"—that Blake sets out to expose. For Blake, Reynolds's is an aesthetic of generalization and abstraction, of "Blots and Blurs," rather than of concrete minute particulars; as such it addresses and even satisfies "Corporeal Understanding" but does nothing for the visionary intellect. Blake's pictures are anti-Lockean in their representation of *mental* acts, events, and conditions.[5] They are the visionary made concrete and particular, for "General Knowledge is Remote Knowledge it is in Particulars that Wisdom consists & Happiness too" (*VLJ*; E, p. 550). Hence Blake's advice that we "Labour well the Minute Particulars" (*J* 55.51; E, p. 203).

Blake saw in Milton an initial embrace of truth in that poet's choice of a Christocentric mythology, a choice recorded in the *Nativity Ode* and explored in Blake's designs to the ode. This embrace is undermined in *Comus*, Blake argues, by the poet's seeming reversion to a moralizing and dogmatic posture more characteristic of the Urizenic Father Blake saw in *Paradise Lost* than of the humanistic Christ Milton had so recently championed. Hence Blake's *Comus* designs deviate from the text they accompany in order to reveal its errors. The strength of Blake's convictions regarding *Comus* is demonstrated by the fact that his initial unfavorable judgment of the masque remained unaltered even when his mature understanding of Milton had led him to reassess his original opinion of *Paradise Lost*. The dogmatic defense of physical and intellectual-imaginative chastity essayed in *Comus* remained an anathema to Blake. Blake's reading of *Paradise Lost* did change as his understanding of its poet matured, prompted both by his rereading of Milton and by suggestions from his well-intentioned but exasperating patron, William Hayley. By whatever process, Blake came to realize that Milton's diffuse epic was not the record of the author's subscription to error he had at first thought it to be,[6] though he never fully approved of Milton's performance in the epic. Blake ultimately perceived the subversion of orthodox doctrine the poet had performed in the epic in engineering the subtle eclipse of the Father by his more attractive and decidedly human-oriented Son. Blake stresses this reorientation in his designs to the poem, shifting the focus to the various aspects of the Son's offer to redeem man. Finally, Blake saw in *Paradise Regained* the strongest evidence of Milton's return to the God of his youth,[7] the humanistic Christ and the system of values he represents, which matter Blake treats in his designs to that work.

In short, Blake saw in the totality of Milton's poetic canon an assertion of, then a falling away from, and finally a gradual reclamation and reassertion of correct vision. Reynolds showed no signs of making a similar reclamation, nor had he *ever*, to Blake's mind, espoused correct principles, and Blake's scorn colors all his annotations to the *Discourses*. Milton emerges both in Blake's illustrations and in *Milton* as finally awakened from his imaginative slumber, while Reynolds remains everywhere among the lost souls of Ulro, a "Liar" and a "Damnd Fool" (Annot. Reynolds; E, pp. 627, 645). In Blake's judgment Reynolds's *Discourses* constituted an enormously dangerous document, a distillation of the artistic "system" of the "Man [who] was Hired to Depress Art" (Annot. Reynolds; E, p. 625). For Reynolds or any other popular artist to use his influence to propound and disseminate such an elaborate system of Lockean error is intolerable to Blake, for because of the influence of just such spokesmen "the most wretched taste ever produced has been upheld for many, very many years" (K, p. 122).

Reynolds's error may, of course, also be viewed as one of choice: he has mistakenly chosen to perpetuate by his practice and by his published speculations a conservative system that appears to Blake to reassert all the worst elements of the past—of convention—at the expense of creativity and progress—of vision—in the present. To systematize as Reynolds does, to move in the direction of a consensus that attempts to enforce leveling generalizations on art and vision, is to approach the matter from the wrong direction altogether, Blake contends: "To Generalize is to be an Idiot. To Particularize is the Alone Distinction of Merit—General Knowledges are those Knowledges that Idiots possess" (Annot. Reynolds; E, p. 630). In the works of the young Milton the generalizing tendency, the immature and complacent inclination to advance untested hypotheses as though they were proven fact, typifies the sort of attitude to which Blake most objects and which he sees most obviously in the Lady's speeches and performance in *Comus*. Blake identifies the same tendency toward indeterminacy in Reynolds's *Discourses*. From his own economically and intellectually pressed position Blake may well have mistaken Reynolds's appeal for a unified and unifying consensus among the arts and artists for a compromising of the integrity of individuality. Yet if this is the case, Blake may perhaps be pardoned, for it is in the nature of the prophet to reject vehemently all compromise of fundamental principles.

Choices and compromises enter also into Milton's work. In choosing to commemorate the Nativity, for instance, Milton identified and entered into implicit competition with the tradition of generally light secular Christmas poems. The poem reveals Milton's characteristic conscious effort to expand the traditional forms and contents of individual poetic modes and genres; he effectively reshapes tradition here, making tradition bend to his needs rather than compromising his own vision in order to force it into preshaped artistic containers. At the same time the *Nativity Ode* announces Milton's first major effort at this sort of radical procedure, it identifies a vital component of his revolutionary poetic, verbalizing there an awareness of the apocalyptic import of Christ's birth as man. For, according to both Milton's poem and Blake's illustrations to it, in the instant of Christ's birth the old pagan mythology is overthrown and its various mythological elements are replaced by their Christian counterparts. Milton's announcement of this reorientation of the mythological system of Western culture parallels the poet's imaginative reorientation. For Milton's ode is also about the poet's own poetry and stands as an assertion of the benevolent and potentially transcendant nature of a poetic vision centered upon a heroic figure who, even in the first hours of his infancy, surpasses the infant Hercules and who,

> to show his Godhead true,
> Can in his swaddling bands control the damned crew.
> [L l. 227–28]

Milton is announcing not only the birth of Christ but also the artistic birth of John Milton; the hero of the poem's *narrative* is Christ, but the hero of the *poem* is the poet.

Even though both Milton's poem and Blake's designs invoke the Christus Victor motif, there is no need for the infant Christ to grapple physically with either the serpents of paganism or the new serpent of Christian mythology, for the infant's mere presence in the world already effects the rout of the former and implies the defeat of the latter. So, too, this infant may be seen to represent the new urge in Milton's poetry toward a serene and humanistic Christocentrism that reaches its apogee in *Paradise Regained*. Milton's act of choice here, then, constitutes his act of faith, an act in which the poet implicitly invites his readers to join.[8] Speaking in his own voice in the four introductory stanzas, Milton draws his audience into the collective voice that then completes the poem, a voice that merges Milton with all humanity. That collective voice celebrates the universal harmony produced by Christ's birth and signaled by the descent of Peace in the third stanza, an integrative harmony that is both intellectual and imaginative.

Blake's designs form an extended visual discussion of the nature and consequences of Milton's critical choice of mythology.[9] Furthermore, they set out to liberate the poem from the errors of previous criticism which tended, when it took notice of the poem at all, to deal only super-ficially with it, generally relating it to the tradition of light Christmas poetry and concluding that it did not fit very well.[10] Approaching the poem from the other direction, on its own terms, Blake demonstrates how the ode goes beyond all previous verbal celebrations of the Nativ-ity, revealing the effects of Christ's birth in both the supernatural or mythological world and the world of men.

For Blake, the Nativity initiates Christ's assumption of the mortal, corruptible body—the mundane, material container of the "human form divine"—which container he then casts off in his Crucifixion. In *Milton*, Milton explains:

> All that can be [can be] annihilated must be annihilated
> That the Children of Jerusalem may be saved from slavery
> There is a Negation, & there is a Contrary
> The Negation must be destroyd to redeem the Contraries
> The Negation is the Spectre; the Reasoning Power in Man
> This is a false Body: an Incrustation over my Immortal
> Spirit; a Selfhood, which must be put off & annihilated alway
> [M 40.30–36; E, p. 141]

Erdman's suggestion that the extra "can be" (or "ann be") in line 30 in all copies of *Milton* is an error (E, p. 730) is unconvincing, for Milton here articulates a central Blakean premise: all that "can *be*"—all that exists or can exist in the mortal, empirically perceived Lockean uni-verse—can be annihilated. "What can be Created Can be Destroyed," Blake writes in *The Laocoön* (E, p. 271). In other words, the natural world can be annihilated through an imaginative last judgment, for "Er-ror is Created Truth is Eternal Error or Creation will be Burned Up & then & not till then Truth or Eternity will appear *It is Burnt up the Moment Men cease to behold it*" (*VLJ*; E, p. 555; my italics). Not at all a concession to Satan, the Crucifixion is for Blake an assertion of the Son's *total* victory over materiality, corporeality, and the selfhood. His exemplary *mortal death* on the cross symbolizes his embrace of *eternal life*, a lesson that Albion is striving to understand on plate 76 of *Jerusa-lem* and that Blake wants Adam and his entire human progeny to recog-nize in *Paradise Lost*, plate 11. At the Nativity the Son enters the same mortal state in which all men exist so that man may join him in eternity by following his exemplary repudiation of his mortal part. This is pre-cisely the point of one of Blake's earliest assertions: "God becomes as we are, that we may be as he is" (*There is No Natural Religion* [b]; E, p. 2).

In the Miltonic context, the celebration of Christ's birth in the *Nativ-ity Ode* represents for Blake the ascendancy in Milton's poetry of the correct Christocentric mythology based upon dynamic, creative imagi-nation rather than the false, retrogressive pagan mythology of neo-classicism based upon the "daughters of Mnemosyne, or Memory" (*Descriptive Catalogue;* E, p. 522). Blake is adamant on this point, in-sisting, "We do not want either Greek or Roman Models if we are but just & true to our own Imagination, those Worlds of Eternity in which we shall live for ever; *in Jesus our Lord*" (*M*, pl. 1; E, p. 94; my italics). In *Milton* Blake has Milton define this change in terms of a ritual purificatory disrobing:

> I come in Self-annihilation & the grandeur of Inspiration
> To cast off Rational Demonstration by Faith in the Saviour
> To cast off the rotten rags of Memory by Inspiration
> To cast off Bacon, Locke & Newton from Albions covering
> To take off his filthy garments, & clothe him with Imagination
> To cast aside from Poetry, all that is not Inspiration
> That it no longer shall dare to mock with the aspersion of Madness
> Cast on the Inspired, by the tame high finisher of paltry Blots,
> Indefinite, or paltry Rhymes, or paltry Harmonies.
> [*M* 41.2–10; E, p. 141]

That the speech Blake assigns Milton is pointedly autobiographical, echoing sentiments and suggestions we have already encountered in the marginalia to Reynolds, is anything but coincidental. Milton's rejection of both the neoclassical pagan mythology and the more traditional Nativity poem had aligned him with the artists of inspiration, the true prophets who in their revolutionary practice trample to dust the altars to the Daughters of Memory at which worship the conservative traditionalists. The autobiographical note in Blake's lines invites us to recognize the poet's assumption of his role as Milton's successor both as prophet and as iconoclastic rejector of the conservative taste-shapers, the enthusiastic proponent of a radically new standard of taste and vision. In making the correct choice indicated in his ode, Milton advanced beyond the sort of wrongheadedness typified later by Reynolds and entered into the line of true prophetic vision.

Blake's *Nativity Ode* designs emphasize the simultaneity of all aspects of the central event they depict. The visual similarity of the first and sixth designs, *The Descent of Peace* and *The Night of Peace*, suggests the completion of the expansion-contraction sequence of the designs and reinforces the dominant sense of simultaneity, the overall harmony and tranquillity introduced in the first design by the descent of Peace also pervading the final design. In the two middle designs Blake depicts the contrary pole of activity: the world overthrown in the instant of Christ's birth. The third design, *The Overthrow of Apollo and the Pagan Deities*, represents the collapse of the old aesthetic order: the design's central figure is a clear visual echo of that great neoclassical ideal, the Apollo Belvedere. Blake's prominent depiction of the figure here suggests the eclipse of Milton's classical poetic by the Christian, an eclipse that also reflects Blake's subversion of the neoclassical aesthetic. The fourth design, *The Flight of Moloch*, proclaims the demise of an Old Testament representative of inhumane chaos and expands Blake's definition of the world overthrown by Christ's birth. It suggests, likewise, Milton's devaluation of the harsh God (Jehovah) of the Old Testament, a devaluation also implicit in the choice of the Nativity as the ode's topic.[11] The fifth design, *The Descent of the Gods into Hell*, expands Blake's definition to its fullest, identifying among the overthrown gods Satan himself, springing outward from a cliff at the lower right. His physical appearance corresponds to that of Satan in the *Paradise Lost* designs and cements his identification here. He is the pagan of the New Testament overthrown at Christ's birth and finally defeated at the Last Judgment. Here he is merely one aspect of the dragon figure Typhon, who himself resembles the figure ridden by the Whore of Babylon in Blake's painting of that subject (B, pl. 584). Blake associates both Typhon and the Whore with the subhuman form of "the Church and State Militant."[12] Blake's fifth design suggests the fall both of the Satan of orthodox Christianity and of the Satan who *is* militant, doctrinal Christianity, the repressive system presided over by the Ancient of Days–Jehovah, the "Accuser of This World" (who, as we shall see, resembles also the Father of *Paradise Lost*) and supplanted now by the revolutionary, benevolent Christocentric faith.

The peace and harmony of the world of Christ and the Nativity stand in marked contrast to the violence and discord of the world it forces down into submission in design 5 and finally replaces. This establishment of order and integration in place of disorder and fragmentation Blake advances as a visual analogy to the imaginative tension involving the two artistic and intellectual worlds between which Milton had to choose. The correctness of Milton's choice of the visionary sublime is underscored visually by the calm symmetry of the Nativity scene with which the designs begin and end. Blake consistently regards as a primary consequence of any individual's correct choice in a crisis some act or phenomenon that is an extraordinary reinforcement of self-assurance based upon that proper choice—in short, a miracle. In the case of the *Nativity Ode* the miracle is both the reigning calm and the composition of the poem itself, a poem that stands as the young Milton's declaration of poetic independence. As Paul Fry remarks, the ode "celebrates the birth of an authentic voice, and the end of speechlessness."[13]

Choice is fundamental to *Comus* as well, and Blake's designs to that work analyze not only the choice faced unsuccessfully by the Lady in her wilderness temptation but also that faced with a seemingly equal lack of success by Milton in composing his masque. Blake considered *Comus* the record of Milton's reversion to oppressive moralizing, a betrayal of the very humanism the poet had so recently embraced. Hence Blake's illustrations alert the reader who knows Milton's text that the victory of the poet claims for the Lady is really an empty one. The Lady's response to Comus's temptation, to which Milton devotes such attention, is exposed as no proper response at all, but rather a paralyzing retreat from salutary psychological conflict.[14] Blake rejects the grounds upon which the Lady is made to resist Comus; he regards the doctrine of chastity articulated in the masque as one of fear and withdrawal, and the virtue so highly touted by all characters as a perverse and unnatural excuse for avoiding the necessary confrontation with experience. As Blake asserted in "The Everlasting Gospel," chastity as the

Lady appears to understand it is foreign even to the ideal man, Jesus Christ:

> Was Jesus Chaste or did he
> Give any Lessons of Chastity[?]
> [E, p. 512]

Rather, it is a hypocritical perversion that blasphemes both love and God, a gesture, not of natural integration, but rather of unnatural separation. Falling back upon a system whose terms are only assumed (that is, learned but still untested), labeling Comus perverse and automatically associating him with evil and sin, the Lady attempts to establish a protective psychological distance between herself and the force that threatens her. The verbal castle she builds to protect herself proves, in Blake's estimation, not a fortress, but a prison, a set of "mind-forged manacles." The immature Lady has not yet comprehended that true temperance is no mere withdrawal from conflict, nor is chastity, which Angus Fletcher agrees includes "a way of living and loving in the world." Chastity and temperance are keys to *functioning* in the world, strengths that facilitate the activities of individuation and self-discovery. In the Lady, in whom they are not yet fully developed, these potential strengths prove inadequate: she is too immature to understand the import of the doctrine she recites.[15]

Milton appears to have intended us to recognize that the Lady fails, in fact, to go far enough in her response to Comus to enable her to win a definitive victory. We note, for instance, that he leaves the Lady still enchanted after Comus is driven out. The Lady's claim that Comus cannot touch her mind is undercut by her continuing immobility; she still requires the external intervention of the Attendant Spirit and his ally Sabrina before she and her brothers can be reunited with their parents. Milton's masque ends with a festive reception, but as perceptive readers we should recognize that what is actually being celebrated at the conclusion is the *restoration* of the children, not the Lady's victory, for we have already observed the Lady's paralysis and the Attendant Spirit's criticism of the brothers' mishandling of Comus's rout. Still, that the festive conclusion was customarily regarded as the commemoration of the Lady's *triumph* is evidenced by the fact that this festivity was preserved—and usually heightened—in eighteenth-century performances not only of Milton's original version but also of the popular stage adaptations by John Dalton and George Colman. In much the same manner, illustrations previous to Blake's tended to stress the Lady's virtuous disdain toward Comus and her supposed eventual triumph over his advances.[16] Too, the outright moralizing Milton had introduced into the masque primarily in the celebrated virginity passages proved particularly attractive to eighteenth-century critics. Dalton's stage version of *Comus*, for instance, ends with the explicit statement of the moral he and countless other critics extracted from the masque:

> What means this wild, this allegorick mask?
> . . . .

> But to be grave, I hope we've prov'd at least,
> All Vice is Folly, and makes Man a Beast.

Blake's response to *Comus* openly disputes such simplistic interpretations. For Blake, Comus is unable to touch the Lady's mind precisely because she herself cannot do so; she is out of touch with her own psychological and experiential state. Blake sees in the Lady's responses the simplistic rejoinder of moral good to moral evil. But such polarized declamation tends to preclude creative, progressive dialogue: neither can truly hear the other under such circumstances. True, the Lady answers Comus's arguments point by point, but the sequence in Comus's hall is actually a skeptical debate in which neither side prevails and which is truncated by the brothers' arrival.

Blake regards *Comus* as a psychological drama of confrontation: the unquestioning faith of an innocent ingenue (that is, a youth not ignorant in the pejorative sense, but merely uninformed), nurtured by a rationalistic doctrine that condemns sensual activity, is brought into direct conflict with an extreme exponent of sensual indulgence. In *The Marriage of Heaven and Hell* Blake tells us that the Last Judgment that will convert the finite to the infinite, the corrupt to the eternal, "will come to pass by an improvement of sensual enjoyment" (*MHH*, pl. 14; E, p. 38). That he sees such a process at work in the temptation in *Comus* explains why Blake appears almost to champion Comus's cause. Blake advocates the rejection of dogmatic orthodox assumptions about the place of sensual activity in man's total life experience; his word in *The Marriage* is "improvement," not "proscription." But the Lady has been taught that such activity—even its serious consideration—is "sinful," as her initial remarks about the activities of the "loose unletter'd Hinds" (1.174) indicate. So she responds immediately and defensively, attempting to resolve the difficulty by berating the threat. Blake never intended that the Lady should yield to Comus, of course, nor did Milton. Neither does he advocate a physical attack by Comus, a totally unsatisfactory resolution of the *mental* crisis the masque explores. But Blake does have a response in mind, and we may gain further insight into his dissatisfaction with the Lady's response by considering an analogous situation.

Blake provides us with an excellent opportunity to observe the disastrous effects of foolish, self-conscious defensiveness in "The Angel" (*Songs of Experience*), which documents the tempering of the "mind-forged manacles" that cripple the poem's virginal "maiden Queen." There her "woful" posturing drives away the angel (who is more likely offended than deceived by her response to his advances) and prompts the "rosy red" blush of morning that betrays Nature's shame and indignation at the woman's unnatural behavior. Firmly entrenched in frustration and self-torment, the speaker again rejects the angel when he returns, repelling him this time on the basis of her mistaken notion that her advanced age prevents her loving him:

Figure 12. William Blake. *Comus*, plate 3B: *The Brothers Plucking Grapes*. About 1805–10. 15.4 cm by 12 cm. *Gift of Mrs. Robert Homans. Courtesy, Museum of Fine Arts, Boston*

Figure 13. William Blake. *Comus*, plate 5B: *The Magic Banquet*. About 1805–10. 15.3 cm by 12 cm. *Gift of Mrs. Robert Homans. Courtesy, Museum of Fine Arts, Boston*

For the time of youth was fled
And grey hairs were on my head
[L l. 15–16; E, p. 24]

Unable to burst the mental shackles of experience and error, she fails to realize that physical age is no factor, that true, integrated love may exist at any time through an assertive act of the imagination. So the aging queen condemns herself needlessly to the hell of preconception she has built in heaven's despite.

As Blake reads *Comus*, the Lady's retreat into the orthodox responses with which Milton provides her prevents her from testing the validity of those responses or the propositions Comus advances, and places her in a state of mental divorce remarkably like that of the "maiden Queen." Rather than engaging Comus's arguments directly, the Lady merely repeats what she has been taught and refuses to hear any counterargument. She is, in fact, not arguing at all, but is merely reciting, and in doing so the Lady demonstrates the extent of her captivity. Hence Blake depicts her immobile during her temptation; her posture is kept identical in designs 3, 5, and 6 (figs. 12, 13, 14), which show her *before*, *during*, and *after* her encounter with Comus.[17]

It has been suggested that Blake's *Comus* designs ultimately *reinforce* the sense of triumph Milton built into the masque.[18] The designs, however, suggest otherwise. Blake essayed in these illustrations to correct the critical tradition *as well as* Milton's original masque by delineating

Figure 14. William Blake. *Comus*, plate 6B: *The Brothers Driving out Comus*. About 1805–10. 15.4 cm by 12.1 cm. *Gift of Mrs. Robert Homans. Courtesy, Museum of Fine Arts, Boston*

Figure 15. William Blake. *Comus*, plate 8B: *The Parents Welcome Their Children (The Lady Restored to Her Parents)*. About 1805–10. 15.4 cm by 12.1 cm. *Gift of Mrs. Robert Homans. Courtesy, Museum of Fine Arts, Boston*

the nature of the error the masque embodies, a mistaken stance that might have been pardonable—or at least tolerable—had it not subsequently been exaggerated and solidified both by Milton himself in his additions to his text and by previous commentators. In separating the masque's essential vision from its internal and external encumbrances, Blake wishes to demonstrate the fundamental error of dogmatism inherent in that vision as it emerged particularly in Milton's revised, published version.

Blake's intentions are made abundantly clear by two central visual assertions. First, by emphasizing the Lady's paralyzed position Blake demonstrates her inability to act, externalizing the mental paralysis brought about by her naïve acceptance of untested doctrine as though it were proven fact. Second, by illustrating the conclusion in distinctly subdued terms (fig. 15) Blake makes a final deliberate effort to deflect attention away from the conventional critical responses to *Comus*, suggesting, not a triumphal return, but a simple family reunion.[19]

Blake expects the perceptive viewer to recognize that the paralysis he sees in Blake's designs finds its basis in Milton's text. Hence the celebration recorded in that final design is at best a qualified sense of satisfaction and relief shared by all parties: the parents who have their children back, the children who are home again after a bewildering night in the forest, and the Attendant Spirit who has managed to extract the children from their predicament and deliver them back to their parents.

Among Milton's illustrators Blake's careful fidelity to the details of the poems is uncommon. Where his visual details deviate from the text, they do so with conscious purpose, to alert the viewer to changes Blake *wants* him to notice. Recognition of difference promotes conscious comparison wherein both original and alteration (or substitution) are evaluated. That Blake's overall fidelity to detail is deliberate is demonstrated by the fact that whenever he made multiple sets of designs to a poem, he customarily altered details of the first set in order to bring particular designs into still greater congruence with the text.[20] This process is visible in the initial designs to the *Comus* sets, where Blake alters the Lady's posture (recalling that she does not see Comus in this scene) and gives Comus his cup (which an attendant had carried before, in violation of Milton's stage direction). While Blake's designs are explicitly corrective in nature, it remains for the viewer to accomplish the actual *process* of correction by participating in the act of comparison. Hence Joseph Anthony Wittreich, Jr.'s assertion—that Blake's second set of designs is faithful to Milton's original performing text (without the virginity passages) and that the second set therefore counters and supersedes the unfavorable estimate embodied in the first set—proves unsatisfactory. The passages Milton added for the printed version reinforce the moralizing, doctrinal elements, certainly, but these elements are already implicit in the original, and they are offensive to Blake's sensibilities in either case. Hence, though Blake revised his original estimate of *Paradise Lost* during the period he was illustrating Milton's poetry, he did not revise his adverse judgment of *Comus*, but, instead, some eight years after first articulating it in a set of designs, actually *strengthened* his original position, reasserting his negative reaction in the second set of designs.[21]

Underlying the two poets' different views about the Lady's trial is, of course, the manner in which they define "testing." Milton's most definitive statement occurs in the *Aeropagitica:*

As therefore the state of man now is, what wisdom can there be to choose, what continence to forbear without the knowledge of evil? He that can apprehend and consider vice with all her baits and seeming pleasures, and yet abstain, and yet distinguish, and yet prefer that which is truly better, he is the true warfaring Christian. I cannot praise a fugitive and cloistered virtue, unexercised and unbreathed, that never sallies out and seeks her adversary, but slinks out of the race where that immortal garland is to be run for, not without dust and heat. . . . that which purifies us is trial, and trial is by what is contrary. [H, p. 728]

Blake seizes upon this very point, telling us in *The Marriage*, "Without Contraries is no progression" (*MHH*, pl. 3; E, p. 34). Milton's Lady responds to Comus with a defense of virtue whose central point seems to be that Comus

> hast nor Ear nor Soul to apprehend
> The sublime notion and high mystery
> That must be utter'd to unfold the sage
> And serious doctrine of Virginity,

> And thou art worthy that thou shouldst not know
> More happiness than this thy present lot.
> ·
> Thou art not fit to hear thyself convinc't.
> [*Comus*, ll. 784–92]

In short, since she judges Comus unworthy of her counterarguments, the Lady will not bother to present them at all, but will, rather, stand on her *rhetorical* conviction that the doctrine she might cast up against Comus, should she choose to do so, would prove unassailable. Though his comment about "some superior power" indicates he knows the Lady is reciting rather than thinking for herself, Comus is misled by the force of her rhetoric into doubting himself. Still he determines to try a diversionary tactic:

> I feel that I do fear
> Her words set off by some superior power;
> ·
> . . . I must dissemble,
> And try her yet more strongly. Come, no more,
> This is mere moral babble . . .
> ·
> . . . Be wise, and taste.
> [*Comus*, ll. 800–813]

At this point the Lady's brothers rush in and drive out Comus.

Several key issues are revealed in these two passages. First, the Lady's principal response to Comus's temptation is her threat to present her doctrine—a threat that, because of the brothers' intrusion, is never carried into effect. Second, though Comus is disquieted by the Lady's rhetoric, he resolves to "try her yet more strongly." He objects to the form of her response, identifying it as *mere* "moral babble" (an identification with which Blake agrees completely). Third, Comus's resolution to try the Lady more severely and thereby heighten the dramatic tension of the scene, driving the Lady nearer the necessary testing of her claims, is also short-circuited by the brothers' arrival. Unlike Jesus in *Paradise Regained*, the Lady never arrives at her pinnacle; consequently, she never does stand. Both Milton and Blake specifically keep the Lady *seated* during her trial, even when her declamatory rhetoric might seem to suggest otherwise. Jesus' assertion of self-sufficiency on the pinnacle in *Paradise Regained* takes on added significance when we recall this matter of posture. For while the imaginative struggles of the Lady and Jesus are clearly related, their critical differences become apparent when we recognize at Blake's visual prompting that unlike the Lady's purely verbal response to temptation, Jesus' response is both verbal and physical: "He said and stood" (*PR* 4.561).

Comus's most pressing temptation, "Be wise, and taste," presents the crisis in precisely the same terms in which Satan appeals to Eve in *Paradise Lost* ("Reach then, and freely taste" [9.732]) and to Jesus in *Paradise Regained* ("What doubt'st thou Son of God? sit down and eat"

[2.377]). In each case the appeal to man's physical appetite is linked to an implicit questioning of man's mental self-assurance or self-sufficiency. Each figure is tempted to confuse the generated and the eternal, to embrace the error that the mortal, vegetable body—with its material appetites—is the real human body. Likewise, this dual appeal of the temptations figures prominently in Blake's designs to these poems.

The crisis in *Paradise Regained* is much like that in *Comus*. Whereas Blake's *Comus* designs document the absence of clear choice, his *Paradise Regained* illustrations stress the nature and consequences of Jesus' correct choices. Blake found in the poem a distinctly human Jesus, the "one greater Man" (*PL* 1.4) who is motivated, not by any set of arbitrary, learned responses of the sort that shape the Lady's character, but rather by a complex inner necessity and an instinctive sense of right that is continually deepening and developing. Jesus' testing is also a psychological one; the Satanic arguments with which he grapples and which he resolves are actually projections of his mind—of his own self-doubts—as had been the case with the Lady and Comus.[22] But Jesus willingly engages in this "Mental Fight" to complete his self-definition, his expansion of consciousness. Finally, in terms of imaginative, aesthetic values, Jesus' victory may be taken to represent the imagination's victory over the Satan of the personal and artistic selfhood, a pattern with which Blake had already worked in *Milton*.[23] In the final temptation Satan offers Jesus the gift of human wisdom. As both Milton and Blake perceive, however, the wisdom Satan offers is the cumulative bulk, not of visionary insight, but of traditional mortal learning, the empirical legacy of the Daughters of Memory. Hence Jesus rightly rejects Satan's temptation, affirming instead a revolutionary new imaginative wisdom and aesthetic. Jesus is, in fact, rejecting more than just "human wisdom": he repudiates the entire material world, the vegetable or corruptible body of generation that impedes man's discovery of his real and immortal spiritual or imaginative self. His eventual return to "his mother's house" and the mortal society it represents is necessary if Jesus' *public* victory over mortal materiality, his crucifixion, is to be revealed to man, but the miracle on the pinnacle marks his *private* discovery of spiritual, imaginative eternity.

Blake's designs reveal the archetypal significance of Jesus' experience in the wilderness. The central consequence of the epic's action, the miracle on the pinnacle, symbolizes Jesus' transformation of being in that process of self-discovery. Stuart Curran rightly regards *Paradise Regained* as the epitome of the internalized epic in which the struggle between good and evil becomes centered in a single exemplary figure who, in his resolution of the internal conflict, provides a pattern for the re-creation of paradise on earth.[24] Jesus' responses to his temptations, culminating in the apocalyptic insight marked by the miracle on the pinnacle, provide a paradigm for man's choice of the spiritual, imaginative world over the mundane and material. For Blake, *Paradise Regained* is a lesson in imaginative regeneration, a lesson demonstrated both by its central character and by its author.

Blake located Jesus at the center of a psychological experience in which he undergoes the traditional epic journey into the underworld. That underworld, like Comus's hall, is psychological: a mental wilderness. Hence, building upon Milton's statement that Jesus "into himself descended" (PR 2.111), Blake portrays Jesus' journey in a series of illustrations depicting his gathering in-sight. The journey proceeds by means of Jesus' repeated rejections of the error implicit in the vain and selfish forms of physical and psychological gratification Satan's temptations represent. Each rejection advances the process. Jesus freely admits at the outset his ignorance of his journey's purpose:

> And now by some strong motion I am led
> Into this Wilderness, to what intent
> I learn not yet. [1.290–92]

He does, however, know that a difficult and trying experience awaits him:

> Straight I again revolv'd
> The Law and Prophets, searching what was writ
> Concerning the Messiah, to our Scribes
> Known partly, and soon found of whom they spake
> I am; this chiefly, that my way must lie
> Through many a hard assay even to the death,
> Ere I the promis'd Kingdom can attain,
> Or work Redemption for mankind, whose sins'
> Full weight must be transferr'd upon my head.
> [1.259–67]

Most significant here is his willingness to confront his temptations, to undertake "many a hard assay," for in these encounters with error his own self-assurance is repeatedly reinforced; his awareness of the nature of his divinity develops accordingly. Jesus proceeds to his major apocalypse by a series of minor ones, each of which increasingly fortifies him for the next temptation. Such incremental progress is the natural result of correct choice in the conflict of contraries. The conviction of truth is invariably reinforced in the imaginatively awakened individual by the active confrontation with, and the repudiation of, error. Thus Jesus succeeds where the Lady fails by participating fully in his trial. He gains a greater self-assurance, facilitating his last judgment, whereas the Lady only increases her self-deception and frustrates any possibility for progress.

Blake's penultimate design, *Jesus Ministered to by Angels* (B, pl. 694), invokes the context of the Eucharist as Jesus blesses the loaves and the cup presented to him.[25] Having rejected the excesses of materiality in Satan's banquet, he now prefigures the Last Supper and the sacramental rite by which man symbolically reasserts his unity with God. Blake's eucharistic allusion is consistent both with his other designs and with the pattern of previous *Paradise Regained* illustration, though he carries the sacramental context further than any previous illustrator had. The first design, *The Baptism of Jesus* (fig. 16) incorporates the other sacramental rite traditionally associated with man's admission into eternity.

Figure 16. William Blake. *Paradise Regained*, plate 1: *The Baptism of Jesus.* About 1816. 17.3 cm by 13.6 cm. *Reproduced by permission of the Syndics of the Fitzwilliam Museum, Cambridge*

The baptism scene was a familiar illustration for *Paradise Regained* (figs. 17, 18); frequently it was the only one accompanying the poem.[26] Yet Blake infuses this recurrent motif with a new significance that is heightened by the eleven designs that follow it. While it immediately invokes the tradition of interpretation his designs are about to supersede, Blake's initial design also announces the universal, symbolic nature of his illustrations, depicting as it does an all-inclusive age group of observers, representations of Satan with his alter ego the Serpent, the Trinity, and John the Baptist, all set against an open background scene. The design both portrays a rite of initiation into the severe temptations that follow and suggests a means of overcoming those temptations.

Traditionally, baptism is an act of cleansing, a symbolic purification and initiation, and Blake's reference to the event in his first design naturally reminds us of the conventional connotations of this *external* ritual.

But in Jesus' case that external act initiates a series of *internally* performed reenactments that constitute the ongoing process of conscious and deliberate purification he subsequently experiences in the wilderness. The spiritual aspect of Jesus' baptism is already reflected in the initial design in his serene posture and facial expression as well as in the accompanying iconography. But the atemporality of that internal act only becomes fully apparent as we view the designs as a series, a progress almost in the Hogarthian sense. Unlike the Lady in *Comus*, Jesus is a mature adult who has consciously chosen to be baptized, who participates willingly and actively in the rite, and who subsequently completes that rite in the withstanding of temptation that leads him to the pinnacle and his assertive act of self-sufficiency. In short, Jesus' external and temporal baptism signals the beginning of the internal and continuing process of his rigorous soul-searching, fortifying him in order that he may make the correct choices in the severe temptations that follow. It is

Figure 17. Pierre Fourdrinier, after Nicholas Pigné. *The Baptism of Jesus.* 1713, 1727. *Stephen C. Behrendt Collection*

Figure 18. E. F. Burney. *The Baptism of Jesus.* 1796, 1817. *Stephen C. Behrendt Collection*

the outward symbol for the washing away of the vegetable body, "the Not Human" that the messianic Milton washes off in *Milton* by bathing in "the Waters of Life" (*M* 41.1; E, p. 141) and that the Son likewise accomplishes in his crucifixion.

The patterns of experience presented in Blake's *Comus* and *Paradise Regained* designs are remarkably similar, and the visual terminology the artist employs is often practically identical, a clear indication of Blake's desire to elucidate the archetypal relationship between Milton's two works. At the center of each poem is a temptation in the wilderness, each involving a symbolic banquet as part of its apparatus. Each poem begins with the separation of the protagonist from his accustomed society and concludes with his reintegration into that society. In each case the temptation proves essentially mental, and the resolution of each trial is followed by a miracle of some sort. Likewise, each poem evaluates the response of its protagonist to the temptations posed by an antagonist who represents the extreme and distorted behavior of physical materialism. The responses of the Lady and Jesus reveal the quality of each character's mental assurance and his ability—or inability—properly to assess the temptations and react to them. Blake agrees with Milton's notice of the Lady's actual failure in her experience with experience, attributing that failure (as Milton might not have done) to her compulsive recitation of dogma as a substitute for creative confrontation and choice. By contrast, he seconds Milton in judging Jesus a success because he confronts Satan openly and chooses insightfully.[27] For Blake the critical point is not that Jesus comes to any understanding that his ultimate welfare, whether on the pinnacle or on the cross, is to be safeguarded by his father. Rather, it is that he recognizes his own self-sufficiency: he makes a fundamental choice regarding the degree to which he feels compelled to rely on external assistance. Hence while Blake's tenth design shows the angels *ready* to assist Jesus, it emphasizes that Jesus stands quite on his own, not even *looking* at the angels: such an assertion of self-sufficiency is totally beyond the powers of the immature Lady. Hence Blake is adamant about showing us her immobility.

The final designs to each set of illustrations clearly underscore Blake's evaluations in their conspicuous departures from Milton's texts. Whereas Milton's *Comus* ends with a festive reception by the parents of the triumphant youths following the miracle of disenchantment performed by Sabrina, Blake's designs conclude with a subdued, rather melancholy reception by elderly, world-weary parents strongly resembling Job and his wife as Blake depicted them in his illustrations to the Book of Job. And whereas Milton's *Paradise Regained* ends on the quiet note of Jesus' unnoticed return to his mother's house following the miracle on the pinnacle, Blake's designs conclude with Jesus' joyful reception by his mother, Andrew, and Simon Peter (B, pl. 695). Blake thus emphasizes the point Milton had made so subtly that his critics had often overlooked it: Jesus' return to human society following his recognition of his divine nature demonstrates his *human* integration—his love for and identification with mankind in order that his experience may prove an effective and credible symbolic paradigm for every man's own miracle on the pinnacle. Jesus' act of human reintegration is of primary importance to Blake, who sees in it another aspect of God becoming man in order that we may be as God (that is, Jesus) is. Thus comparative study of the two series of designs reveals that the latter poem, not the former, records the gathering insight of the exemplary human being, the deeds "Above Heroic" (*PR* 1.15) worthy of celebration and emulation.

Blake does not condemn the Lady or her brothers for their inaction, though, but merely suggests that an opportunity has been lost. The Lady's release from her mental paralysis is effected by an external agent; she is freed by Sabrina in an act iconographically suggestive of baptism. That the Lady's is not a hopeless case is indicated by the rainbow—a traditional iconographical suggestion of hope Blake employs elsewhere in his work—Blake added above Sabrina and her attendants in the second set of designs (B, pl. 630). Sabrina's act is not depicted until the penultimate design, however, just as it occurs late in Milton's text (unlike the enactment of Jesus' baptism early in *Paradise Regained* and Blake's designs). The Lady's baptism contrasts sharply with Jesus'. Her facial and bodily gestures in all the designs indicate that she is, in fact, consistently bewildered by the events. Abruptly freed from her paralysis, she looks about her for external guidance and reassurance. Blake would have us understand that the *external* baptismal rite is of little value unless it reflects internal, mental awareness and integration and is followed up by the sort of *internal* reenactments Jesus accomplishes in *Paradise Regained*, in which case baptism becomes an assertive act of self, not of external agent. The solution to crisis, the choice in temptation, must originate within, not without.

The *Comus* designs respond to what Blake regarded as Milton's own implicit suggestion: that the opportunity for creative choosing had been lost and that the Lady must now be returned home unenlightened, to mature and to await some future trial in which she might participate more successfully. Her overconfidence in her ability single-handedly (or single-mindedly) to withstand temptation—and the paralysis that results—is viewed sympathetically by author and illustrator alike, both of whom recognize the considerable disparity between the depth of her understanding and that of the doctrine she advances. *Paradise Regained* is another matter, however; there we encounter a hero equal to the demands placed upon him. Hence the *Paradise Regained* designs *begin* with the initiatory baptismal rite, after which Jesus moves into the wilderness—into experience—to meet his adversary, where the process is repeated in the hero's conscious choices.

A striking number of visual parallels exist between individual designs from the *Paradise Regained* and *Comus* sets. *The Baptism of Jesus* (*PR*, pl. 1), for instance, corresponds to *Sabrina Disenchanting the Lady* (*C*, pl. 7). Both *The First Temptation* (*PR*, pl. 2) and, to a lesser extent, *The Second Temptation* (*PR*, pl. 7), recall *Comus Disguised as a Shepherd*

Addresses the Lady (C, pl. 2). *Andrew and Simon Peter* (PR, pl. 3) and *Mary Watched by Two Angels* (PR, pl. 4) represent the mortal associates of the protagonist—the equivalent of the Lady's brothers and the parents, respectively—watched over by attendant spirits (note the presence of the Attendant Spirit in C, pls. 2, 3, 4, 7, 8). *Satan in Council* (PR, pl. 5) is related to the upper portion of *Comus and His Revellers; The Lady Lost in the Wood* (C, pl. 1). *The Banquet Temptation* (PR, pl. 6) is related to *The Magic Banquet* (C, pl. 5), *The Tempter Inspiring Jesus' Ugly Dreams* (PR, pl. 8) to the depictions of the Lady in captivity, and *Morning Chasing away the Spectres of the Night* (PR, pl. 9) to *The Brothers Driving out Comus* (C, pl. 6). Finally, *Jesus Returning to Mary* (PR, pl. 12) corresponds to *The Parents Welcome Their Children* (C, pl. 8). Two designs, *The Third Temptation* (PR, pl. 10) and *Jesus Ministered to by Angels* (PR, pl. 11), have no counterparts in the *Comus* designs. This is to be expected, since these two designs record the central character's triumph and its implications, a triumph Blake feels has no counterpart in *Comus*.

Blake's reading of the two poems is sensitive and perceptive, and his designs alert us to the important relationship between the two. Both protagonists are tempted by figures of disorder and excess who indulge in intellectual warfare for the vain and perverse motive of self-gratification (and who first appear to each, incidentally, in the guise of ingratiating old men). While the Lady is essentially powerless to counter Comus's advances and is both enchanted and released by external forces she never fully understands, Jesus resists Satan's advances from the first and rejects his arguments on the basis of his own gathering inward awareness of himself and his capabilities. Both central characters are tempted sensually, at crucial moments, with banquets prepared by their adversaries. For her part, the paralyzed Lady ironically admonishes Comus that he cannot touch her mind, demonstrating in the intemperate nature of her refusal of the banquet her inability to deal correctly with the sensual, physical aspect of her temptation it represents. Jesus, on the other hand, emphatically chastizes Satan on the basis of his own inner conception of right and wrong, rejecting the banquet, in spite of his hunger, because he recognizes the impropriety of Satan's appeal to the vegetable body.[28] After their experiences in their respective wildernesses, the central characters return, as we have seen, to their accustomed societies, the Lady a failure, Jesus a success.

The sort of reception Blake depicts for each protagonist reflects his final evaluation of that character's performance, but it also implies a judgment of Milton's performance in each poem. While Blake may have glimpsed in the Ludlow Castle *Comus* the intimations of the Lady's inadequacy he makes central to his designs, the moralistic passages Milton subsequently added to the masque surely dismayed Blake, who must have seen in them an inappropriate response to a critical aesthetic temptation.[29] *Paradise Regained*, on the other hand, stood for Blake as an example of the perfected work embodying all the correct choices (by both author and protagonist) and consequently fulfilling its visionary, prophetic obligation. The final illustration to each poem reflects the mental condition of its poet as Blake apprehended it, and so do the two protagonists. The flawed heroine of *Comus* and the sublime hero of *Paradise Regained* epitomize the poetic vision of John Milton, flawed at first but ultimately perfected, for as Blake had noted, "As a man is, So he Sees" (K, p. 30). Hence Blake's designs to *L'Allegro* and *Il Penseroso* demonstrate that the creations of any poet reflect that poet's imaginative condition at the moment of composition. This being the case, we cannot doubt that the Milton of *Paradise Regained* is, in Blake's estimate, the sublime visionary whose enlightenment is finally complete and who, having through creative conflict and correct imaginative choice attained the fullness both of his years and of his vision, stands triumphantly atop the poetic pinnacle in a miracle of creative insight and self-assurance.

The temptation-choice theme is, of course, central to *Paradise Lost* as well, and Blake's designs explore that theme carefully from a variety of perspectives. Blake was one of the first critics to apprehend the degree to which the entire epic is governed by a series of critical choices. Eve's temptation and fall and Adam's subsequent willful participation in that fall are not the only trials in the epic but are, in fact, uninformed counterparts to the central trial and choice: the Son's conscious choice first to assume and then to renounce materiality and the vegetable body. The Son's offer to die for man antedates the actual Fall, but since in heaven—as in the mind of the Blakean visionary whose archetype is Jesus—chronological, narrative time does not exist, that offer is both made and completed on the cross in the same instant. The Son's "death out of Death" for man is assured, not by man's fall, but by the tender of the offer made out of love and identification with mankind. In this humanistic sense the Son in *Paradise Lost* is the early prototype of the Jesus of *Paradise Regained*. That Blake apparently undervalued this point in his early reading of the epic is demonstrated by his original aversion to the Son, whom he at first considered merely a surrogate agent for his unattractive Father. But by the time he came to create his illustrations for *Paradise Lost* Blake had reevaluated Milton's diffuse epic and had perceived the radical and subversive restructuring of the Trinity the poem advanced. Hence Blake's designs set about redirecting critical response to the poem, refocusing our attention on the essential truth the epic embodies. Blake engineers this reorientation most subtly, portraying the activities of all the central characters, giving most attention to Adam and Eve, to Satan second, and to the Son seemingly least of all. But in highlighting the Son's offer to redeem man in the illustration to book 3, Blake effectively prepares us for the recognition that his crucifixion, shown in the penultimate design and visually suggested in the third design and elsewhere, is an integral part of the original offer that both anticipates and enfolds the activities in Eden depicted in the intervening designs. Blake's *Paradise Lost* designs visually explore the action and consequences in temptation sequences both of incorrect choices (Adam and Eve, as well as Satan in *his* fall) and of the exemplary correct choice (the Son) in a systematically developed juxtaposition that mutually illuminates all participants in the drama.

A number of points must be made immediately. First, the pattern of temptation in the wilderness we see in *Comus* and *Paradise Regained* (and to a lesser extent in intellectual and aesthetic terms in *L'Allegro* and *Il Penseroso* and the *Nativity Ode*) is by necessity varied in *Paradise Lost*. The other poems involve the movement of the protagonist from his accustomed, relatively integrated and secure mental and social environment into a wilderness in which the trial "by what is contrary" occurs and from which that protagonist emerges (successful or not) and is reintegrated with his previous environment. But in *Paradise Lost* the trial of Eve (and then Adam) occurs *within* the familiar environment, within the Garden of Eden, from which the fallen pair are subsequently expelled into the wilderness. Upon further examination, though, the difference proves slight. Satan himself provides the key hint for understanding the situation when he declares in book 4, "myself am Hell" (l. 75). Like *Comus* and *Paradise Regained*, *Paradise Lost* is reducible to mental, imaginative terms, and Blake's designs clearly indicate his intention to treat all three as symbolic psychodramas illustrative of the range and depth of man's experience. Just as Satan recognizes hell as an internal condition, so must Adam and Eve discover that paradise is likewise internal.[30]

Adam and Eve are tempted and fall within a familiar setting, but their respective falls are facilitated by the disintegration and disorientation of Eve from Adam in book 9 that enables Satan in the guise of the Serpent to confront Eve alone. Blake correctly perceived in Eve's desire for separation and Adam's assent, however grudging, the breakdown of the couple's primal unity. Their psychological separation anticipates—indeed, assures—their physical separation. Once Eve has tasted the fruit and has fallen, Adam, with Eve encouraging him, responds in improper and irrational fashion to the natural human impulse toward reintegration by tasting of the fruit himself. In his seeming reassertion of oneness with Eve, Adam ironically and erroneously participates in the Fall. Basing his response to Eve on mistaken physical and material motives, he effects, not the psychic reintegration he desires, but, rather, an even further disintegration. The entire matter is then set straight (as best it can be) in the Expulsion by which the pair are finally reunited physically in the joining of hands (12.648) and psychologically in their common attitude and destiny as they make their solitary way into the wilderness of the world outside Eden where the only paradise now available to them is internal and spiritual. Their trial occurs, like the Lady's and Jesus', in a mental wilderness. The external geography is indeed different, the internal similar.

So, too, may we regard the other conspicuous example of incorrect choice: Satan's rebellion and his subsequent expulsion from heaven.

Satan's rebellion is another instance of improper response to trial. His physical rebellion is symptomatic of the psychological disintegration that has *already* occurred and that triggers his erroneous and exaggerated view of himself, his power, and his position in heaven.

Blake acutely observes the similarities between the tyrannical egotism of both the Father and Satan, concluding that Satan's expulsion from heaven occurs because heaven is not big enough for two tyrants. This suggests why Satan's hell is such an obvious parody of heaven, as we see in Blake's painting, *The Fall of Man* (fig. 51), where Satan and the Father—in their two domains—are visually similar. So close is this remarkable similarity between the Father and Satan that, as Blake writes in *The Marriage*, "it indeed appear'd to Reason as if Desire was cast out, but the Devils account is, that the Messiah fell. & formed a heaven of what he stole from the Abyss" (*MHH*, pls. 5–6; E, p. 34). In short, each thinks the other has fallen.[31] The further to the extreme right and left of center two factions draw, the nearer they approach one another: the extreme rational legalistic self-indulgence, or reason, of the Father is for Blake neither more nor less depraved than the extreme irrational sensual self-indulgence or excessive desire of Satan. Hence, though both appear to claim otherwise in *Paradise Lost*, neither is fit to dictate the rules of human conduct. For Blake, as for other Romantics like Shelley, the deck appears to be stacked against man from the start. The significance of the Son's example to man lies in its suggestion of a personal, internal alternative by which man may yet build "a Heaven in Hells despair." The Son's repudiation of mortality is like Milton's in *Milton*: while conventional empirical thought may regard his crucifixion as his entry into eternal death, we know that the lesson is valid, that the unveiling of the natural body through physical death is the means of exposing the spiritual body previously confined therein. The speaker in "To Tirzah" recognizes that going to eternal death (from the mortal perspective) is actually going to eternal life (from the eternal perspective), and he correctly proclaims that "the Death of Jesus set me free" from "Mortal Life" (E, p. 30).[32]

The Son's decision to die for man is based upon the sort of self-sufficiency we see in Jesus in *Paradise Regained*. His decision is based upon a clear and healthy understanding of who and what he is in relation to both God and man; it is an act of love and humility intended to show his fellow men the appropriate means of achieving a personal apocalypse and admission into eternity. But in the cases of both Satan in heaven and Adam and Eve in Eden the incorrect response to temptation stems from a faulty self-definition, a definition based in each instance upon inflated pride and self-esteem rather than upon the proper motives of humility and self-awareness—of mental wholeness—epitomized in Jesus.

A corollary deserves mention here. Since the temptations in *Paradise Lost* occur within externally familiar environments rather than in unfamiliar wildernesses, we tend naturally to regard the tempters more as interlopers than we do Comus or the Satan of *Paradise Regained*. That is, in the most conspicuous instance, Satan must *enter* Eden in order to tempt Eve. Yet if Satan tempts Eve into her fall, then who tempts Satan into his? The answer, of course, is Satan himself. His self-esteem, a natural trait carried to a perverted excess of inflated pride, underlies his own fall, just as Eve's fall stems from the induced inflation of her pride. Adam's fall, likewise, derives from a form of prideful self-aggrandizement by which he puts his vainly heroic, masculine self-image and his desire for companionship at any cost before his maturer sense of right and wrong. The interlopers prove, in *Paradise Lost* as in Milton's other poems, not only characters but also representatives of the "contrary states of the human soul,"[33] essentially the forces of reason and desire carried to distorted extremes.

Blake's critical reading focuses upon the characters who must decide and choose. In her way Eve accepts the banquet the Lady of *Comus* and Jesus of *Paradise Regained* had rejected for different reasons. Eve gets beyond the canting paralysis of the Lady in choosing, though her choice is wrong. Adam does too, though his choice is also wrong. These faulty external choices advance the pattern of division that has already begun and cut them off still more from the "garden of delight" that is the "inward form" of the "Generated Body" (M 26.31–32; E, p. 122). Since Adam and Eve are rapidly proving themselves unequal to the conflict of contraries in Experience née Eden, they require a paradigm for their own self-rescue. When they receive it in the vision of the Son's crucifixion, a miracle occurs in their physical and psychological reintegration as they leave Eden. Thus Blake reads *Paradise Lost* as a psychodrama of man's imaginative disintegration—a history symbolically articulated in the narrative mythology of the Fall—and his potential self-redemption by emulation of the Son's symbolic example. Thus in exploring *man's* progress in his designs, Blake does not neglect the "profound cosmic optimism" surrounding the Son's role in the epic.[34]

Milton's Father asserts that he has provided his creations, both angelic and human, with free will in order that they may demonstrate their allegiance to him:

> I made him [man] just and right,
> Sufficient to have stood, though free to fall.
> Such I created all th' Ethereal Powers
> And Spirits, both them who stood and them who fail'd;
> Freely they stood who stood, and fell who fell.
> Not free, what proof could they have giv'n sincere
> Of true allegiance, constant Faith or Love,
> Where only what they needs must do, appear'd,
> Nor what they would? what praise could they receive?
> What pleasure I from such obedience paid,
> When Will and Reason (Reason also is choice)
> Useless and vain, of freedom both despoil'd,
> Made passive both, had serv'd necessity,
> Not mee. . . .
> . . . .

> . . . they themselves decreed
> Thir own revolt, not I.
> [*PL* 3.98–111, 116–17]

Significantly, Milton has the Father employ the crucial word: "choice." For the poet takes great care throughout his epic to demonstrate that the various characters act freely and of their own volition in choosing their responses to temptation. That Milton does so emphasize the concept of free choice, and indeed that he articulates it explicitly through the Father, underscores the importance of the Son's offer, which follows so close upon the heels of the Father's words. In a daring maneuver, Milton has the Son respond to the Father's promise of grace and mercy in a manner that seems implicitly to suggest dissatisfaction with the Father's solution to man's dilemma and a recognition of its fundamental inadequacy. The Father promises grace to man in order

> that he may know how frail
> His fall'n condition, is, and to me owe
> All his deliv'rance, and to none but me.
> [3.180–82]

But the Father's promise has a curiously condescending ring to it, and a troubling suggestion that he plans to use man to remind himself of his own omnipotence. His decree would put man at the mercy of mercy, so to speak, making him dependent solely on the Father's will for all things and rendering him essentially incapable of doing anything on his own to better his lot.[35] While this situation would doubtlessly be strictly *just*, since man *has* fallen by his own choosing, it would effectively negate any possibility for man to regain any sense of fundamental personal dignity, keeping him subserviently dependent upon the Father's promise.

Then, too, the Father's call for a hostage to die for man arises from his strict sense of retributive justice: man is destined to be eternally unredeemed

> unless for him
> Some other able, and as willing, pay
> The rigid satisfaction, death for death.
> Say Heav'nly Powers, where shall we find such love,
> Which of ye will be mortal to redeem
> Man's mortal crime, and just th' unjust to save,
> Dwells in all Heaven charity so dear?
> [3.210–16]

Only the Son, "in whom the fulnes dwells of love divine" (3.225) proves willing to undertake the sacrifice. And he embraces the role of redeemer upon the latter terms specified by the Father: love and charity.[36] The Son's offer seems less concerned with satisfying the Father's demand for legal justice than with enabling man to help himself. His loving and charitable offer is undertaken by deliberate choice.

Recognizing the Son's correct motivation, the Father accepts his offer and blesses his choice, reaffirming that it is his human nature, not his divine, that will underscore the Son's act of redemption. As happens regularly in Milton, this correct choice is followed by a miracle of sorts: the qualifier the Father appends to his acceptance initiates the celestial ceremony while specifically identifying the complementary qualities that underlie the Son's offer:

> Nor shalt thou by descending to assume
> Man's Nature, lessen or degrade thy own.
> . . . .
>   . . . because in thee
> Love hath abounded more than Glory abounds,
> Therefore thy Humiliation shall exalt
> With thee thy Manhood also to this Throne;
> Here shalt thou sit incarnate, here shalt Reign
> Both God and Man, Son of both God and Man.
> [3.303–4, 311–16]

Directly contrasting the motives informing the Son's offer to participate in man's fallen nature in order to redeem it are those underlying Adam's decision to taste the fruit proffered by Eve. When he learns of Eve's transgression, Adam reacts with acute disappointment, but that initial disappointment is quickly tempered by a resolution to join with her fallen state, a resolution made both inwardly and outwardly:

>   Some cursed fraud
> Of Enemy hath beguil'd thee, yet unknown,
> And mee with thee hath ruin'd, for with thee
> Certain my resolution is to Die.
> . . . .
> However I with thee have fixt my Lot,
> Certain to undergo like doom; if Death
> Consort with thee, Death is to mee as Life.
> [9.904–7, 952–54]

Eve's response is understandably one of relief and gratitude, expressed ironically in terms of love:

> O glorious trial of exceeding Love
> Illustrious evidence, example high!
> [9.961–62]

The references to love telescope here: "linkt in Love so dear" (l. 970), "this happy trial of thy Love" (l. 975), "so faithful Love unequall'd" (l. 983), as do the references to "trial" with which they are linked in tragic irony. In fact, Milton carefully dwells on the ironic invocation of love in these circumstances, continuing,

> So saying, she embrac'd him, and for joy
> Tenderly wept, much won that he his Love
> Had so ennobl'd as *of choice* to incur
> Divine displeasure for her sake, or Death.
> In recompense (for such compliance bad
> Such recompense best merits) from the bough
> She gave him of that fair enticing Fruit
> With liberal hand: he scrupl'd not to eat

> Against his better knowledge, not deceiv'd,
> But fondly overcome with Female charm.
> [9.990–99; my italics]

Clearly, Adam's "love" is of a far different sort than the Son's, with which Milton so obviously wishes us to compare it. It is, as Eve's own line suggests, a *trial* of *exceeding* love engendering a consequent incorrect choice arising directly from the excess of Adam's physical self-concern, his mistaken subscription to the false and divisive sexual materialism of the natural, vegetable body. Adam's fall *is* "illustrious evidence" and "example high"—of error. The Son and Adam both offer to "die," freely to offer themselves up for another. But while the Son's love is proper, motivated as it is by charity and humility, and by a desire to provide man with a paradigm for self-sufficiency, Adam's is grievously inappropriate, induced by pride and selfishness. Adam makes it abundantly clear that his decision to join Eve in the Fall is based, not upon any sense of right, though he clothes his responses in the posturing garb of chivalric self-sacrifice, but purely on his overwhelming desire not to be alone again, deprived of Eve. In the terminology of *Milton*, he chooses, not to redeem his emanation, but to second her depravity by joining in her error. Adam's question to Eve is not, as we might expect, "How can I live with you now that you are fallen?," but, rather,

> How can I live without thee, how forgo
> Thy sweet Converse and Love so dearly join'd,
> To live again in these wild Woods forlorn?
> · · · · · · · · · · · · · · ·
> So forcible within my heart I feel
> The Bond of Nature draw me to my own,
> My own in thee, for what thou art is mine;
> Our State cannot be sever'd, we are one,
> One Flesh; to lose thee were to lose myself.
> [9.908–10, 955–59]

Adam reveals his engagingly human—but nonetheless selfish—motivation in these passages. Confronted with Eve's transgression and the plain fact that at this point their state is not "one," but is, in fact, one of diametrical separation—she fallen, he unfallen—Adam's first concern is for his own interests. That he casts his lot, not with his God, but with his fallen wife indicates the degree to which he has foolishly ("fondly," 9.999) mistaken his priorities. This is precisely Milton's point in observing that Adam *chooses*, in complete awareness, "not deceiv'd" (9.998), to share in the Fall. He has not the excuse of deception Eve is reasonably to claim later (10.162). Rather, he offers to die with Eve (even though neither of them has any real idea yet what death is) because of the supposed inseparability of their natures. This declaration of solidarity—of *seeming* integration—proves merely the prelude to further disintegration of their union, for Adam's declarations are still ringing in our ears when, called to account by the Son in book 10, he abjures his own responsibility and places the blame for his own fall squarely and unchivalrously upon Eve:

> This Woman whom thou mad'st to be my help,
> And gav'st me as thy perfect gift, so good,
> So fit, so acceptable, so Divine,
> That from her hand I could suspect no ill,
> And what she did, whatever in itself,
> Her doing seem'd to justify the deed;
> Shee gave me of the Tree, and I did eat.
> [10.137–43]

After this truly horrible speech the Son properly reminds Adam of the correct priorities: "Was shee thy God, that her thou didst obey / Before his voice [?]" (10.145–46). But it is already too late: man is in the wilderness.

Blake's comment to Crabb Robinson about Milton's desire that he correct the error of *Paradise Lost* that sexual pleasures arose from the Fall is relevant here because Blake's view is that "the Fall produced only generation and death, not pleasure." Robinson noted that after making this comment Blake "went off upon a rambling state [ment?] of a union of sexes in man as in God—an androgynous state in which I could not follow him."[37] Presumably Robinson's difficulty lay with Blake's notion of the androgynous union. Blake's point, as both the *Paradise Lost* designs and his own writings remind us, is that in his fall into division and generation man abandoned the Eden of his spiritual body to live in the diminished wilderness of his natural body. Eve's creation from Adam's side begins the separation of Adam's emanation, which rupture then broadens throughout *Paradise Lost*. Like Milton and Ololon, Albion and Jerusalem, Adam and Eve must learn what the Son demonstrates to them in his liberating example: that the essence of fallenness lies in the spectre, the error of separated selfhood.[38] This is an error of the natural, sexual body; external differences among individuals distract them from the universal reality of eternity: that all men are one man in the human imagination "Which is the Divine Body of the Lord Jesus" (*J* 3.59; E, p. 147).

The punishment prescribed by the Father and administered in Eden by the Son for man's fall demands, in the Father's eyes, atonement. But Blake's sense of the Atonement conflicts with what he regards as Milton's view:

Listen! Every Religion that Preaches Vengeance for Sin is the Religion of the Enemy & Avenger; and not of the Forgiver of Sin, and their God is Satan, Named by the Divine Name. . . . The Glory of Christianity is, To Conquer by Forgiveness. [*J*, pl. 52; E, p. 199]

Forgiveness of Sin is only at the Judgment Seat of Jesus the Saviour where the Accuser is cast out. not because he Sins but because he torments the Just & makes them do what he condemns as Sin & what he knows is opposite to their own Identity. [*VLJ*; E, p. 555]

In the strict view, the Atonement inherently exacerbates the rift between accuser and accused and makes the Son's death appear a concession to

Satan's power.[39] But Blake's idea of forgiveness of sin points directly to a mutualism between the Son and man that effectually eliminates the accuser. So for Blake in *Paradise Lost* the Son's death on the cross provides the symbolic key by which man may unlock his mind-forged manacles and render irrelevant both his accusers, the Father and Satan, and reintegrate his own personality in that spiritual-imaginative androgyny Blake must have tried to explain to Robinson. But if he is ever to reach this self-sufficiency, man must stop warring with himself, repudiate his spectre, redeem his emanation, and reenter his fourfold Edenic wholeness. Since "The Spiritual States of the Soul are all Eternal" (*J*, pl. 52; E, p. 198), man must "Distinguish therefore States from Individuals in those States" (*M* 32.22; E, p. 131). Self-knowledge, as it was for Jesus in *Paradise Regained*, is crucial to Adam and Eve in *Paradise Lost*, as Blake attempts to show us in his designs.

As the Son's correct choice in heaven was followed by a miracle of sorts, so too are the incorrect choices of Adam and Eve marked by physical phenomena. Seeing Eve returning, Adam recognizes the change in her bearing; when she addresses him, he drops the garland he had made for her (9.838–52, 887–93). This is a slight miracle, to be sure, but a number of illustrators including Blake incorporated it into their illustrations to book 9. After Adam joins in the Fall, the couple's incorrect choices are followed by the miraculous disruptions in nature, in which the animals turn upon one another (another point frequently noted by *Paradise Lost* illustrators), and by the subsequent appearance of the Son in the garden, come to judge them.

Paradise Lost, then, involves a complex and interrelated series of mutually illuminating choices. The faulty motivations that lead Satan, Adam, and Eve to choose incorrectly are all grounded in pride, pride that plays upon vanity and false values and that manifests itself in declarations of selfish posturing. Against this spectrum of distorted motives and faulty choices is placed the exemplary self-sufficiency of the Son, whose loving offer to redeem man places the gesture of self-sacrifice through the repudiation of the vegetable body in its proper context.

Blake's doctrine of contraries affects his reading of all Milton's poems. In responding to *Comus* Blake notes that while the activities of the three youths are consistently manipulated by higher, suprahuman beings, in the world of men it is the choices made (or *not* made, as in *Comus*) *by men* that determine the consequences of men's activities. The higher beings, Comus (with his crew), the Attendant Spirit, and Sabrina (with her attendants), engage throughout the masque in intellectual warfare. Comus's primary objective is psychological self-reinforcement, which he sets out to accomplish by intellectual conquest. His temptation of the Lady clearly involves more than the liquid in his cup. He has nothing to gain from the purely physical aspect of the temptation: of what use to Comus is an animal-headed Lady? Rather, the advantage desired is psychological; the victory sought is simply that she should accept the cup (and hence Comus's arguments) and taste. The Attendant Spirit's motivation is also, to some extent, self-serving in that he wishes to reinforce his own self-esteem by preserving the Lady. To thwart Comus's plan is to reinforce his own standing as defender and patron of conventional moral good. The power struggle in *Comus* centers, then, upon the efforts of the two principal powers to upset one another's designs. The resolution of the conflict in *Comus* is a temporary one: Comus is not annihilated, but is merely driven out. The Attendant Spirit has the upper hand in this encounter, and with matters in this state he leads the youths out of the wilderness, their lesson unlearned. The contraries are preserved, to remain free and active in the world and to engage in the inevitable retesting.

The similarity of the power struggle in *Paradise Lost* ought to be obvious. Once again the contending powers engage in a battle to thwart one another's designs. Satan declares his selfish motive early on:

> To do aught good never will be our task,
> But ever to do ill our sole delight,
> As being the *contrary* to his high will
> Whom we resist. If then his Providence
> Out of our evil seek to bring forth good,
> Our labor must be *to pervert that end*,
> And out of good still to find means of evil.
> [1.159–65; my italics]

As Blake clearly perceived, man becomes the pawn in this battle. He is both the battlefield and the prize, for the psychological fall Blake discerns in the epic is played out within the individual mind. In poems like *Comus* or *Paradise Regained* the dialectic is easily recognized. But *Paradise Lost* presents us with an added complication. To Blake's way of thinking the Father is himself an unattractive and fallen figure. The representative of moral good, or virtue, as perceived by rationalistic orthodoxy, the Father is as distasteful to Blake as the moral evil he casts out. The standard of rigid retributive justice espoused by the Father and that of selfish destructiveness personified in Satan represent, from the Blakean perspective, a definition of the limits of the fallen world, a world in which true liberty is forced to submit to the dictates of law and in which the impulse toward integration and love is perverted into a desire for triumph and domination accomplished at the expense of the suffering and even death of other parties who may be totally innocent. The proper antidote to this spiritual and imaginative poison is the return to unselfish love and integration epitomized in the Son's redemption of man. Hence Blake remarks in *A Vision of the Last Judgment*:

Thinking as I do that the Creator of this World is a very Cruel Being & being a Worshipper of Christ I cannot help saying the Son O how unlike the Father   First God Almighty comes with a Thump on the Head   Then Jesus Christ comes with a balm to heal it[.] [E, p. 555]

Blake here identifies Christ's function specifically as that of healer or restorer. For Blake, resolving the conflict of contraries in every individual's experience involves establishing an informed and balanced perspective on humanity, a prophetic vision that encompasses and resolves the dialectic through an ongoing series of apocalyptic insights. To maintain this enlightened stance is, for Blake, to enter into one's imaginative divinity, becoming one with Jesus Christ, the "Human Form Divine."

Blake recognized the radical stance Milton had adopted in his epic regarding the myth of the Fall. In his mature assessment of *Paradise Lost* he perceived Milton's elevation of the Son and the rationale behind that elevation. Blake seconded placing the Son at the center of the epic activity and regarding him more favorably than the Father. In his illustrations Blake sets out to demonstrate, in a subtle but deliberate manner, the sorts of comparisons Milton invites us to draw about the poem, its action, and its characters. He likewise corrects Milton in a number of important ways, particularly in terms of the sexual symbolism of his designs. The designs form a distinct departure from the manner of seeing the poem that had arisen in the eighteenth century, even while they refer frequently and incisively to the iconography the poem had accumulated in its previous illustration. Henry Fuseli's Milton paintings notwithstanding, Blake's illustrations provide the first full and systematic exploration of the poet's symbolic achievement. We discover early on that Blake's *Paradise Lost* designs, like those for *Comus*, set out not merely to interpret the poem but likewise to correct misunderstandings that had resulted both from what Blake regarded as doctrinal and aesthetic errors on Milton's part and from the mistaken criticism of previous commentators, verbal and visual. This is a monumental task to undertake within the scope of an interpretive essay on so major and influential a poet as Milton. The critical task was complicated—for Blake no less than for us—by its execution, not in the conventional verbal medium, but in pictures. Yet if we are willing to take Blake on his own terms and read his designs carefully, we will discover a rich vein of sensitive criticism awaiting our exploration.

Chapter 3: Blake's Reading of *Paradise Lost*

By the time he completed his first set of *Paradise Lost* designs in 1808, Blake had already illustrated Edward Young's *Night Thoughts* with more than five hundred watercolor page illustrations and Thomas Gray's poetry with more than a hundred. The illustrations to Young and Gray are, to be sure, of an entirely different nature from the Milton designs: they were designed as page illustrations, each surrounding a block of text, some line or image of which they illuminate. By nature sequential, they are tied physically to the text in a way that Blake's Milton designs are not. Too, many of the more than six hundred watercolor illustrations, particularly those to Young, may properly be considered essays rather than finished illustrations. For the actual printed edition of *Night Thoughts* Blake was subsequently commissioned to engrave some of his original designs as page illustrations. The technical demands of engraved printing imposed an entirely different set of restrictions upon Blake than did even the initial watercolors, and the finished products must be assessed with the limitations of the medium in mind.

The illustration of Milton's poetry, however, demanded of Blake a different critical procedure. Unlike Young or Gray, Milton was generally accounted a surpassing literary figure, and his works, *Paradise Lost* in particular, had become prime forces in all the arts, contributing heavily to the shaping of eighteenth-century tastes. Working with *Paradise Lost*, the conscientious illustrator was obliged to consider not only the text itself but also both previous verbal commentary and the richly complex accumulated visual iconography developed in previous illustrations, an iconography that had blended with that of Genesis illustration to the extent that by 1800 it was often difficult to ascertain whether a particular depiction of, say, the Garden of Eden, was derived from Milton or the Bible. Inevitably, the epic had inspired many separate works of art not strictly conceived as textual illustration; often such works are related only tangentially to the epic. The outstanding example of this tendency in Miltonic art is Henry Fuseli's Milton Gallery, although many Milton pictures had been made and exhibited previous to Fuseli's exhibition.[1]

These difficulties and complications will be explored in detail later. We need to be clearly aware at the outset, however, that by 1800 *Paradise Lost* imposed upon its serious illustrators two particular defining limits: Milton's text itself and the accumulated iconographic tradition of its illustration, though individual artists had already begun to take increasing liberties with both. Once John Baptist Medina and Henry Aldrich created the first illustrations to the poem in 1688, subsequent illustrators could typically count on the reader's general familiarity both with the text and with a fair number of prior illustrations. As is his usual custom, Blake operates upon these bodies of material in revolutionary fashion, systematically dismantling them in order to reassemble them in his unique and rigorous evaluation both of Milton's poem and of its critical tradition. And because *Paradise Lost* was so much more widely illustrated than the earlier poems, Blake's designs form a more obvious response to and critique of those previous illustrations than do his designs for the earlier poems. Blake refused to accept the two limits—text and iconographic tradition—as absolute, regarding them rather as points of departure and indicators of specific verbal and visual contexts he wished to invoke for his critical statements.

A proper evaluation of Blake's designs requires that we recognize the artist's change in response to *Paradise Lost*. It is most convenient to divide the artist's attitudes into two periods, marking the division at 1800, the year of Blake's removal to Felpham and the beginning of his most intimate association with William Hayley. As we have seen, Hayley was an important figure in the Romantic reassessment of Milton's achievement, a determined proponent of discovering Milton the man and revolutionary artist and thinker concealed within the conventional estimate of the poet.[2] Hayley's influence undoubtedly figured in Blake's reassessment of his prophetic predecessor; Blake's mature statements on Milton document critical judgments that are in many ways at odds with his early statements and in accord with many of Hayley's convictions. The intellectual and imaginative disparity between the two men, which Blake deplores in his notebook and letters, should not distract us from his critical agreement with Hayley on the nature and significance of Milton's achievement.

While Bernard Blackstone's assertion that Blake saw in *Paradise Lost* "the record of Milton's submission to error" is appropriate to the period of *The Marriage of Heaven and Hell*,[3] it is less immediately applicable to the poet's view in 1804–18, the period of *Milton* and many of the Milton illustrations. One of the dangers inherent in Blake scholarship is the occasional temptation to make sweeping generalizations about the artist's opinions as if they were held with equal firmness at all points of his career, all his ideas and works being part of "a great, coexisting corpus."[4] This is a hazardous way to approach *any* artist, for to impose blanket statements of this sort, implying that the artist began his career with his ideas fully developed and that they never changed significantly, effectively precludes appreciation of that artist's intellectual and artistic progress. It is particularly foolish to suggest such stasis in terms of so complex and meticulous an artist as Blake, an artist whose critical assessments and appreciations are continually evolving, continually deepening. The very process of revision, clarification, and amplification that Blake's verbal and visual canon evidences ought to alert us to the pitfalls of all such hasty generalization about Blake's views.

Blake himself provides the definitive statement on intellectual evolution in *The Marriage:* "The man who never alters his opinion is like standing water, & breeds reptiles of the mind" (*MHH*, pl. 19; E, pp. 40–41). This is good advice to artist and critic alike: as one progresses in intellectual or imaginative maturity, old opinions are naturally replaced by new, altered ones the individual consciously chooses to embrace. To Blake, this is entirely as it should be; it is pointless to judge any individual on the basis of earlier opinions and beliefs he has subsequently renounced. The "reptiles of the mind" are generated in those stagnant states like the vales of Har (*Tiriel, The Book of Thel*) in which there is no opposition, no creative conflict of contraries, no "Mental Fight." The shift in Blake's perspective on Milton substantiates the point.

Blake initially regarded *Paradise Lost* as the greatest embodiment in Milton's poetry of the repressive Puritan ethics to which that poet appeared mistakenly to have subscribed. The magnitude of Milton's error and its effects upon the reader, Blake likely felt, could only be increased by the wide dissemination of this enormously popular poem. Hence Blake's earlier verbal responses to *Paradise Lost* always possess a particular sense of urgency, an impetuosity more than usually pronounced, that reminds us of the tone of the artist's annotations to Reynolds.

Blake's most extensive verbal criticism of *Paradise Lost* is *The Four Zoas,* his own experiment in the diffuse epic form which S. Foster Damon incorrectly called Blake's rewriting of *Paradise Lost.*[5] Not a rewriting at all, *The Four Zoas* is to Milton's epic what *Europe* is to the *Nativity Ode:* a carefully executed independent work that continually invokes the previous work as its context. Blake employs this procedure, not to rewrite Milton's epic, but to show most dramatically how his own epic differs from Milton's, leaving it for the perceptive reader to recognize first the similarities and then the differences, thus achieving through his own comparative critical involvement with both poems the insightful perspective on them Blake wishes to generate. The difference between the two epics is most apparent in Blake's conclusion to *The Four Zoas.* Blake's epic presents as contending powers, not God and Satan, but Urizen and Orc, the rationalistic lawgiver and the fiery, energetic rebel, cast as contrary powers in a complex drama. Urizen and Orc both degenerate in the poem, each becoming a dragon, much as the figure of Albion's Angel does in the context of *America* in a similar variation upon the demonic old dragon theme in Revelation. The fall of one necessarily involves the fall of the other. But in the final stages of the poem Urizen renounces his own quest for unnatural domination and rational order, and his renunciation triggers his immediate transformation into a radiant, youthful, naked figure:

> I alone in misery supreme
> Ungratified give all my joy unto this Luvah & Vala
> Then Go O dark futurity I will cast thee forth from these
> Heavens of my brain nor will I look upon futurity more

> I cast futurity away & turn my back upon that void
> Which I have made for lo futurity is in this moment
> Let Orc consume let Tharmas rage let dark Urthona give
> All strength to Los & Enitharmon & let Los self cursd
> Rend down this fabric as a wall ruin'd & family extinct
> Rage Orc Rage Tharmas Urizen no longer curbs your rage[.]
>
> So Urizen spoke he shook his snows from off his Shoulders & arose
> As on a Pyramid of mist his white robes scattering
> The fleecy white renewd he shook his aged mantles off
> Into the fires   Then glorious bright Exulting in his joy
> He sounding rose into the heavens in naked majesty
> In radiant Youth. [*FZ* 121.17–32; E, pp. 375–76]

In thus repudiating his repressive tendencies, Urizen achieves an individual last judgment, an apocalypse that initiates his resurrection. His correct choice is immediately commemorated by his miraculous transfiguration into the radiant, naked youth. This is the same pattern of miraculous reinforcement of correct choice we see again, for instance, in *Milton*, plate 16, and in the *Paradise Regained* illustrations.

Blake's sharpest criticism of *Paradise Lost* and its author occurs more than a dozen years earlier, however, on plates 5 and 6 of *The Marriage of Heaven and Hell* (1790–94).[6] Blake's analysis includes a succinct evaluation of the theological foundations of the poem as well as of their proponent, John Milton. The comments on plates 5 and 6 are voiced by the Devil, who we should take care to distinguish from Blake: he may speak *for* Blake on occasion, but his voice is not therefore identical to Blake's. His comments represent an extremist view, albeit a view possessing an element of truth and penetration. The Devil's deliberately provocative and inflammatory words are calculated to shock readers, not into self-righteous and blind defense of the received orthodox opinion they customarily accept without question (as the Lady does in *Comus*), but, rather, into productive dialectical examination of that customarily untested opinion. At the heart of the Devil's comments lies Blake's early assessment of the castrating effects of religious orthodoxy upon the intellectual and imaginative vision of even a strong poet like Milton when that poet attempted to incorporate its dogma into a work of prophetic art.

Linking prophecy with patriotism in its purest sense, Shelley later wrote in *A Philosophical View of Reform* that

the true patriot will endeavor to enlighten and to unite the nation and animate it with enthusiasm and confidence. . . . the patriot will be foremost to publish the boldest truths in the most fearless manner.[7]

Blake contends that Milton's duty as prophet was to participate in such an activity of enlightened leadership. But his early reading of *Paradise Lost* suggested to Blake that Milton had eschewed that responsibility and had instead devised an elaborate apology for the repressive orthodoxy that had reduced man to the debility of the sick, sleeping Albion. In setting out to "justify the ways of God to men," Milton appeared to have sided with the oppressor, forsaking his bond of humanity with his fellow men.

The first of Blake's original disagreements concerns the Trinity. Blake's Devil finds that in *Paradise Lost* "the Father is Destiny, the Son, a Ratio of the five senses. & the Holy Ghost, Vacuum!" (*MHH*, pl. 6; E, p. 35). His ironic opinion is strikingly perceptive of Milton's anti-Trinitarianism. The Holy Spirit is never identified explicitly in Milton's poem, nor is he ever specifically associated with his traditional function in Christian doctrine as the grace that proceeds between Father and Son.[8] Milton invokes as his "Heavenly Muse" (1.6), not the Holy Spirit, but Urania, though the poet hints at a fusion of their identities and functions that recalls the pattern Milton had already employed in the *Nativity Ode* of replacing traditional pagan figures with their Christian counterparts. Invoked even by the early Christian poets as the patroness of inspiration, Urania is introduced here in a verbal structure that, in the opening passage of book 7, conflates allusions to allow the poet to associate his own inspiration not only with that of the great bards of antiquity (whom he claims to be in the process of surpassing) but also with that of Moses and the biblical prophets who wrote under the direct inspiration of the Holy Spirit. Milton's allusions reveal the Holy Spirit's *implied* presence in the poem; yet, compared to the other members of the Trinity, he is kept remarkably well hidden. The impetuous young Blake could easily enough have missed the allusive suggestions Milton employs in dealing with the Holy Spirit. More likely, Blake found the connection Milton draws between his own inspiration and that of the *classical* bards distasteful and artificial, a taming of his prophetic vision to meet the expectations of convention, as his remark in *Milton* suggests:

Shakspeare & Milton were both curbd by the general malady & infection from the silly Greek & Latin slaves of the Sword. [*M* pl. 1; E, p. 94]

Blake enthusiastically asserts the incompatible natures of the Daughters of Memory and the Daughters of Inspiration. Annotating Reynolds's *Discourses*, he wrote:

A Work of Genius is a Work "Not to be obtained by the Invocation of Memory & her Syren Daughters. but by Devout prayer to that Eternal Spirit. who can enrich with all utterance & knowledge & sends out his Seraphim with the hallowed fire of his Altar to touch & purify the lips of whom he pleases." Milton[.] [Annot. Reynolds; E, p. 635]

But, as Blake informs us in the following paragraph of this note, the "Eternal Spirit" that enlightens and purifies the prophets is the divine power (or god) of inspiration. If Blake did, in fact, annotate his copy of the *Discourses* between 1798 and 1809—perhaps even by 1802—as Erdman suggests (E, p. 801), then we may properly place with this passage a remark from Blake's famous letter to Dr. Trusler (1799):

What is it sets Homer, Virgil & Milton in so high a rank of Art? Why is the Bible more Entertaining & Instructive than any other book? Is it not because they are addressed to the Imagination, which is Spiritual Sensation, & but mediately to the Understanding or Reason? [K, p. 30]

Clearly, the primary characteristic of inspiration would appear to be this infusion of imagination, a conclusion all of Blake's work supports. Blake regards imagination as a gift of the "Daughters of Inspiration." As he tells us (significantly, in the preface to *Milton*), "when the New Age is at leisure to Pronounce," proper values will be reasserted and "the Daughters of Memory shall become the Daughters of Inspiration" (*M*, pl. 1; E, p. 94) in a transfiguration like that of Urizen in *The Four Zoas*. Blake again implies that the latter are already implicit in the former, the same principle we have noted elsewhere in Blake's works.

We might, of course, see Milton's muse as what Blake terms "that Eternal Spirit," divine inspiration, an identification that, in terms of the Holy Spirit, does have a basis in Christian art. We might, in fact, extend the point and see Blake's own muse functioning in a manner that suggests Christ's role as creative principle in the artist's mind. Viewed in terms of the artist and his inspiration, the Son and the Holy Spirit are for Blake, as Northrop Frye points out, very nearly the same thing.[9] Still, we ought to be wary of working so hard to read this all into *Paradise Lost* merely to supply the missing member of the Trinity whom Milton has so deliberately reduced in his poem.

God the Father, on the other hand, is very much in evidence in *Paradise Lost*, and he epitomizes for Blake the poem's flaws. The clearest indication of Blake's regard for him as archetypal rationalist is his related painting and frontispiece to *Europe, The Ancient of Days*, (fig. 19), which portrays the Creator at work with his compasses, "the almost invariable attribute of the Creator in the European imagination,"[10] performing what was to Blake the abhorrent act of separation and division. Separation was for Blake the essence of the fall of man; the establishment and assertion of separate individuals was an act of fragmentation grounded in pride and totally destructive to unity, integration, and wholeness.[11] The painting, which Blake copied at various times in his career (including one copy on which he worked on his deathbed) is deliberately paradoxical. The powerful visual *form* of the picture, so immediately attractive, seems initially at odds with the inherently negative *content*. Yet in this marriage of contraries Blake subtly demonstrates how an implicitly evil figure, act, or principle may, by its seeming attractiveness, deceive the unwary whose doors of perception have not yet been cleansed. Blake's picture reflects the ironic ambiguity that lies at the heart of traditional Christian concepts of morality: the deceptive beauty of "evil." Roland Frye's comment on the physically attractive Satan of Renaissance art who replaced the earlier monster-devils of Bosch and Brueghel is particularly appropriate to Blake's Ancient as well:

Both in what he presents and in what he represents, Satan is essentially a perversion and distortion of created good, and therefore should be understood as a distortion of created beauty. In the Christian understanding of this tension, the

demonic is essentially hideous and destructive, but perennially appeals to man under appearances which are both attractive and tempting.[12]

Blake's Ancient of Days testifies to the ambivalent nature of the Creator and provides us with another instance of Blake's characteristically paradoxical visual treatment of conventional themes.

To Blake, the Father is an emotionless legalist, deserving of contempt not so much because of his tyranny as because of his rationalism, which *makes* him a tyrant instinctively dependent upon hierarchies and systematization. At the same time, the Ancient in Blake's picture is a figure of great energy, albeit energy turned to incorrect purposes. Working with his draftman's compasses, he is "the God of This World," parceling out infinity into definable, empirical spheres of existence in time and space, circumscribing man's mind even as he defines his natural world. Like Urizen in *The Four Zoas*, he *ought* to be capable of self-renewal through annihilation of his spectre. The *potential* for imaginative regeneration exists in the Father-Ancient, but it is never fulfilled there. Blake recognized the self-defeating strictures Milton had imposed upon himself in setting out "to justify the ways of God to men." For Blake, the Father's ways could *support* no justification or apology. In attaching the massive doctrinal superstructure to his poem, Milton obscured his own vision and misled generations of readers. Much of Blake's reaction here depends upon his notion that man's relation to his God is a matter, not of rationalistic doctrine, legal strictures, and unquestioning acceptance, but of love, imagination, and enlightened choice. Hence he argues that in its substitution of the kind of self-righteous "Moral Hypocrisy" Blake hears from Milton's Father, Christianity has become anti-Christian: "The Modern Church Crucifies Christ with the Head Downwards" (*VLJ*; E, p. 554).

Commenting on both the character and the performance of the Father in the epic, Desirée Hirst claims that Milton reveals himself in the long run as a slave to the Daughters of Memory:

In spite of Milton's concern for spiritual things, and his powerful imagination, his mind was too matter of fact to hold the genuine prophetic quality. He remained precise and concretely materialistic even when speaking of heavenly matters, so much the scholar that his respect for abstract reasoning limited his vision and made him produce a very prosy deity, for example.[13]

This comment, however, betrays a misreading to which even Blake would object. Blake agreed that Milton had needlessly and foolishly imposed a debilitating burden of narrative and doctrinal detail upon his epic, but he never doubted that Milton possessed "the genuine prophetic quality." Rather, Blake contends that Milton mistakenly obscured that quality, mantling it with the "rotten rags" of orthodox thought. As for the "very prosy deity," Blake *would* agree with Hirst to a certain point, but would surely remind us that the deity—the Father—*is* prosy and that his prosiness originates in his own unsatisfactory rationalism. To make the Father's performance the measure of the

Figure 19. William Blake. *The Ancient of Days*. 1824 (?). 23.4 cm by 16.8 cm. *Whitworth Art Gallery, University of Manchester*

entire epic is akin to the error Blake observed in his copy of Swedenborg's *Heaven and Hell*, in which someone had penciled in as half title Theseus's line from *A Midsummer Night's Dream:* "And as Imagination bodies forth y[e] forms of things unseen—turns them to shape & gives to airy Nothing a local habitation & a Name." To this notation Blake replies,

Thus Fools quote Shakespeare The Above is Theseus's opinion Not Shakespeares   You might as well quote Satans blasphemies from Milton & give them as Miltons Opinions[.] [Annotations to Swedenborg's *Heaven and Hell;* E, p. 590]

Blake was acute enough to understand that to regard the Father as Milton's spokesman, to assume *his* views are the poet's, is to misread the epic just as surely as we misread Blake's poems if we regard Urizen's opinions as Blake's. To a considerable extent, as Blake would recognize, both the Father and Satan function as foils to the Son, as points of contrast against which we may measure the Son's superiority.

Against the grim aspect of the Father Blake came finally to place the heroism of the Son. C. A. Patrides believes that Milton differentiates between Father and Son essentially for dramatic purposes, separating them to facilitate dialogue and dramatic action and fusing them whenever "God" acts outside the confines of heaven. It is this fused Son whom the Devil equates on plate 5 of *The Marriage* with the Satan of the Book of Job, for reasons that will become apparent shortly. While Patrides would have us believe that Father and Son are essentially one and the same, A. S. P. Woodhouse, pointing to what he regards as Milton's subordinationist tendencies, contends that the Son's relationship to the Father is one of "perfect submission": "not only is the role in creation which Milton assigned to the Son an example of this subordinationism, but . . . nowhere in orthodox thought is the 'subordination of persons' . . . more often implied than in the account given of the creation." Yet Barbara Lewalski has demonstrated that Milton's view of the Son's relationship to the Father, especially as we find it elaborated in his *De Doctrina Christiana* (with which, naturally, Blake would not have been familiar), is neither perfectly Trinitarian nor subordinationist but is, rather, a heterodox view that defies precise classification, though it most nearly approximates Arianism.[14]

Milton's Son is a created divinity (*PL* 5.603–4), unlike the eternal Father, and possesses only such divine attributes as the Father sees fit to bestow upon him. Hence, when the Son is called upon to act as the Father's agent, as when he effects the creation, routs Satan, or judges Adam and Eve, Milton suggests that he accedes to a portion of the Father's divine power, later to relinquish that higher power and glory. Interestingly, these acts in which the Son participates in the Father's divine power are precisely those for which Blake most actively criticizes him, as he does in *The Marriage*. All are limiting acts that point away from eternity and oneness, toward mortality and division. It is as if the Son's accession to that portion of the Father's "divine power" is actually a proportional fall by which he assumes, not a divine, but a demonic trait, for the added authority by which he acts in these three instances is the rationalistic, tyrannical authority of the Father's system to which Blake so objected. By his accession to and participation in the Father's deeds the Son becomes, in Blake's early estimate, a party to the Father's misrule, a servant to what appears the sort of blind fate or destiny that predestines man to a life of suffering in experience.

After his offer to die for fallen man, the Son appears in three disintegrative situations that seem to Blake to reveal a dangerous paradoxicality about him. First, in an act we recognize as antecedent to his offer, he participates in the creation as the Father's agent, thus falling heir to a portion of the antimechanistic criticism implicit in *The Ancient of Days*. Second, his participation is the decisive factor in the expulsion from heaven of Satan and his crew, the only real opponents of the Father's tyranny. Third, after the fall of Adam and Eve, he participates in man's judgment, again as the Father's representative. Hence, acting as a surrogate for the Father, he appears to Blake ultimately to assume the role Satan plays in the Book of Job, becoming a dispenser of afflictions.

In his most distinctively integrative act—his act of redemption, from initial offer to Crucifixion and Resurrection—the Son receives the very curious praise from the Father we have noted previously:

> Nor shalt thou by descending to assume
> Man's Nature, lessen or degrade thy own.
> [*PL* 3.303–4]

Like so many of the Father's speeches, this one suggests, not that the Son's offer to redeem man reflects the Father's power, glory, or real concern for man's welfare, but, rather, that it will *not degrade* his Son—or, by extension, himself. He is essentially damning with faint praise here, implying that the heavenly family name will survive even this. He dissociates himself verbally from the Son's most heroic act, and in having him do so Milton cleverly reveals the Father's ambiguous nature. The Father's case is not helped, elsewhere, by references to him as "the great Work-Master" (3.696) and "Our great Forbidder" (9.815). We become uncomfortably conscious of the Father as a figure rather too much concerned with his status, even at the expense of his own Son.

Milton wishes his reader to recognize that the hero of *Paradise Lost* is the Son: not a lesser God but "one greater Man" (1.4). Perhaps in his early reading of the poem Blake missed this point, as his remarks in *The Marriage* imply. Perhaps he simply felt Milton had obscured this point as well. Whatever the case, Blake's initial response to *Paradise Lost* was unmistakably harsh, for it seemed to him that Milton had sided with the orthodox churches that "exalted the Decalogue and its author, the 'Angry God of this World,' while presenting Jesus as a secondary figure, cast in a sentimental light, far removed from his revolutionary role as the advocate of forgiveness."[15] Blake seems to have felt at first that Milton had denigrated the very hero he ought to have exalted, presenting in the Son's "Filial obedience" (3.269) "a masochistic willingness to be sacrificed by the father" in conformity to the bitter tradition of the Atonement.[16] Only later did Blake come to understand the degree to which Milton's epic actually subverted traditional orthodox Christian patterns of expectation in its implicit conferral of heroic status upon the Son.

In altering his original negative reading of the Son's role, Blake rejected as well the sort of reading suggested by Desmond Hamlet's argument that "divine justice lies at the very heart of the creative and restorative processes of the poem's world because of its inherent and inextricable connection with the Son, in whose person and function, throughout the poem, God's righteousness or justice is most fully expressed."[17] To the contrary, Blake would finally argue that the Son performs *his* creative and restorative (or reintegrative) function *despite* the righteousness or justice of the Father which Blake continues to regard as repressive and destructive principles of an archetypal restrainer of desire. At first, though, particularly in his participation in the judgment of Adam and Eve, the Son seemed to Blake to controvert his own nature, for as Blake later tells us in *Jerusalem*, "The Spirit of Jesus is continual forgiveness of Sin" and "Every Religion that Preaches Vengeance for Sin is the Religion of the Enemy & Avenger; and not of the Forgiver of Sin" (*J*, pls. 3, 52; E, pp. 144, 199).[18] Blake's view of *Jesus Christ* (the "God" of his own personal, radical Christianity as distinct from either the Son of *Paradise Lost* or even the Jesus of *Paradise Regained*) seems to have been largely a stable one: he tells us flatly that "God is Jesus" (*Laocoön*; E, p. 271). Hence when we consider Blake's assessment of the Christ in whom he personally believed, we can more easily understand why he seems originally to have seen in *Paradise Lost* the fall not just of man but of *all* the characters. Northrop Frye's suggestion that Blake regarded *Paradise Lost* as a poem without a hero, an illustration of that stage in the "Orc cycle" in which all characters are "caught in the same quicksand of fatalistic morality,"[19] quite accurately reflects Blake's early reading of the epic.

Blake apparently took to heart Raphael's point about love:

> Freely we serve [God],
> Because we freely love, as in our will
> To love or not; in this we stand or fall.
> [5.538–40)

Here Raphael presents Adam with the Father's view, that obedience is a valid measure of love and that the Fall (when it occurs) is a clear matter of disobedience: *a lack of love*. Blake claims the Father bases his relations with fallen men, not on love, but on justice, a psychologically distancing factor. Employing the standard Milton enunciates through Raphael, Blake judges the Father to have fallen through his own rejection of love. And in initially judging the Son a surrogate for the Father, Blake discovers in him a fall not unlike the falls suffered by all the epic's characters. Further, Blake locates *Milton's* fall in his apparent endorsement and justification of the actions of Father and Son, and the *reader's* fall in his subscription to and perpetuation of the mistaken principle of retributive justice represented in the conventional religious notions assembled behind the Father's role.

We cannot say precisely when or how Blake's reading of *Paradise Lost* changed. Surely it was a gradual process, perhaps related to the general shift in his own poetry away from the pessimistic note of the early and middle nineties. Certainly his altered conception was solidified during his stay at Felpham. Blake's letters from the period, for instance, remark on the artist's work on the Cowper projects Hayley had undertaken, projects which would have made available to Blake Cowper's comments on Milton, if in fact Blake was not already familiar with them.[20] Likewise, *Milton*, plate 49,[21] suggests the Felpham period, for it is from his garden there that Blake commemorates the awakened Milton and the descent of the redeemed Ololon as "Moony Ark" into "Felpham's Vale" (*M* 42 [49].7–9; E, p. 142). This moment, as we have already seen, is an integral part of the poet's reappraisal of Milton and his works.

However the change in attitude came about, as his understanding of *Paradise Lost* deepened, Blake decided that Milton's conception of the Son accorded well with his own notion of Christ and that the poem had actually set out to exalt the Son, particularly in terms of his example to man, in fulfillment of the promise of the poem's fourth line. The orthodox doctrine of the Atonement Milton calls up in the poem is actually subverted by the Son, who is motivated by true love, the perfection of desire.

Against the Father's repeated offer of "mercy"—of "judicial clemency"—to man, an offer whose condescending terminology implies and reinforces the vast difference in stature between accuser and accused, the Son offers *himself*, basing his offer on a principle, not of separation, but of unification and integration. The Son is, of course, the perfect man. He is at once the particularized epitome of the self-assured and the insightful hero—as *Paradise Regained* was to demonstrate—and the sum of human and divine perfection. His offer to die for man expresses, as Ronald Grimes has noted, his concern that the individuality of man be preserved.[22] Unlike both the Father and his demonic parody Satan, the Son has no desire to dominate, correctly recognizing that any such arbitrary and external domination deprives man of that necessary freedom to choose among alternatives upon which his imaginative progress depends. The Father's offer of mercy, magnanimous as it may be, still reinforces his posture of superiority and dominance. The Son's offer of *himself* more than fulfills the demands of the mediatorial function; more importantly, it reduces the gulf separating God and man and asserts his identification with man and man's consequent potential for participation in divinity. The central identity of the Son lies in his humanity, his knowledge of himself as man in relation to the Father.[23] Blake's *Paradise Regained* designs, as we have seen, celebrate not only

Jesus' discovery of his divine nature but also his reassertion of human dignity in his return to "his mother's house" and the society of his human associates, the world of men in which his offer to die for man reaches its fruition. Thus Marcia Pointon is correct in asserting that "the true crucifixion is Christ's voluntary adoption of flesh, not his enforced release from it."[24] The Son's offer epitomizes his exemplary heroism: "God becomes as we are, that we may be as he is" (*There is No Natural Religion* [b]; E, p. 2). Blake's Jesus reveals his understanding of the necessity of his example insightfully for Albion in *Jerusalem:*

> Unless I die thou canst not live
> But if I die I shall arise again & thou with me
> This is Friendship & Brotherhood without it Man Is Not
> . . . .
>
> Wouldest thou love one who never died
> For thee or ever die for one who had not died for thee
> And if God dieth not for Man & giveth not himself
> Eternally for Man Man could not exist! for Man is Love:
> As God is Love: every kindness to another is a little Death
> In the Divine Image nor can Man exist but by Brotherhood[.]
> [*J* 96.14–16, 23–28; E, p. 253]

The Son could justifiably adopt the Father's strictness and likewise call for retribution and reparation. He opts, however, to cast his lot with man, choosing the "many a hard assay" his experience as redeemer will entail. Likewise, in his crucifixion he provides man with the lasting symbol that epitomizes true Christianity. But Blake recognizes that the Son's death is a death out of the state of living death ordinarily called life, or the vegetable body of the natural man. As we have already seen, the death of the Son's natural body on the cross points to an eternal reality: "The Natural Body is an Obstruction to the Soul or Spiritual Body" (Annotations to Berkeley's *Siris;* E, p. 653).

Blake's reaction to Satan and his crew can tell us much about the way he viewed *Paradise Lost,* once we reject the simplistic assumption that Blake was entirely a champion of Satan. While Blake exhibits obvious admiration for certain qualities of Satan, he also shows clear distaste for him as he subsequently appears in the poem. Blake's view of Satan resembled that voiced by Shelley in the preface to *Prometheus Unbound:* whatever dramatic interest Satan may possess is undermined by his perverse motivations, by the "taints of ambition, envy, revenge, and a desire for personal aggrandisement."[25]

Satan had rebelled for some of the right reasons. The Father seems arbitrarily to have altered the heavenly order, inserting the Son into the hierarchy by fiat and demanding universal reverence for him. The Father's action, taken with his insistence on preserving the heavenly caste system he has set up (he speaks continually, we recall, in terms of orders and hierarchies), constitutes in Satan's view insupportable tyranny, against which the first duty seems, not humble acquiescence, but, rather, defiance and rebellion. We might at first thought expect Milton's own libertarian tendencies to have prompted him to side with the rebels. But the poet is dealing with a doctrinal matter here, and in allowing the case against Satan to be rendered from the viewpoint of the Father, the "supreme authority," he sacrifices the insight into the situation Blake felt it in his power to provide us as "inspired seer." Instead of offering a balancing perspective upon the revolutionary power struggle in heaven, Milton simply gives us the word of the Father, followed by the deed of the Son. John Beer has stated—perhaps overstated—the case against the Father's behavior:

God [the Father], already given a perfect case against Satan, emerges in his speeches as an ancient legalist, bound, to a ridiculous extent, by the laws of his own universe. The central being of a heaven of light and music and love reveals himself as a faceless idol of Necessity, caught within the cobweb of his own abstractions.[26]

If we regard the Father, as Blake appears to have done, less as *person* than as *principle* or *state*, we may glimpse considerable truth in Beer's assertions. Rather than focusing upon what is *implicitly* wrong— indeed, as Dr. Johnson correctly perceived, what is immoral and blasphemous—in Satan's vain, self-centered resistance to his orders, the Father instead bases his case upon his whole rationalistic order of systems, hierarchies, "justice," and obedience, thereby betraying his own critical flaw. Hence, for his opposition to the Father's imposed order, Satan is expelled, as are his followers. In Milton's view, the Father's action through the Son (book 6) is justified, for he has demanded only "voluntary obedience, with love and gratitude, and with the consent of reason and of the whole being, like that of a son; so that the act of obedience is itself an exercise of liberty, and God's service is found to be indeed perfect freedom." Blake, of course, could scarcely accept such reasoning, for in his view the struggle in heaven finds its parallel in the mind of man, and to accept Milton's justification of the Father's action is to accept a priori that "the free man's mind is a dictatorship of reason obeyed by the will without argument."[27] This is the sort of line to which Blake objected so strenuously in *Comus*.

Milton does not argue the justice of the Father's actions, after all, but probes by implication the ethical aspect of the question: the relative humaneness of the Father's conduct judged in light of the Son's. Besides, regarding the power struggle in terms of the Father and Satan actually confuses the real issue, for, as Blake reminds us, the real contrast proves to be that provided by the son to *both* the Father and Satan who are, ironically, alike in so many ways. Particularly in the matter of the interrelation of these three characters, Milton's inferences are often provocatively at variance with the conventional understanding of that very orthodox doctrine from which the poet draws his material. Milton's own practice, it then appears, was much like Blake's in its subversive determination to encourage the reader to test the validity of principles and beliefs he had hitherto accepted without question. Milton proves to have been in search and service of truth and vision, even when he occasionally was misled. Blake's contention, after all, is that Milton, like

Jesus in *Paradise Regained*, returned enlightened and fortified from his experience in the wilderness of self-doubt.

Blake recognizes that Satan's seemingly heroic resistance to dictatorship rests, finally, upon incorrect—indeed, indefensible—motives that directly influence his own mental, imaginative fall. While Satan does initially represent a form of passion (or desire) in revolt against restrictive reason, any favorable assessment of Satan as hero is quickly undercut by the recognition—Blake's and ours—that he is motivated, as Shelley observes, by pride and self-aggrandizement, isolationist impulses of division and separation closely related to the narcissism Blake so abhorred. Satan, we discover, rebels, not because he recognizes the oppressive rationalism of the Father, but simply because his pride is injured.

The paradoxical result of Satan's fall is that he sets up, both in hell and in himself, a parodic counterpart to the arrangement in heaven. In *Milton* Blake has the awakened Milton accuse Satan of monstrous deceit and perversion at plate 38. Satan's audacious retort is fraught with massive, self-delusive irony that reveals his parodic situation:

> Satan heard! Coming in a cloud, with trumpets & flaming fire,
> Saying I am God the judge of all, the living & the dead
> Fall therefore down & worship me. submit thy supreme
> Dictate, to my eternal Will & to my dictate bow
> I hold the Balances of Right & Just & mine the Sword
> Seven Angels bear my Name & in those Seven I appear
> But I alone am God & I alone in Heavn & Earth
> Of all that live dare utter this.
> [*M* 38.50–57; E, pp. 138–39]

Still, even after this revelation, Satan is "permitted . . . to imitate" the God of Eternity (*M* 39.25–26; E, p. 139). That he *is* so permitted to exist by the Father cements still further the connection between the two. As Blake frequently observes, the two figures are nearly interchangeable; hence Blake can address them in the epilogue to *The Gates of Paradise* as "The Accuser who is The God of This World" (E, p. 266). This crucial dilemma of identification sets up for every man the eternal possibility—indeed the absolute necessity—for drawing the distinction between the genuine and the false: every individual must define and repudiate his own Satanic selfhood in order to integrate his personality as Milton does in Blake's epic.

In *Paradise Lost* the perversion of Satan's reasoning is illustrated by his institution in hell of all the evils of the heaven he has vacated. Ideally, his gesture of resistance ought to have been the correct one; further, he ought to have been able to subvert heaven by turning its terms against themselves and thereby exposing the shortcomings of the original. But subversion carried on for the sole purpose of irritation and disruption is an ignoble end in a heroic struggle of the proportions of *Paradise Lost*. Subversion of the sort Satan undertakes involves only a niggling attempt to frustrate the opposition; it offers no positive, constructive action, no viable alternative. By engaging in such subversion simply for self-gratification, as Comus had done in Milton's masque with equal disregard for the consequences to the humans involved, Satan demonstrates his littleness. Satan's hell and the Father's heaven are both fallen states, organized on elaborate hierarchical principles and governed by fiat. Thus we are told in *The Marriage* that "it indeed appear'd to Reason as if Desire was cast out, but the Devils account is, that the Messiah fell. & formed a heaven of what he stole from the Abyss" (*MHH*, pls. 5–6; E, p. 34). From this perspective the Son might appear culpable in his mere acceptance of the position assigned him by the Father, were it not that in his performance in the epic—and by extension in the world of man—he transcends the narrowness of both systems, replacing them with one that venerates him instead.

Blake could not fail to appreciate Milton's use of the aesthetic pattern of parallel with difference, a pattern that is, in fact, one of the most consistent structural devices in Milton's poetry.[28] This pattern inherently suggests the sort of dynamic tension Blake developed and elaborated in his doctrine of contraries. The war in heaven, continued on earth, becomes a convenient metaphor for the "Mental Fight" Blake perceives as the essence of the conflict of contraries in the human soul. In this context we can see that man in *Paradise Lost* becomes very much the dramatic equivalent of the Lady in *Comus*, though the stakes are infinitely higher: he becomes the object of the warring contraries, both the battleground and the prize. As had been the case in *Comus*, the active opposition here of the superior, supernatural forces (which are essentially still man's own psychological inclinations or selves) is absolutely essential if man is to progress by the internal and imaginative process of recognizing and rejecting error, externalizing his embraces of truth in assertive physical acts.

The difference between the Lady, on one hand, and Adam and Eve, on the other, is that while Blake considers the former mentally paralyzed and therefore incapable of making the requisite choice entailing recognition and rejection of error, he recognizes the latter's innate ability to choose. Adam and Eve make wrong choices, of course, and they fall as a result. But the insight they gain from their wrong choices helps them to make the correct choices later on. Having departed Innocence and struggled with Experience, they can now properly attempt a marriage of the contraries, a reconciliation that will enable them to enter the superior imaginative state wherein they are more likely to choose wisely and informedly. Yet neither are Adam and Eve the hero and heroine in Blake's reading of the poem, though they are the principal beneficiaries of the poem's action. In their original, unfallen state their affairs are governed by the unity and integration represented in their mutual, selfless love. With the Fall, that loving unity disintegrates into focus upon self, into lust and resultant shame and accusation, all manifestations of separateness. Milton resolves the imbalance, to Blake's dissatisfaction, by invoking the doctrine of temperance, "the legitimacy of restrained enjoyment being duly defended and the real temptation in *Paradise Lost* being interpreted simply as that of sinful excess."[29] In this respect *Paradise Lost* would appear to be both an echo and an expansion of *Comus*, another point Blake surely perceived with considerable dismay.

The culpability of the act of separation is built into the poem, but it has too often been overlooked by those attempting to oversimplify the Fall by associating it carelessly with the sexual activity of Adam and Eve. Blake was painfully aware of this latter tendency, as his remark to Crabb Robinson on 17 December 1825 indicates: "I saw Milton, and he told me to beware of being misled by his 'Paradise Lost.' In particular, he wished me to show the falsehood of the doctrine, that carnal pleasures arose from the Fall. The fall could not produce any pleasure." Milton had, after all, dealt explicitly with the healthy prelapsarian sexuality of Adam and Eve (8.500–520). For Blake, the Fall is a matter of dis-integration, of separation and division that destroys the imaginative unity represented in the prelapsarian mutualism of Adam and Eve's experience. It is, as Anne Mellor has suggested, a private mental event that occurs whenever man subscribes to error, "contracts his imaginative vision, denies his mortal body as sinful flesh, and represses or perverts his Energy."[30] When man's creative, integrative energies—the manifestations of the healthy imagination—are mistakenly channeled into the creation and perpetuation of guilt, man enters his fallen state, typically demonstrating his fallenness by further overt acts of physical or mental disintegration and alienation. Hence in *Paradise Lost* their mental separation and fall is paralleled by the physical separation of Eve from Adam in book 9. The suggestion of a reconciliation by a taming of the passions ("take heed lest Passion sway / Thy Judgment to do aught, which else free Will / Would not admit" (8.635–37), a curbing of natural mental and physical desire, is also distasteful to Blake, for in his discussion of the circumstances of their repentance in book 9, Milton states a doctrine of abject subordination of man before God, a doctrine of limitation Blake identifies as puritanical, orthodox, and therefore to be resisted. Besides, Blake has already told us in *The Marriage* that the key to seeing the world correctly lies in "an improvement of sensual enjoyment":

> If the doors of perception were cleansed every thing would appear to man as it is, infinite.
> For man has closed himself up, till he sees all things thro' narrow chinks of his cavern. [*MHH*, pl. 14; E, p. 39]

If this cleansing is ever to be accomplished, desire cannot arbitrarily be limited in the manner Raphael suggests to Adam in book 8, even in the interests of what the moral establishment regards as temperance.

We have already seen in the case of the Lady in *Comus* that temperance is a virtue to be *discovered*, an alternative to be chosen insightfully: it cannot be *imposed* externally and in violation of man's natural right of free choice. The compound fall of Adam and Eve is one of incorrect choices: excess is chosen over moderation, the choice is condemned, and the participants are punished. Having learned their lessons painfully, Adam and Eve emerge from Eden fallen but better prepared to choose again in the further temptations that must inevitably await them in the wilderness that is their new home. The pair do learn from their experience, though, validating Blake's Devil's proverb that "the road of excess leads to the palace of wisdom" (*MHH*, pl. 7; E, p. 35). The renewed progress of Adam and Eve is indicated by their reintegration at the poem's conclusion. That reintegration, we should recall, is externally represented by a purely sensual detail, the joining of hands, an act that looks forward to the spiritual and imaginative reintegration we assume is yet to come as Adam relates to Eve the vision of salvation Michael has presented him.

The suggestion that Blake *originally* read *Paradise Lost* as a poem without a hero, then, proves legitimate. As he saw it, all characters displayed flashes of heroism, but none was able to maintain his heroic posture uncompromised, not even the Son. Blake placed the blame on this seeming deficiency squarely on Milton. As noted earlier, one can regard Milton the poet as the one and only possible hero of the poem. But in Blake's early reading Milton proves not a complete hero—a true prophetic bard—but rather a bard gone astray—a prophet in captivity. If we accept Milton's conception of the role of the poet as that of the prophet of God, the herald of ideals that know no compromise with evil, then we are right to examine his role in *Paradise Lost*, where he speaks within the dramatic logic of the poem as "the inspired seer whose transcendental vision extends beyond the limited, fallen experience of the reader."[31] As part of his narrative posture, in other words, Milton assumes his place in the succession of visionary poet-prophets.

Blake initially objects strenuously to Milton's performance, however, accusing him of deliberately taming his vision, corrupting its purity, and reducing it to an allegory of moral good and moral evil, forcing upon it the fetters of unimaginative orthodoxy. It seemed to Blake that Milton exhibited in the poem the Puritan tendency to view in every aspect of human experience a moral conflict.[32] These conflicts he resolved by calling into play rationalistic doctrines that seemed to Blake to deny their imaginative import, much in the manner in which the Lady responds to Comus.

For Blake, the imperative for independence of vision is both clear and legitimate. Henri Peyre has commented insightfully on this point:

Let us not cherish the illusion that an artist is great because he imitates or expresses his own times, and thus adds sociological value to his idle imaginative creations: nonconformity, or even bitter revolt against their age and environment, has been a far more common characteristic of great artists than acceptance or sympathy.[33]

In Blake's eyes Milton would have done better simply to have declared his poetic and intellectual independence as he had in the *Nativity Ode*, for Milton's decision to work within the intellectual and theological system, reorganizing from within, seems ultimately to produce infidelity to the very vision that motivated the decision and informed the epic. It was not until *Paradise Regained*, in Blake's opinion, that Milton achieved that genuine fidelity. All the major poetry preceding it had been, to a significant extent, written in fetters. Even when he came to reassess *Paradise Lost*, Blake could not bring himself to credit Milton with a wholly flawless and successful work, but maintained his contention that the poet had needlessly and detrimentally obscured his vision.

Blake has been regarded all too frequently as a literal Satanist, particularly by those who misread works like *The Marriage* by assuming that the voice of the Devil is Blake's voice. But to categorize Blake in such an easy manner is mistakenly to ignore the context of those supposedly Satanist remarks. The speaker in plates 5 and 6 of *The Marriage* is, after all, the Devil; naturally enough, he delivers his ironic commentary from the demonic point of view. With a masterful sense of dramatic irony, Blake allows his Devil to present an extreme view that is, in its own way, as far left of the truth as Milton's epic is right of it.[34] Blake leaves it to the perceptive reader to work out the disparities correctly in arriving at the truth. If we are to call Blake a Satanist at all, we can only do so in the same sense in which we can term Milton also a Satanist: we must expand our definition beyond the conventional. Wittreich reminds us that "in its earliest historical meanings . . . 'Satanism' was employed as a pejorative and referred to anyone who challenged prevailing religious opinions or moral values, to *any* inquiring spirit, whether he was a religionist or atheist."[35] In this sense of radical mentality the term legitimately applies to Blake and Milton alike, as it does to any of the "great artists" to whom Peyre alludes.

What, then, was the nature of Milton's captivity? His fetters were imaginative ones, comprised of dogmatic conceptions the poet sought to weave into the fabric of his poem, conceptions that generations of critics had further reinforced in readers' minds by their disproportionate attention to them. Leland Ryken makes the important point that "in writing his poem doctrinal to his nation, Milton was using as his material an established story and theological system. He did not have to prove that God is good and Satan is evil."[36] But while he did not *have to* do so, conventional commentary on the poem reveals a widespread belief that Milton had in fact set out to do just that. Certainly he seems to have felt that the ways of God needed to be "justified" to a puzzled and doubting humanity, as the famous lines at the end of the invocation indicate. Still, in order to "assert Eternal Providence" Milton had to subvert the established theological system upon which he drew because that system itself was the product of a fallen mentality that had come to focus upon retribution and wrath rather than upon integration, love, and "forgiveness of sins." Doing so created an underlying ambivalence sometimes characterized as schizophrenic that attempts to reconcile the orthodox views of the Fall, the Atonement, and the deprecation of sensual activity with an enlightened and benevolent visionary perspective on Milton's part.[37] Given these limitations, Milton's success is necessarily only partial. As Blake at last realized, though, Milton goes a long way toward accomplishing his revolutionary subversion by subtly implying the primacy of a strongly Christocentric faith as an alternative to the more conventional Christianity that, in exalting the wrathful God of retributive justice, "Crucifies Christ with the Head Downwards" (*VLJ*; E, p. 554). While in Milton's poem the Father is proven *legally* right in his dealings, the ethical and humanistic implications of the poem make a stronger case for the more humane, more attractive Son.

Milton, and Blake after him, perceived that the Fall and its consequences are not reducible to simple terms. Gradations of guilt and accountability, degrees of good and evil, of right and wrong, are complicated matters, and invoking the old absolutes—Satan equals evil, the Father equals good—grossly oversimplifies a most complex situation. Even the blanket use of the nondifferentiating term *God* troubles the two poets. *God* proves a reducible term in both poets' work, dividing into the stern Jehovah–Father–Ancient of Days and the immediately attractive Christ-Son-Jesus and further demonstrating the limitations of inherited polarized nomenclature (God versus Satan) and value judgments (good versus evil). Particularly in Blake, there can be no refuge in a priori assumptions: everything must be tested *now*, on its own inherent merits and deficiencies, within a context of continually fluctuating intellectual and imaginative values. "The God of This World" is not necessarily *the* God: it all depends on who is doing the naming and from what mental condition. Milton set about recasting Christian mythology to bring it into line with his own visionary perception of the nature and values of eternity. That Milton worked with the mythology of the Bible does not indicate his automatic enslavement to it, but merely identifies his principal source. Blake finally recognized Milton's perceptive reading of the central episode of man's fall and redemption, and he sought to free it from the conservative and mistaken critical tradition that had labored to demonstrate Milton's endorsement of much of orthodoxy the poet had actually renounced.

In writing of Satan and his crew, for instance, Milton could draw upon very little from the Bible itself, for the bulk of writings concerning them consisted of secondary theological and exegetical documents, though as Roland Frye has demonstrated, he also drew to a large extent upon the iconography of visual art. Because these were not primary source materials—because they were not Scripture—Milton willingly appropriated and transformed them for his own artistic purposes. For the rest of the materials on the rebels, Milton's own imagination was the primary source. For passages dealing with God and the heavenly scene, however, Milton draws a proportionally greater amount of material from the Bible and makes significantly fewer changes in it, seemingly asserting an a priori acceptance of much that he found there and a reluctance to embroider upon the Bible in this area.[38]

To the extent that Milton was unable or unwilling to overcome his Puritan ethical and theological heritage, even in the interests of his own poetic vision, which he seemed to recognize as conflicting with much of that heritage, to that extent was he in fetters. In his unwillingness to repudiate the Father explicitly, Milton seemed to Blake originally to side with the repressive forces against the figure and values of the Son, whom his visionary imagination strove to proclaim hero.

There is a curious irony here that suggests a new perspective on Blake's note that Milton "was a true Poet and of the Devils party without knowing it" (*MHH*, pl. 6; E, p. 35). We should consider whether Blake may have intended, in using the word "and" as he does in this line, to suggest that the designations on either side of it were simultaneously applicable; that is, that Milton was at the same moment both a true poet—a bard of prophetic insight—and a fallen angel—a slave to and victim of a destructive mental system based upon the debilitating false premises of pride, self-gratification, and separation. In *The Marriage* Blake's Devil is not the traditional, totally negative figure; this we might expect in light of the devil's advocate point of view from which *The Marriage* is written. Besides, to a devil the revolutionary poet appears a devil and comrade himself: he is a Satanist in the sense of nonconformity to which Wittreich and Peyre allude. Hence Milton is a true poet in that *Paradise Lost* does attempt to subvert orthodoxy in the interests of vision and truth. But to undertake the composition of a poem like *Paradise Lost* is to walk a very tricky tightrope. To be at once a "good, God-fearing" (notice the implicit suggestion there) Christian in the traditional sense *and* a radical, subversive prophet asserting a system grounded in love, not fear, involves imaginative gymnastics of the most extraordinary and exhausting sort. When he wrote *The Marriage*, Blake felt that the subversion had misfired, that Milton had ended up in service to "God and Angels."

Viewed from Blake's early perspective, Milton appears in *Paradise Lost* the apologist for a proud, rationalistic definer of justice based upon an abstract system of hierarchies. Instinctively opposed to traditional and restrictive systematization, Milton is, like Satan, still bound by his own imaginative fall, so that he likewise becomes narrow and intolerant, unable to make the correct aesthetic and intellectual choices. Rebelling for the right reasons, Milton at first seems to Blake to become a mouthpiece for the orthodox doctrinal tradition he ought to be undermining. He is himself a parallel to the Son he appears to create: a visionary, humanitarian figure who falls through his unquestioning and subordinate devotion to the Father away from heroism and into error. Blake's paradoxical note in *The Marriage* provides both a basis for and an explanation of Blackstone's comment that the remark lays bare the contradiction the reader senses in Milton's poetry "between the Puritan and the man of the Renaissance, or between the imaginative artist with all his love of beauty and the ascetic for whom chastity is the prime virtue."[39] The conflict involves as always the eternal and salutary conflict of contraries, culminating in repeated aesthetic and intellectual choices, choices in which Blake initially judges Milton to have erred significantly.

In assessing Blake's response to book 3, particularly his early response, we should entertain the possibility that he, like so many of Milton's other critics, may have misread the book and underestimated the degree to which Milton actually elevates the Son. The picture we get of the Son in book 3 is surely more innately attractive than any we get of the Father. Milton seems to have invited his readers to make the comparison themselves and to recognize thereby that it is the Son whom the poem elevates to heroic stature. The Son, finally, is the one who makes the really critical choice. That the choice is made quickly, without the elaborate preparation we see for the choices of Adam and Eve, should not mislead us into underestimating either its correctness or its absolute centrality to the poem. In further comparing Father and Son, Milton's readers would also have been led to the related perception that the Son is motivated by the demands of love, not justice, and that his concern for man's salvation is what elevates him. Milton invokes orthodox doctrine to subvert it, to be sure. But because there is so much of that doctrine to be invoked and so much narrative detail to be marshaled, the actual subversion tends to become obscured in the process.

Blake chastizes Milton verbally for the reversion to dogma that subsequently diverted the epic's focus away from the Son. The *Paradise Lost* designs aim at liberating the epic's central vision from its encumbrances. Two designs, *The Son Offers to Redeem Man* and *Michael Foretells the Crucifixion*, serve to emphasize the point. While the Son's offer is the climactic event of book 3, Milton surrounds it with so much additional detail, so much celestial celebration, however appropriate, that its real significance was clouded for many of the poem's verbal and visual commentators. That this is so is proved by the illustrations to book 3 before Blake's, a considerable number of which abandoned the Son's offer altogether in favor of some depiction of Satan and Uriel, whose meeting at the end of book 3 was apparently more congenial to the artists' desire to depict dramatic or sentimental tableaux. Those illustrators who depicted the scene in heaven often did so only in a generalized fashion, again at the expense of the specific moment of choice Milton sought to underscore. Rejecting previous visual misreadings and reasserting the overwhelming significance of the Son's offer, Blake directly isolates and emphasizes that offer in his design for book 3. Similarly, while Milton devotes relatively little space to the fulfillment of the Son's offer in the course of Michael's long narrative, Blake singles it out dramatically in his design. By means of such visual isolation and highlighting Blake removes the obstructing narrative and the misdirected visual responses to it so that we may clearly discern the foci of Milton's poem.

Blake did not number his *Paradise Lost* designs, nor did he inscribe on them any quotations from the text, another fashionable practice, particularly with engraved book illustrations. Neither did Blake bind his designs, nor, since they were not executed as book illustrations in the usual sense, did he make any notation as to where they might stand in a printed text. Strongly antichronological in nature, Blake's designs resist strict narrative organization. While we can arrange them in an order that approximates that of the text, we quickly discover that

Blake's subtle repetition of visual motifs—themes, gestures, postures, and compositional techniques—suggests a complex interrelationship among designs and characters. Northrop Frye's observation concerning *Milton* is relevant here as well: what is said in *Milton*, as in the *Paradise Lost* designs (and in the other Milton illustrations) presents the context of the poet's or the illustrator's moment of insight "as a single simultaneous pattern of apprehension. Hence it does not form a narrative, but recedes spatially, as it were, from that moment."[40] As is the case in some of the earliest known depictions of the Fall, Blake abandons the narrative separation between the Fall and Redemption, fusing the two in such a way as to imply that nothing be interposed between them. Blake recognizes the essential paradox epitomized in the poem's title: the poem that takes its name from the *loss* of paradise takes as its most important episode, not the loss, but the *regaining* of paradise through the Son's paradigmatic act of self-annihilation and spiritual reintegration. Blake perceived this essential truth and sought to emphasize it in his designs. Likewise, he ultimately realized that the perception was indeed Milton's, but that the poet himself had seemingly lost track of it. Recognizing that Milton had been his own worst enemy, Blake set about liberating Milton's original vision by correcting, through verbal and visual means, the elements of error with which Milton had obscured that vision.

Chapter 4: The Tradition of *Paradise Lost* Illustration

The tradition of *Paradise Lost* illustration that Blake inherited is a rich and complex one, occasionally brilliant, but more often fraught with the sort of critical errors that characterize the verbal tradition of criticism. Too often, illustrators failed to study Milton's text or, when they did examine it, fell victim to the sort of misreadings being advanced by careless verbal critics. Placed in the awkward position of frequently having the style or content of their designs dictated by editors or tampered with by engravers, either or both of whom were often insensitive or misinformed, illustrators sometimes produced visual hybrids indebted more to the interpretation—or taste—currently in vogue, or to peripheral and irrelevant matters, than to either the letter or the spirit of Milton's epic. Few illustrators were as fully in control of the execution of their designs as Blake was of his. Once completed, their designs were customarily handed over to another artist—the engraver—for reproduction. Often, significant corruption of the original occurred at this stage. The engraved illustrations would then be placed in the printed copy as the editor directed, and it was not at all unusual, apparently, for designs to be bound in the wrong places within a volume or even in the wrong volumes altogether. Some illustrations appeared on pages opposite the passages they were intended to illustrate; others were considerably separated from the relevant lines. Most commonly, illustrations were placed at the beginning of each book of the epic, or when the epic was issued in several volumes, a single design might stand as frontispiece to each individual volume in the set. Obviously, the most effective *and faithful* placement of a particular illustration would seem to involve locating the design opposite the passage it illustrates, though this procedure generally disrupts the formal order of a uniform volume because the pictures appear at irregular intervals.

To place a book's illustration at the beginning, as frontispiece to a particular book of *Paradise Lost* (or of any other work, for that matter), is to imply that the scene represented in the picture possesses particular importance, that it is an epitome or a synopsis of that book's action or vision, a forecast of what the text will reveal. This hazardous procedure is clearly undertaken for aesthetic purposes of consistency in format—for mechanical or editorial rather than for interpretive reasons—and generally in violation of the spirit of the text. Being a graphic representation in a different and more sensually immediate medium, any illustration tends automatically to underscore the significance of the scene it depicts. Receiving such a visual stimulus at the outset of a book, the reader frequently proceeds in expectation of having that same scene unfolded for him in the text, and he quite naturally recalls the illustration when he encounters Milton's verbal account. If the illustration is indeed an epitome of the book, its utilitarian purpose is fused with its aesthetic impact: it instructs even as it emphasizes and delights. Unhappily, however, a significant number of the eighteenth-century Milton illustrations are quite out of balance with the text they accompany.

Perhaps the most glaring examples of this sort of critical imbalance occur in the illustrations for books 3 and 12. Unquestionably the key to book 3, indeed to the entire epic, involves the Son's offer to die for man. Yet illustrators favored, almost unanimously, the scene at the end of the book in which Satan approaches Uriel disguised as a young angel. Presented as the only illustration to book 3, as it generally was, this depiction of Satan and Uriel necessarily deflects attention away from the Son's offer, especially when it is placed as frontispiece to the book. This sort of critically inappropriate illustration stems from a desire on the illustrator's—or publisher's—part to portray moments of dramatic potential in the theatrical sense. Rather than grapple with the difficult imaginative abstractions of the Son's offer—or, for that matter, of the speech of the Father that occasions it—illustrators turned to a concrete scene easily represented in terms of conventional heavenly iconography, replete with the inevitable wings and fluffy clouds. Since most illustrators focus upon Satan in their designs for books 1 and 2, repeating him again in book 3, even in his disguise, perpetuates his presence for the reader despite Milton's clear emphasis in this book upon the introduction of the Son and his paradigmatic offer of self-sacrifice.

The case of the Expulsion scene, for book 12, is somewhat different. Here most illustrators portray the obligatory moment of eviction from Eden. But for nearly a century that moment is depicted in visual terms that are clearly at variance with Milton's poem. While Milton concludes his poem on a note of hope, detailing the mental and physical reintegration of Adam and Eve (who leave holding hands) and the promise of redemption, illustrators of this scene customarily show the pair violently driven out in suffering and despair. Not until the end of the eighteenth century do any illustrators return to this scene any real measure of that strong sense of hope Milton makes central to his poem's conclusion. And it remains for Blake fully to elaborate the promise of redemption and the sense of hope generated therein. While hope may not be readily apparent in the conventional Puritan view of life in the mortal world, and while illustrators before Blake may have neglected Milton's hopeful conclusion as a result of their own contrary conditioning by orthodoxy and convention, we must note that Milton specifically rejects the traditional hopeless view of man's fallen state. In fact, he places his assertion of hope in the highly visible *closing lines* of his epic, where it registers as a final impression in the reader's mind. Whether the conventional violent Expulsion illustration is placed at the book's head, then (suggesting epitome), or opposite the lines it purports to illustrate and therefore at the very end of the poem (suggesting the conclusion), such an illustration misinterprets Milton's poem at a decisive pass and further ensures the reader's misreading.

The critical power and influence of the illustrator is exceedingly great, perhaps greater even than that of the verbal critic whose essays were frequently subjoined in editions of *Paradise Lost*. While the reader might well ignore an essay tacked on at the end or parceled out in fine print at the base of the pages, he can scarcely avoid the illustrations. Hence the illustrator is intimately involved in shaping the reader's perceptions, and to the same degree that his visual representations are inaccurate or misleading, the interpretations of the reader are likely to be confused or mistaken. It becomes necessary, then, for us to undertake both general and particular observations on the whole tradition of *Paradise Lost* illustration in order to assess Blake's designs more accurately. This tradition has been tentatively surveyed by C. H. Collins Baker, within the larger context of Milton illustration in general by Marcia Pointon, and in the area of Milton's own visual sources by Roland Frye.[1] The present discussion sets out to assess the import and direction of that visual tradition particularly as it relates to Blake's designs to *Paradise Lost*.

Paradise Lost illustration began with Jacob Tonson's edition of 1688, which contained twelve full-page designs, one for each book. Those designs to books 1, 2, and 12 were done by Henry Aldrich, the design to book 4 by Bernard Lens, and the others by John Baptist Medina.[2] Medina, in particular, appears to have taken his role very seriously, attempting not merely to decorate the text but to interpret it as well. His reading of the poem is thorough and generally accurate, and all his designs reflect careful attention to Milton's details.

Involved as he was in a pioneer project, preparing the first illustrations for the epic, Medina found himself in a unique position. Having no direct visual precedent upon which to base his designs to the poem, he turned naturally to an element of iconographic tradition that *was* readily available: the tradition of biblical illustration, from which he appropriated elements of both form and format, of conception and detail. A number of his designs are synoptic: they combine several scenes or episodes, often depicting the same characters but in different postures or situations, within single designs. Synoptic illustration is common in traditional biblical illustration, particularly for scenes from Genesis and the Fall, and is exemplified, for instance, by Michelangelo's Sistine depiction of the Fall, in which Adam and Eve are shown both before and after their fall, on either side of a single tree. As J. B. Trapp tells us, there exists in the early iconography of the Fall the tendency to contract or telescope the episodes of the temptation of Eve, the temptation of Adam, the actual Fall, and the hiding of nakedness into one or at most two scenes. This tendency, particularly apparent in early Christian art, never really disappears in the Western tradition.[3] Medina telescopes scenes repeatedly to summarize all the major events of individual books. He thus avoids the danger of disproportionately elevating one scene over another that inevitably results when an episodic design, representing only a single scene, is employed. But the synoptic technique is generally less successful visually, tending to become cluttered or confusing.

Medina seems to have preferred the synoptic technique, for he employs it for his designs to books 5, 7, 9, 10, and 11. Lens's design for book 4 is also synoptic.[4] Medina's other designs employ a related technique of composition best described as mixed. These designs—to books 3, 6, and 8—depict centrally one event or incident, surrounding that central depiction with visual references to details, contexts, and implications drawn from elsewhere in the poem and not immediately present in Milton's description of the central scene. Such mixed designs attempt to invoke a wider context than the scene illustrated might ordinarily suggest; they invite the reader into this broader perspective by presenting the particular incident within a visual environment of its related (or accumulated) iconography. Through this mixed technique Medina draws together in single visual statements details separated in narrative time. In this respect the mixed designs are like the synoptic ones in their attempt visually to overcome the limitations of narrative time with its consequent isolation of linearly separated incidents. The mixed techniques of illustration gained popularity in the eighteenth century both for the illustration of *Paradise Lost* and, more particularly, for the detailing of various portraits of Milton which typically involved surrounding Milton's likeness with elements of the iconography derived from his poetry.

Compared to the productions of the illustrators who followed him, Medina's designs are stiff and archaic, almost crude in nature. Still, as first illustrations to the poem they are adequate and indeed display an admirable fidelity to Milton's purpose. The same cannot be said of Aldrich's designs to books 1, 2, and 12. Those to books 2 and 12 are episodic: they depict a single event only, with no repetition of characters or details, and employ large figures that dominate the designs. Even the design to book 1 (P, pl. 9), though it includes in the background a scene of Satan in Pandemonium, is essentially an episodic rather than a mixed design. All three of Aldrich's designs deviate significantly from the details of Milton's text and exhibit clear indebtedness to recognizable visual sources. The design to book 1, for instance, is very similar in conception to an engraving of Raphael's *St. Michael and the Devil* that Aldrich had in his collection. Likewise, Aldrich's design to book 2, (P, pl. 4) is based upon Andrea Mantegna's *The Descent into Limbo*, with the figures of Satan, Sin, and Death substituted for Mantegna's figures and with the background revised.[5] It is from Mantegna's picture that Aldrich most likely drew the three incongruous, demonic *putti* (or winged infants) that hover over Satan, Sin, and Death.

Aldrich's infidelity to Milton in his design to book 12 is far more

Figure 20. After Henry Aldrich. *The Expulsion 1688. By permission of the British Library, London*

significant. In his version of the Expulsion scene (fig. 20), Aldrich ignores Milton's text and simply copies Raphael's Expulsion scene, providing, not a creative, interpretive illustration, but, rather, an entirely inappropriate and misleading one. Aldrich's design subscribes to the conventional conception of the woeful, despairing state in which Adam and Eve supposedly had been evicted from paradise.[6] Aldrich unwisely illustrated the traditional view of the Expulsion, the orthodox ending the reader *expects* to get because of what he has been taught about the Fall, and in so doing he distorted Milton's conclusion, which subverts those customary expectations by positing the relative optimism provided by faith and hope, by physical and psychological reintegration. Aldrich misses, or chooses to ignore, this positive note. Aldrich's erroneous visual conclusion tends significantly to obscure and undermine the verbal conclusion Milton provides us. Hence the final illustration both stimulates and reinforces the reader's confused or incorrect reading of the poem's conclusion. Depictions of the Expulsion between Aldrich's and Blake's demonstrate that the theme of woeful banishment predominates for over a century. Illustrators turn repeatedly, not to the appropriate precedent of Milton's text, but to the precedent within the tradition of their own visual medium: Aldrich's misleading design and the Renaissance iconography of the Expulsion that stands behind it.

One other point concerning the designs of Medina and Aldrich deserves mention here: their treatment of Satan. With no visual precedent upon which to draw in depicting Milton's Satan, they evolved a figure combining the traditional devil of biblical illustration and an Italianate satyr (P, pls. 3, 4, 9).[7] Here, once again, Medina and Aldrich established a precedent widely followed by their successors. They were likewise followed in their choice of antique Roman military garb and equipment for Satan; traces of this iconographic tradition persist even in Blake's designs, though Blake quotes the tradition only in the weaponry of his naked figures.

Although the designs by Medina and Aldrich were reengraved and republished, in increasingly deplorable condition, through 1784, the next set of illustrations for *Paradise Lost* appeared in 1720. Jacob Tonson's new edition of Milton's works included twelve headpieces, twelve tailpieces, and twelve detailed initial letters of the poem. Sir James Thornhill designed the headpiece to book 1 (P, pl. 16); all other designs are the work of Louis Cheron. Tonson's edition was a lavish and expensive one, which may account for the fact that it never again appeared in its original form; a 1724 edition, for example, incorporates only the twelve headpieces.

The designs reflect the style of French classicism and tend to be repetitive in visual arrangement. They are less faithful to Milton's textual details than Medina's illustrations, exhibiting if anything an even greater dependence upon the iconography of biblical illustrations. This reliance is scarcely surprising, though, since Thornhill and Cheron had done the illustrations for an Oxford Bible that had appeared in 1717.[8] Cheron's appropriation of visual suggestions from the Bible illustrations for use in his *Paradise Lost* designs is both inevitable and perhaps even fitting in some respects. But the important point is that his designs display Cheron's consistent effort to fuse the iconography of *Paradise Lost* with the more firmly established and traditional iconography of the Bible, thus visually reimposing upon the epic the conventional visual apparatus of the very religious system upon which Milton had worked his subtle but significant variations. This fusion, of course, broadens the context within which *Paradise Lost* is presented visually, but it contributes at the same time to the infidelity to Milton's text and purpose that was increasingly to characterize eighteenth-century illustrations.

The use of three illustrations per book enabled Cheron to approach his task as illustrator in a different manner than had Medina and Aldrich. Most notably, he was able to abandon the synoptic technique, employing instead designs that are entirely episodic. Likewise, utilizing major designs at both beginning and end of each book allowed him a greater flexibility in subject selection, a fact that also explains some of the designs' repetitive nature. For some of the books, Cheron appears to have been hard pressed to devise illustrations. Hence we occasionally encounter designs that are more decorative (although iconographically related) than illuminative. Such designs occur as tailpieces, as for instance those to books 1, 2, and 5: a display of the wrecked armory of the rebel angels, a vignette assembling the iconography of Milton's Sin, and a pair of interwoven cornucopias. These designs are, however, the exception to the rule of generally pertinent scene depiction that characterizes Cheron's tailpieces.

Cheron's headpieces (and Thornhill's) portray the central episode of each book, with the exception of that to book 10, "Sin and Death in the Garden" (P, pl. 22), showing the angels leaving Eden and deflecting attention away from the far more significant act of the Son's judgment of Adam and Eve. While Cheron attempts little background detail in his views of heaven and hell, he depicts in considerable detail the lush Edenic landscape both before and after the Fall. This concern with the landscape is important in the overall consideration of *Paradise Lost* illustration as it was, for the most part, maintained by succeeding illustrators like Thomas Stothard and E. F. Burney and subsequently developed as a *central* and predominating feature by such nineteenth-century illustrators as John Martin and Gustave Doré, a point that finds an interesting parallel in the eighteenth- and nineteenth-century interest in landscape and gardening.[9] Cheron's headpieces, however, possess little intrinsic dramatic value. They typically include only a few figures (Thornhill's depiction of Satan's legions for book 1 is the single exception), and these figures are generally presented in academically static and statuesque tableaux. Cheron's infidelity to Milton's text is most obvious in his designs to books 2 and 12. The first, *Satan, Sin, and Death* (P, pl. 17), is even more inappropriate than Aldrich's illustration. Cheron's Death is merely a skeleton holding a scythe, his Sin a muscular, blindfolded female figure struggling with a number of serpents that coil about her. Satan's confrontation with them is anything but dramatic. Further, Satan appears to have risen out of a rift in the earth, trapdoor fashion, from which flames belch up behind him. Behind Satan we glimpse yet another demonic figure, wingless but with pointed ears like Satan's, though book 2 nowhere suggests the presence of any other figures than the customary trio during the confrontation at the gate of hell. The design for book 12 (P, pl. 24) is also more unfaithful to Milton than Aldrich's, portraying the same Raphaelesque Expulsion scene but suffusing it with an even more violent and despairing atmosphere. Indebted to the originals of both Raphael and Aldrich, Cheron's designs add to the iconography of this scene, slithering away behind Eve's feet, a coiling serpent.[10]

Both the potential advantage and the practical disadvantage of using tailpieces as well as headpieces are demonstrated in book 12. While the headpiece depicts (however mistakenly) the violent Expulsion, the tailpiece, appearing as it does after the final lines of the poem, provides yet another shift in critical emphasis, a shift that proves in this case also to be essentially inappropriate. Cheron's tailpiece (fig. 21) shows a scene in heaven in which the Son appears seated upon a cloud, surrounded by reverential angels, looking and extending his arm upward—presumably toward the Father. His left hand supports a large cross that occupies the right center of the design, while its base rests upon the crushed head of a serpent that coils about the base of the design. The intent of the design is ambiguous, perhaps intentionally so; it may be meant to suggest the Son risen after his crucifixion and death, or it may be a reference to either his offer to redeem man (book 3) or the promise of that act's completion (book 12). Most likely we are expected to recall all three interrelated aspects of the single act. The tailpiece also makes visual reference to the headpiece to book 3 (P, pl. 18) and the tailpiece to book 6, both of which include the Son, the cross, and a group of attendant angels. While Cheron's tailpiece does perform a final unifactory function, redirecting the attention of the reader-viewer back to the promise of man's redemption, it remains a critically unsatisfactory visual cue, for it overlooks Milton's intentional concluding focus upon the departure of Adam and Eve from Eden.

Figure 21. After Louis Cheron. Tailpiece, *Paradise Lost*, book 12. 1720. *By permission of the British Library, London*

Figure 22. After Louis Cheron. Initial letter, *Paradise Lost*, book 4. 1720. *By permission of the British Library, London*

Numerous advantages derive from the use of multiple illustrations for each book, of course, and Cheron's designs for book 4 provide a good example. His headpiece (P, pl. 19) depicts Adam and Eve peacefully conversing in Eden, surrounded by placid animals and the pleasant landscape. Beneath this design, on the same page, appears the initial letter: a Roman capital O (fig. 22). The expanded letter itself constitutes an oval frame within which we see in a close-up view Satan disguised as the cormorant, perched on a tree branch. Outside the letter we see in wide-angle view the tree in which Satan perches. Thus the initial letter adds interestingly to the iconography of this particular book a detail that could not easily and strikingly be worked into the headpiece. Finally, the tailpiece represents a scene from the end of book 4 (essentially ll. 866–76), showing Ithuriel and Zephon presenting the cowering Satan to Gabriel (P, pl. 15). Though the awkward, animal fear manifested in Satan's appearance conflicts with the suggestions of Milton's text, this scene, taken with those scenes in the headpiece and the initial letter, does effectively remind the reader of the dual presence in Eden in book 4 of both Adam and Eve, on one hand, and Satan in his various forms, on the other. This visual reminder is, of course, quite appropriate to book 4, particularly since Cheron's next headpiece (P, pl. 32) returns the reader visually to the peaceful setting of Eden in book 5 which is so soon to be subverted.

Similarly, the headpiece to book 3 (P, pl. 18) shows the Son in heaven with attendant angels genuflecting at the right and supporting the cross—into the base of which one nail has already been driven—at the left. This iconographic suggestion of the Crucifixion is then followed in the tailpiece to book 3 by a version of the scene that was to supplant it among most eighteenth-century illustrators: the meeting of Satan and Uriel.

Cheron's treatment of book 9 is particularly striking. The headpiece (P, pl. 21) depicts the temptation and fall of Adam and Eve, assembling in a single design details from the entire temptation sequence. At the center of the design Eve holds in her right hand the fruit she has apparently taken from the jaws of the serpent wrapped around the tree at the left. With her left hand Eve offers the fruit to Adam, who is about to accept it, despite a warning glance from the open-mouthed dog lying beside him.[11] This design is followed by the initial letter *N*, behind which stands an open songbook with a lyre-shaped branch of thorns growing over it. The tailpiece to this book (fig. 23), though, is of greatest interest as an early example of symbolic interpretation. Adam and Eve are perilously separated by a female figure whose breasts and Medusa-like snaky hair (like that in the tailpiece to book 3) identify her as Sin. She extends a pair of flaming torches or brands before her in visual anticipation of the flaming brand Michael places at the gate of Eden in book 12. Adam and Eve recoil from Sin and her torches, their mutual shrinking gestures further emphasizing their physical separation from one another, which would appear to be Cheron's point. Cheron

Figure 23. After Louis Cheron. Tailpiece, *Paradise Lost*, book 9. 1720. *By permission of the British Library, London*

effectively represents here the guilt-induced division of Adam and Eve resulting from sin, from the Fall. Cheron's visual comment on the psychological consequences of the Fall adds a new element of symbolic significance to *Paradise Lost* illustration. But an illustration of this sort is atypical of the period; Milton's symbolism was only scantily explored by eighteenth-century illustrators. It was left for Fuseli and Blake to unlock this dimension of the poem.

The next major illustrations of *Paradise Lost* were executed by Francis Hayman in 1749 and were reengraved and republished frequently through 1818, an indication of their considerable popularity. Known less as a literary illustrator than as a decorative painter and a member of theatrical circles, Hayman nonetheless furnished a series of lively, striking designs, all episodic in nature. Hayman's designs exhibit two stylistic tendencies that undoubtedly reflect his theatrical orientation. First, he illustrates from each book the moment of greatest external dramatic action or potential, as he had done in the case of his single illustration to *Comus* (P, pl. 41). Hayman clearly prefers action to tableau. Hence his depiction of Satan, Sin, and Death (fig. 24) presents, not simply the familiar arrested action of the moment of confrontation, but rather the dramatic denouement: Satan's departure from his demonic kin. As in the *Comus* design, a dais figures in this design, further indicating Hayman's familiarity with the conventions of set design and the use of levels in the theatre. Second, his designs involve consistently fewer figures than previous illustrations had involved, generally portraying only two or three figures. Group scenes occur only in the designs for books 1 (and even there Satan and one companion predominate), 6 and 10 (P, pls. 42, 44, 45). The latter two involve the only depictions of God: the war in heaven and the Son judging Adam and Eve, scenes in which we naturally expect to encounter the conventional stage regalia befitting celestial royalty.

Hayman's insistence upon portraying smaller groups of characters stimulated a new tendency in pictorial criticism of *Paradise Lost*. Subsequent illustrators increasingly favored such stagings, which resulted in a growing number of dramatically conceived but academically executed figure studies. Even in Hayman's designs we can already see one important consequence of this tendency. For his illustration to book 3 (fig. 25) Hayman replaced the scene of the Son in heaven that Medina and Cheron had depicted in their designs (P, pls. 8, 18) with a scene that originates with Cheron's tailpiece to book 3: the meeting of Satan and Uriel. The great popularity of Hayman's designs firmly established this interview scene as the standard alternative—indeed the practical substitute—to the heavenly scene. The real importance of this change becomes apparent only when we realize that in replacing *The Son in Heaven* with some form of *Satan and Uriel* illustrators like Hayman shifted the focus of book 3 for readers, maintaining, in a book given over largely to heaven whose central incident is the Son's offer, the continued visual presence of Satan. With changes of this sort *Paradise Lost*

Figure 24. After Francis Hayman. *Satan, Sin, and Death*. 1749–53. *Stephen C. Behrendt Collection*

Figure 25. After Francis Hayman. *Satan and Uriel*. 1749–53. *Stephen C. Behrendt Collection*

illustration began to focus attention—mistakenly, to be sure—upon the figure of Satan at the expense of the Son.

Still, Hayman introduces some interesting new visual suggestions that exerted considerable influence on succeeding illustrations. His version of the rout of the rebel angels (P, pl. 45) substantially diminishes the overt militarism of the scene, suggesting that the routed angels are falling away from the very *presence* of the Son. Standing amid the clouds at the top of the design, the Son grasps a cluster of thunderbolts in his upraised right hand, while the unarmed angels around him look on in admiration and awe. Hayman's illustration anticipates the sort of symbolic interpretation of this episode that emerges in Fuseli's design and reaches its fullest articulation in Blake's. Likewise, his illustration for book 9 (fig. 26) introduces a new concern with Eve's temptation of Adam, a scene effectively rendered later in a separate work by James Barry (fig. 27). In depicting Adam recoiling in horror from Eve and the fruit she offers, Hayman invites his readers to participate in the sense of horror at sin discovered. Rather than showing Eve tasting the fruit—her fall—he shows Adam's (and by implication the reader's) *reaction* both to the act and to its immediate consequence: the brazen invitation to share in the sin and the Fall. Though the design is rather too contrived, too melodramatic, it does effectively deflect attention away from the immediate external action and toward both the motivation and the subjective responses of the participants.

Finally, Hayman's Expulsion (P, pl. 52) presents the conventional military Michael leading Adam and Eve from Eden, but several visual curiosities in this final design contribute to further undermining Milton's verbal suggestions. For one thing, though Michael leads the couple gently, holding Adam by the wrist and Eve by the hand, Eve shows a curious and uncharacteristic lack of reluctance to leave, considering that it is Adam, not she, who has been provided with the optimistic presentiment of redemption and restoration. Eve is, in fact, walking a step or two *ahead* of Michael, and, while her face expresses some slight sadness, she displays little of the acute despair previous illustrators had emphasized. Oddly enough, it is Adam who buries his head in his hands, dragging his feet as he attempts to slow the Expulsion and prolong the last moments in Eden. Inserted at the beginning of book 12, where it clearly breaks the continuity of Michael's prophecy, this design generates pessimistic expectations that must surely have misled many

Figure 26. After Francis Hayman. *Adam Tempted by Eve*. 1749–53. *Stephen C. Behrendt Collection*

Figure 27. James Barry. *Adam Tempted by Eve*. About 1771. *By permission of the British Library, London*

readers, negatively coloring their perceptions of the positive content of the poem's conclusion. The effect of such a misdirection of response cannot be overstated in any consideration of the trends in visual criticism of a literary work.

We should take note here also of the Milton illustrations of Hayman's contemporary, William Hogarth. Hogarth's exaggeratedly theatrical *Council in Hell* and its intensely rococo counterpart, the *Council in Heaven* (P, pls. 38, 39), done about 1724, represent a baroque extension of the sort of effects we observe in Cheron's illustrations. Though the two engravings are, as Pointon observes, "treated in the lofty manner considered suitable by painters in the grand manner for the depiction of noble literary subjects," [12] their ornate, grandiose style only distracts one from Milton's text. Hogarth's only other Milton illustration, a painting done some forty years later, is an essentially romantic and again rather melodramatic depiction of Satan, Sin, and Death (P, pl. 53). Significant, though, is Hogarth's use of a Satan whose facial expression clearly reveals his intense mental conflict, a technique Blake was to employ throughout his *Paradise Lost* designs.

Hogarth's painting of Satan, Sin, and Death—larger and executed in color in a substantially different visual medium—is naturally more striking than the engraved book illustrations that preceded it. Because of the virtual impossibility of illustrating a long and complex narrative with a single episodic picture, any artist must necessarily arrive at some compromise that allows him to reconcile the great quantity of potential source material with the particular aesthetic effect he sets out to achieve. The scene he represents is, consequently, often considerably altered for visual and dramatic purposes from its original state in the text, and this alteration typically involves far more than simply omitting details irrelevant to the scene depicted. In virtually every case, separate paintings purporting to be based upon *Paradise Lost* are far less faithful to the letter and spirit of Milton's poem than are the illustrations customarily printed with it. Infidelity of this sort is perhaps inevitable when the iconography employed in the picture is associated not just with the literary text itself but also with a much broader and more complex verbal and visual tradition. But such infidelity becomes the more apparent in the separate works based upon *Paradise Lost*. The fundamental events with which *Paradise Lost* works had been depicted many times by illustrators of printed Bibles as well as by countless artists in separate biblical paintings. Just as the Bible is inextricably woven into the fabric of *Paradise Lost*, so too is the tradition of biblical illustration inherently involved with illustrations to the epic. Hence it should come as no great surprise that underlying Aldrich's Expulsion scene, for instance, is, not Milton's text, but Raphael's painting—not Milton criticism but Genesis illustration.

Of equal concern, though, is the more conscious infidelity already mentioned: that deviation from the text undertaken for purely aesthetic purposes, in the interest of creating an independent and largely self-illuminating work of visual art. Hogarth's *Satan, Sin, and Death*, for instance, by definition constitutes a different sort of aesthetic entity from the conventional book illustration of the same scene, since it is designed to stand alone, to be a self-contained dramatic subject even as it depends tangentially upon *Paradise Lost* for allusive context. At about the same time Hogarth was painting *Satan, Sin, and Death*, Lessing was speculating in the *Laokoön* about the aesthetic possibilities of the "pregnant moment" in visual art: the moment just before the climax of the action, whose representation effectively suggests both the temporal past (what has happened) and the temporal future (what is going to happen).[13] Lessing's theory urges the visual artist to represent a moment of considerable dramatic potential rather than an academically posed tableau. Clearly, this dramatic component, this "pregnant moment," is more essential in the separate work of representational art than in the illustration that is physically attached to a supportive and mutually elucidatory text. It is, however, subject to much greater pictorial variation than is the illustration which is so attached.

In exploring the many pregnant moments with which Milton's poem supplies them, however, visual artists increasingly introduced highly personal, subjective, and un-Miltonic material into their pictures, making Milton conform to their own intellectual and artistic preconceptions and intentions rather than the reverse. Still, as these works were in their own time at least tentatively regarded as attempts at a sort of Milton illustration, if only because of their Milton allusions or the Miltonic labels and quotations frequently attached to them, so also must we then add, however grudgingly, their often un-Miltonic content to the growing iconography of *Paradise Lost* illustration. Inevitably, inexorably, subsequent illustrators of the epic confronted an ever-increasing mass of verbal and visual commentary through which they had to wade on their way to the poem itself. All too frequently illustrators took this backward approach, beginning with the commentary rather than with Milton's poem. It remained for Blake to perform the proper acts of discrimination in correcting the gathering web of misreading, rejecting the accumulated critical errors and refocusing our attention upon the pages of *Paradise Lost*.

New illustrations to *Paradise Lost* appeared with increasing frequency as the eighteenth century drew toward its close. A number of major artists were involved with the creation of book illustrations as well as separate drawings and paintings based on the poem. The first of these was James Barry, an artist whose work Blake knew and admired.[14] His imaginative Milton pictures, most of which date from the 1770s, employ very large figures that totally dominate the pictures. Edmund Burke, Barry's patron and the author of a dissertation on the sublime and the beautiful, undoubtedly influenced Barry's choice for illustration of episodes from *Paradise Lost* Burke had himself identified as "sublime"; these episodes Barry rendered in designs that are "vast, sombre, grandiose and violent."[15] His *Satan Summons His Legions* (P, pl. 98) is a powerful design, its titanic figures of the rallying angels strikingly lighted from below by the fierce fires of hell, a technique of lighting Aldrich had employed in his design for book 1 (P, pl. 9). Barry's *Satan, Sin, and Death* (fig. 28) likewise depicts the three principals as large, violent figures. Sin is the most successful figure, a hellish voluptuary struggling to hold Satan and Death apart. Barry's skeletal and un-Miltonic Death, enfolded in a cowled robe, and his rather heavy Satan are less successful visually than the striking figure of Sin because of their somewhat contrived postures of arrested action. While Sin's posture is obviously active, Satan and Death seem frozen in artificial tableau; this visual disparity results in the generally unsatisfactory effect on the picture as a whole.

Barry's depictions of Adam and Eve are more intriguing. Their heavy figures reflect a definite sensuality, a physical aspect quite new to *Paradise Lost* illustration. *Adam Tempted by Eve* (fig. 27), for example, emphasizes the pair's nudity in a manner previously unattempted. The expression of grave sadness Barry gives Adam is likewise an innovation. Blake himself must have known either Barry's painting or its engraved version, for the manner in which Barry's Eve "insinuates herself in gesture and expression into the mind of her partner" is echoed in Blake's drawing for his *Tiriel* of *Har and Heva Bathing*.[16]

Henry Fuseli's Milton illustrations date from as early as 1776, the year he drew *Satan Starting at the Touch of Ithuriel's Spear* (P, pl. 101).

Figure 28. James Barry. *Satan, Sin, and Death*. About 1771. *By permission of the British Library, London*

Fuseli admired Milton's poetry and found it a stimulus for his own genius. His interest in Milton led to the creation of his Milton Gallery, the 1799 exhibition of paintings based on Milton that was the logical but largely unsuccessful successor to Boydell's Shakespeare Gallery and the "culmination of the eighteenth-century cult of the Miltonic sublime." Of the forty-two pictures in the gallery, thirty were related to *Paradise Lost*, suggesting Fuseli's particular preoccupation with that poem and particularly with Satan, who epitomizes for Fuseli the Romantic tragic hero.[17]

Fuseli's visual style is a striking fusion of theatrical and symbolic tendencies. He learned early on to depict moments of great dramatic potential, underscoring their inherent drama by carefully avoiding the sort of visual clutter that characterizes and cripples, for instance, Thornhill's 1720 headpiece to book 1 of *Paradise Lost* and concentrating instead on the full expressive potential of the figures themselves. Even though there is much of the theatrical in Fuseli's work, he is not to be classed with theatrically oriented artists like Hayman, but rather with sensitive critics like Blake who sought to isolate and articulate the underlying *symbolic* and *psychological* essence of the text they illustrated. Like Blake, Fuseli sought to accommodate the conventions of his visual medium to the inner necessity of a subjective critical interpretation. This approach involved enlisting both the visual and verbal traditions. Consequently, we discover that Fuseli's Milton illustrations invoke iconographic suggestions from a broad spectrum of visual precedents. Again like Blake, Fuseli worked both with interpretive concepts familiar to many of his contemporaries and with the existing tradition of Milton illustration, frequently adapting or modifying scenes that had come to be an established part of the illustrator's repertoire. Fuseli unhesitatingly quotes figures, gestures, scenes, and details from established iconography to expand the circumference of meaning he sets out to delineate.

Particularly in his Milton Gallery paintings—which were, after all, exhibited as a unified collection rather than being reduced, engraved, and inserted into a book—Fuseli embroiders freely upon Milton's text. We are told, rightly, that for Fuseli "poetic painting" of this sort "did not mean a slavish illustration of a literary text, but the adoption of 'every ornament that will warm the imagination.'"[18] While Blake subscribed to much the same general theory, we shall see that Blake rejected the un-Miltonic elements we find so frequently in Fuseli's work, moving in precisely the opposite direction, toward the most faithful representation of the letter *and* the spirit of the text he can manage. Fuseli's procedure leads, as one might expect, away from the text and toward some rather serious interpretive errors. Fuseli's insistence on Satan's heroism, for instance, maintained even as the artist records his gradual degeneration, reinforces the critical error of hero substitution. From the Milton Gallery subjects, one would scarcely deduce, as Blake deduces from his own reading of *Paradise Lost*, that the poem is most importantly and centrally about the Son of God and his significance for man.

Figure 29. After Henry Fuseli. *Eve Tempted by the Serpent.* 1805. *By permission of the British Library, London*

Figure 30. Henry Fuseli. *The Creation of Eve.* 1793. 207 cm by 207 cm. *Courtesy, the Kunsthalle, Hamburg*

Fuseli's paintings and his designs for the 1802 Du Roveray edition of *Paradise Lost,* both of which Blake undoubtedly knew, are all striking productions. They are highly dramatic (P, pls. 97, 101, 105, 119), often to the point of melodrama (P, pls. 99, 103), and are often overtly erotic, like *Sin Pursued by Death* (P, pl. 127), another instance of considerable free embroidery upon Milton's conceptions. While those dramatic designs tending toward the immense, statuesque style recall designs of Barry and Richard Westall, other designs, like *Eve Tempted* (fig. 29) and the *Creation of Eve* (fig. 30), move in the direction of symbolism, a movement clearly enunciated in Blake's designs and foreshadowed in the lesser-known verbal criticism of unconventional Milton commentators like Robert Lowth, Anselm Bayly, William Hayley, and Thomas Taylor.[19] Yet we ought to recall that even so suggestive a design as *Eve Tempted* was originally painted an astonishing seven by ten feet for the Milton Gallery. Clearly, the difference in effect between a painting of such dimensions and a two-by-three *inch* engraving (in which form it later appeared) is enormous. A small engraving in an equally tiny copy of *Paradise Lost* is rather easily overlooked, its drama and suggestivity being reduced along with its size and its critical function proportionally diminished for the average reader. With much less ease is a viewer able blithely to ignore seventy square feet of strikingly painted canvas. In

any case, it is instructive to note that by 1802, well before Blake's *Paradise Lost* designs, both Fuseli's paintings and his engraved designs had considerably developed the previously latent impulse toward symbolic reading of the epic and had added a number of new and distinctly symbolic elements to the iconography of *Paradise Lost* illustration.

George Romney's Milton drawings may be considered with Barry's and Fuseli's. Blake and Romney became well acquainted, and it is quite reasonable to suspect some reciprocal influence.[20] Though none of them ever resulted in finished paintings, Romney's many sketches for Miltonic subjects exhibit a consistently violent visual agitation. Romney was fond of chaotically falling or driven masses of figures (P, pls. 116, 117, 121) and violently threatening gestures (P, pls. 114, 115, 120), both of which fall naturally into the prevailing orientation of eighteenth-century *Paradise Lost* illustration. The profusion of figures in sketches like *The Fall of the Rebel Angels* (P, pl. 117) and *Satan Summons his Legions* (P, pl. 121) suggests the sort of dynamic visual arrangement Blake was to utilize in large pictures like *The Last Judgment* (fig. 49) and *The Fall of Man* (fig. 51), as well as in designs like *The Fall of the Rebel Angels* for *Paradise Lost*. Pointon's comment that the turbulence and violence we see in Romney's drawings indicates evidence of manic depression or paranoia may serve to suggest as well why the sketches never grew into finished pictures.[21] Perhaps the Miltonic subject matter served catalytically in some sort of personal and expressive self-therapy. Perhaps finished paintings were for Romney simply incapable of reproducing the violent dynamics of the rapid sketches, too liable to tame these wild visions. In any case, both the visual dynamism and the inherent sense of threatened innocence in the sketches likely made a deep impression on Blake if he saw any of them.

Another artist of Blake's acquaintance who produced a large number of Milton illustrations was Thomas Stothard. Stothard's are not particularly good designs; they are generally inconsistent in style and organization, indicating that the artist may have had little understanding of or sympathy for Milton's poem. Stothard generally treats Satan as the muscular, military hero we have seen elsewhere (P, pls. 66, 67, 75, 76). Yet he also portrays him as a sort of Roman senator, arguing in Pandemonium (P, pl. 65). Stothard's designs for scenes in Eden are lush, undramatic affairs: *Eve and the Serpent* (P, pl. 68), for instance, employs such a sentimental format that the whole import of the scene is lost. Stothard's designs are significant mostly as an indicator of the degree to which the illustrations of the period had become interrelated in choice and concept of scene and detail (fig. 31).[22] Mutual borrowing among the illustrators perpetuated the visual misreadings of *Paradise Lost* we have already noted, the artists turning for their precedents to one another's visual statements rather than, as prose criticism was by the end of the eighteenth century at last beginning to do, back to the proper source: the poem Milton had written.[23]

In their designs for the 1794 Wilkins edition of Milton's poems, Malpas and Wilson followed convention in their stiffly anachronistic,

Figure 31. After Thomas Stothard. *Satan Summons His Legions.* 1792–93. *Whitworth Art Gallery, University of Manchester*

winged Satan, armed and outfitted in classical military accoutrement and copied directly from Hayman's designs. His confrontation with Sin and Death in book 2 becomes with Malpas and Wilson a dull and static scene, as are most of the scenes represented in this edition. Their designs are generally nothing more than slavish and often careless copies of previous illustrations; they fail, for the most part, to capture either the emotion of Milton's epic or the animation of Hayman's visual models. Despite being copied directly from Hayman's more successful figures, Adam and Eve first appear here an ordinary, mundane couple in a pastoral setting, peered at from behind a tree by Satan (book 4; this scene appears to draw heavily upon the scene from conventional *Comus* illustration in which Comus peers out from behind a tree at the Lady). Adam and Eve are similarly lackluster in the following designs, generally aping Hayman's most melodramatic poses (Adam recoiling in horror in book 9, both figures posturing in anguish in book 10, Adam despairing in book 12) and only calling attention in the process to the artificial and postured visual arrangements of the illustrations, a deficiency further exacerbated by their poor workmanship.

The next major illustrations were those of J. and H. Richter, which appeared in 1794–95. These designs exerted relatively little direct influence on subsequent illustrations and are, in fact, often disappointing as pictures. Continuing the eighteenth-century tendency toward careful visual particularization of that vast "landscape garden," Eden, the Richter designs present us with an increasingly lush and visually dominant landscape, amid whose luxurious vegetation we discover Adam and Eve in their various pastimes and conditions. They are not a handsome couple; indeed, they are rather clumsily and coarsely executed. The forte of the Richters was apparently a combination of landscape and academic figure tableaux. Still, the designs are probably relevant to Blake's work, for the artist may well have seen them in Hayley's library during his years at Felpham.[24] While the Richter designs appear at first glance to display little sensitivity to Milton's suggestions, closer study reveals that their immediately apparent visual deficiencies tend to obscure what is frequently an insightful reading of the epic.

The headpiece to book 9 (fig. 32), for instance, attempts something new in foreshadowing the Fall. Eve is shown kneeling before the seated Adam; both have their heads inclined in pensive, perhaps troubled, attitudes. The implication that this scene is meant to represent the moment of Eve's insistence that they separate (9.205–384) is strengthened by the presence of the ominous leopard peering out at them from the unusually dark forest at the left. The visual effect of the entire design—a scene not previously depicted in any illustration—is appropriately heavy and foreboding.

While the Richters' headpieces are elliptical designs occupying less than half a page, their interspersed designs occupy entire pages and are not rationed out one per book, but are clustered in crucial books, leaving other books with none. The three full-page illustrations to book 9, for instance, form an interesting triptych outlining the Fall which the headpiece foreshadows. The first design of this triptych (fig. 33) is similar in symbolic suggestivity to the best of Fuseli's designs. It portrays a malevolently visaged Satan rising up from the misty surface of a stream in Eden, looking about for a place to hide (9.74–76). The ominous, ghostly atmosphere of this design further underscores the sense of deadly peril being engineered in text and illustrations alike. The obligatory temptation scene is divided in the following two full-page designs. The first of these (fig. 34) specifically isolates the central aspect of Eve's temptation, the Serpent's appeal to her vanity, interestingly representing the moment of *temptation*—Eve's conversation with the Serpent— rather than the more conventional act of the Fall: the plucking or tasting of the fruit. The innocent whiteness of Eve's body and her open-armed gesture of defenseless folly is juxtaposed with the erect coils of the small and gracefully poised Serpent on the ground, both figures neatly set against the lush calm background of unfallen Eden. Finally, the third design (fig. 35) represents Adam's reluctant participation in Eve's sin. Gravely concerned, Adam reaches out to Eve's hip with his right hand, his left raised in caution and reproach, as Eve offers him a bough; the garland he had been weaving for her lies at Adam's feet. The background is now firmly and inexorably darkened as the Fall is completed. Illustrating book 9 with multiple designs affords the Richters a greater opportunity to represent the series of crucial steps in man's fall. Likewise, of course, it adds significant critical and dramatic weight to the events of this book, further emphasizing an act already familiar to readers and perhaps, in the process, deemphasizing other equally important books that get significantly fewer visual reinforcements. In this edition, for instance, book 3 gets only a headpiece depicting Satan and Uriel, and no view at all of the Son.

The Richters' final illustration presents an interesting variation on the conventional representation of the Expulsion. While previous illustrators had shown Adam and Eve driven or led out of Eden by a Michael physically near or in contact with them, the Richter design (fig. 36) shows Adam and Eve *by themselves*, descending the path from Eden, a visual arrangement later elaborated in John Martin's 1827 painting (P, pl. 159). In the upper right background a group of angelic sentinels guards the gateway to Eden. The scene, then, portrays the final lines of the poem, as

> They hand in hand with wand'ring steps and slow,
> Through Eden took their solitary way.
> [9.648–49]

Removing the customary figure of Michael permits the artists to suggest that Adam and Eve are now leaving of their own volition, reluctantly and sorrowfully, but resigned to the fate they have so unwisely chosen. Their clasped hands imply the physical and psychological reintegration Milton's text suggests; their gestures, their sorrow and resignation. Curiously, like Hayman, the Richters also show us an Adam whose sorrow seems clearly greater (as the gesture of head buried in left hand indicates) than Eve's. Though its visual dynamics are subdued and perhaps less than fully effective, this version of the Expulsion is one of the more faithful to both the letter and the spirit of Milton's poem and suggests that the Richters were, indeed, cognizant of their critical responsibilities as visual interpreters of the poem, even though their technical abilities in this particular variety of illustration may have been limited.

Richard Westall's designs appeared in the sumptuous Boydell edition of 1794–97, another edition that Hayley owned. Pointon places Westall in the general category of "artists of the Miltonic sublime," artists whose work exemplifies in Pointon's view the melodramatic qualities of the sublime as Burke defined it in a visual style that is at once neoclassical, heroic, and emotionally charged. Westall further develops the tendency inherent in Hayman's designs to concentrate on one or two figures per picture, thereby increasing their suggestions of awesome magnificence.[25] The effect of this conception was intensified by the size of the plates in the Boydell edition, issued in folio. But if Westall follows Hayman in dramatic figure isolation, he departs from him in what he does with those figures. Westall's preference for academic tableaux—indeed almost, at times, for statuary—is apparent in *Satan Alarmed*, his design for book 4 (P, pl. 108). Westall shifts the moment of many of his designs, depicting a different stage in the events than had his predecessors and thereby further expanding the iconography of *Paradise Lost* illustration. Hence from book 2 Westall gives us, for example, not the customary scene of Satan, Sin, and Death at the gates of hell, but, instead, the birth of Sin (fig. 37), a moment both dramatically interesting

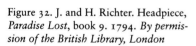

Figure 32. J. and H. Richter. Headpiece, *Paradise Lost*, book 9. 1794. *By permission of the British Library, London*

Figure 33. J. and H. Richter. *Satan Hovering over the Stream.* 1794. *By permission of the British Library, London*

Figure 34. J. and H. Richter. *Eve Conversing with the Serpent.* 1794. *By permission of the British Library, London*

Figure 35. J. and H. Richter. *Eve Tempting Adam.* 1794. *By permission of the British Library, London*

Figure 36. J. and H. Richter. *Adam and Eve Leaving Eden.* 1794. *By permission of the British Library, London*

and symbolically suggestive. Again, he introduces a new scene for book 8, taking his cue from John Hamilton Mortimer's 1777 design, *Eve amongst her Flowers* (P, pl. 54), and elaborating upon this scene for his illustration (fig. 38). Westall's views of Eden, incidentally, repeat and expand the complex lushness of vegetation, a tendency that is even further developed and reworked in the designs of his successors, including Blake.

The designs done by Corbould and Singleton for J. Parsons's 1796 edition of *Paradise Lost* are dramatically conceived episodic illustrations. The figures occasionally seem mere exercises in academic figure drawing, but even so, these large figures that take up much of the visual space are certainly more successful than those Wilson and Malpas had produced the year before. Following Hayman's early lead, Corbould and Singleton focused in their illustrations upon moments of dramatic potential, as in Corbould's temptation scene for book 9 (fig. 39), which echoes that of the Richters (fig. 35). But the result was much like that we observe in Westall's designs: the rather academic visual arrangement, coupled with the often dominating figures, results in designs that reproduce not so much arrested action as artificially posed tableaux. Once again, critical designs—like those to books 10 and 11—become merely stylized studies in the posturing of woe.

Perhaps the most interesting of Corbould's designs (Singleton's are those to books 3 and 11) are those to books 4 and 6. For book 4, Corbould depicts Eve observing her reflection in the pool (fig. 40). She is portrayed amid lush vegetation, and her semifetal position as she lies on the bank reduces her proportional size so that, while she is still a large figure, she appears somehow smaller than she is, a small but lovely part of an immense and still unfallen paradise. The point is subtly underscored by the presence in the middle background of two comparatively large rabbits. The design for book 6 takes the interesting approach of eschewing literal depiction of the Son in conflict with the rebels, showing instead the arrival of Abdiel to deliver his message to the Father (6.1–55). The heavenly forces are represented by two ranks of helmeted, armed warriors rising out of the clouds at the top, while the Father's presence is effectively suggested in the upper right corner by the folds of a robe falling about the lower legs and feet of an otherwise unseen figure.

On the whole, Corbould's designs exhibit greater fidelity to Milton's poem than do Singleton's illustrations for books 3 and 11. In the book 3 design (P, pl. 81), Satan does not strike the viewer as a young angel. Certainly he is not the cherubic youth other illustrators had customarily portrayed. And while he deviates from the typical scene for book 11, Singleton makes an unfortunate selection in the alternative scene he chooses to illustrate. Rather than representing Michael's vision of the future, Singleton gives us the moment at which Michael announces his role in the coming eviction of Adam and Eve (11.258–62). Consequently, the illustration awkwardly repeats Corbould's design for book

Figure 37. After Richard Westall. *The Birth of Sin.* 1794–97. *By permission of the British Library, London*

10, with Adam and Eve again in their postures of woe and with Michael substituted now for the Son as the immediate agent of their suffering. In producing successive illustrations so narrowly similar in content and concept, Corbould and Singleton sacrificed the infinite variety of Milton's text for a restrictive and misleading visual reduction, thereby perpetuating—even as they elaborate upon it—the erroneous, pessimistic critical response to the epic's conclusion.

Thomas Kirk's eleven *Paradise Lost* illustrations (and W. H. Brown's one) for Cooke's pocket edition of Milton's works are superior to designs like those of Wilson and Malpas and even Westall in that they obviously prefer action to frozen tableaux. The figures are more fluid, less statuesque. In assessing any illustrations, though, we have to bear in

Figure 38. After Richard Westall. *Eve amongst Her Flowers.* 1794–97. *By permission of the British Library, London*

mind the pertinent data about the size and format for which they were designed and in which they subsequently appeared. For instance, visual action and fluidity is far more important in a physically small illustration; expanded to the size of Westall's folio pages, Kirk's designs begin likewise to take on a forced appearance, becoming at that expanded size *less* successful visually than Westall's, which were *designed* for the larger page.[26] Adam and Eve are, perhaps, a bit too bucolic in Kirk's designs, especially in their first appearances. Physiognomy appears not to have been among Kirk's artistic strengths: all characters tend to have peculiar and unnatural facial expressions most of the time. Too, Kirk introduces a bothersome number of distracting visual inconsistencies into his designs. First seen bareheaded, bearing an oval shield and a

Figure 39. After Richard Corbould. *Eve Tempting Adam. 1796. Stephen C. Behrendt Collection*

fringed spear (book 1), Satan subsequently confronts Sin and Death wearing an impressive helmet and carrying a spade-shaped shield and a nearly bare spear (book 2). And while Adam's hair appears rather straight in book 4, it becomes increasingly curly and abundant in books 8 and 9.

Much in the manner of portrait artists who surround the generally oval portrait of Milton with a framing set of iconographic references to the poet's life and works, Kirk surrounds his individual scenes with

Figure 40. After Richard Corbould. *Eve Observing Her Reflection*. 1796. *Stephen C. Behrendt Collection*

frames (sometimes repeated from design to design) containing iconographic suggestions associated with the particular scene. His depiction of Eve tempting Adam (fig. 41), for instance, shows a cloud-enfolded skeletal death figure peering over the oval containing the temptation scene, right index finger touching its skull, over which is suspended a snaky crown. Lightning flashes from the dark cloud and falls beside the oval. Beneath the oval are inscribed the appropriate lines from the text, framed by the figure of the Serpent. This technique of illustration should probably be associated with the mixed technique we glimpse in Medina's designs. But the manner in which this type of illustration attempts to draw together various narrative moments and suggestions within a single design should also be assessed in light of the techniques of iconographically elaborated portraiture.

Kirk's designs are indebted to those of his predecessors, but they also reveal an originality that enables them to add significantly to the iconography of *Paradise Lost* illustration. For example, while Kirk's design for book 9 follows Hayman's in basic scene arrangement and in Eve's posture, it portrays Adam in a different, less horrified manner. Adam leans backward as Eve offers him the fruit; his right hand is raised, palm inward over his breast, as if questioning whether Eve seriously intends the fruit for him. His left arm extends straight down, his hand held stiffly out with palm downward in a gesture of rejection and seeming search for support upon which to fall back. Over Adam's right wrist is draped the long and elaborate garland he had woven for Eve. Departing from Hayman's original conception in this scene, Kirk replaces the previous sense of Adam's moral repugnance with one of moving incredulity and indecision. This slight shift in perspective, this alteration of the exact moment depicted, generates a considerable difference in the visual and psychological impact of the illustration upon the reader. It indicates the growing tendency of Romantic criticism to respond to the poem in terms, not of a simplistic set of dialectical choices that can be securely articulated and explained in terms of moral good and moral evil, but rather of a complex continuum of psychological and experiential alternatives demanding difficult choices of all participants, including the reader and the critic. In this scene Kirk's designs, like Fuseli's, move in the direction of the sort of suggestive, psychosymbolic perspective brought to bear on the poem in its most sensitive and concentrated form in Blake's illustrations.

Blake certainly also knew and may have been particularly influenced by the illustrations of E. F. Burney, whose thirteen designs appeared in 1799 and were republished in 1802. While Burney's designs are perhaps most immediately like Westall's, the typically sweeping drama of Westall's large illustrations is replaced in Burney's by an ornate domesticity. The scenes in Eden exhibit an even greater lushness of detail; indeed, at times the human figures are lost in the scenery. This owes partly to the nature of Burney's Adam and Eve, who are portrayed as more simply and youthfully pastoral than even Westall's pair, and who are consequently not very striking figures (P, pls. 85, 87). Burney's Satan is once again the elaborately costumed, winged Roman warrior in the designs for books 1, 2 (P, pl. 86), 4 (P, pl. 87), and 6. Like most of its predecessors, Burney's design for book 3 (fig. 42) portrays Satan and Uriel, repeating that troublesome shift in critical emphasis and visual interest from the Son to Satan. But Burney makes Satan a comically chubby, effeminate angel. This absurd, affected design marks the low point of Burney's abilities as a sensitive and perceptive Milton illustrator, for it

Figure 41. After Thomas Kirk. *Eve Tempting Adam.* 1795–96. *Courtesy of the Newberry Library, Chicago*

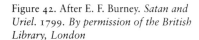

Figure 42. After E. F. Burney. *Satan and Uriel*. 1799. *By permission of the British Library, London*

totally misrepresents both the content and the import of book 3, and even of the Satan-Uriel meeting itself, visually transforming this crucial book into what the illustration might lead the reader to regard almost as a comic interlude. This distortion is even more glaring in light of the instant popularity of Burney's designs and their powerful influence upon the manner in which the poem was perceived by countless end-of-century readers.

In another important anticipation of Blake's treatment of the Expulsion, Burney's design for book 12 (fig. 43) further develops the suggestion evident as early as Hayman's design of an essentially gentle eviction from Eden. Modifying his predecessors' treatments of the scene, Burney rejects the idea of Michael's violently driving out Adam and Eve like profane animals, showing him instead leading them out, holding each by a wrist as they look back ruefully at their lost Eden. Though the pair

Figure 43. After E. F. Burney. *The Expulsion.* 1799. *By permission of the British Library, London*

obviously resist their enforced departure, the sense of compassion with which Burney endows the scene is suggested by the gentle—albeit insistent—manner in which Michael leads the couple.

Like Hayman's designs, Burney's became popular immediately upon their publication, and William Hayley may well have specifically directed Blake's attention to Burney's designs, being in his well-intentioned way "anxious to help Blake by persuading him to work in a style better suited to the public taste."[27] Blake's designs do, indeed, draw upon Burney's, just as they draw upon the entire visual tradition of *Paradise Lost* illustration. But as is typically the case where Blake appears indebted verbally or visually to a predecessor, he takes only the icon itself, infusing it with different values and new implications that leave him less a debtor than a genuine original. We need to remember that Blake regularly invokes verbal and visual conventions deliberately in order to suggest those conventional readings to which he is taking particular exception. Blake works, as we have seen in the previous chapters, with a highly *allusive* visual language, fully exploiting the accumulated connotations of the iconography upon which he draws. The verbal and visual echoes are there for a purpose: to alert the reader-viewer to certain familiar (or, sometimes not so familiar) conventions and expectations Blake wants embraced, rejected, or revised.

Finally, it seems likely that by the time he came to make his *Paradise Lost* designs Blake was already acquainted with those of Stephen Rigaud, published in 1801.[28] Rigaud's designs are related in a number of ways to Blake's in terms of imaginative suggestion. His design for book 3, for instance, showing the angels praising the Son, attempts to refocus the book as Milton had intended. Indeed, several of Rigaud's illustrations essay new and important interpretive statements. While many illustrators dealt with book 5, either as a rather repetitious visual reference to Adam and Eve—who customarily appear in Eden also in designs for book 4—or as a scene of Abdiel's renunciation of Satan, Rigaud gives us Satan scorned by the faithful angels among whom he passes, who point accusingly at him.

More important is Rigaud's treatment of the final two books. The design to book 11 (fig. 44) shows, not the customary prospect scene of Adam's view of the future, but rather the moment that anticipates that prophetic vision. Eve lies asleep in the lower foreground; behind her, Michael leads Adam away, supporting him with his right arm while his left hand gestures heavenward. The reclining figure of Eve significantly anticipates Blake's treatment of her in *Michael Foretells the Crucifixion*, in which he fuses this scene with an entirely new aspect of Adam's view of the future. Though it is a visual failure, Rigaud's Expulsion also pursues previous suggestions of a gentle eviction. A ludicrously winged Michael leads the sorrowing couple slowly from Eden, his right hand grasping Eve's wrist, his left arm around Adam's shoulder. This latter gesture is considerably more familiar and consolatory than any gesture employed by previous illustrators of the Expulsion and may, in fact, be *too* intimate, suggesting a greater camaraderie with Adam and a greater reluctance toward his role than Michael ought properly to have. Although Blake maintained the sense of gentleness and compassion in his own Expulsion scene, he eschewed such a gesture of friendliness, recalling the immense distance between the fallen and the unfallen. Only the Son, Blake will show us, is capable of bridging this gulf.

We should also note, in passing, William Craig's designs, executed in 1804 and conservatively anachronistic in their reliance upon conventional iconography that was by this time largely being replaced. The militaristic portrayals of Satan (books 1, 2, and 6), the outworn military rendition of the war in heaven (book 6), and the views of Adam and Eve in Eden (especially books 4 and 5) are hopelessly redundant. Craig's designs are unframed vignettes, those representing Eden softly curved with lush vegetation, those showing hell choked with flames and smoky

Figure 44. After Stephen Rigaud. *Michael Leading Adam to View the Future.* 1801. *By permission of the British Library, London*

clouds. They seem closest in style to the whimsical illustrations of John Mortimer, whose 1777 illustrations *Eve amongst Her Flowers* (P, pl. 54) and *Satan Flying* (P, pl. 57) scarcely reflect that artist's infatuation with the Romantic sublime.

Of other illustrations that preceded Blake's, little need be said. They are, for the most part, repetitions of previous conceptions that introduced nothing new to the visual critical tradition. Small, cheap editions of *Paradise Lost* or Milton's complete poems that appeared were frequently adorned with frontispiece plates, so that the entire epic or even the complete works might be prefaced by a single design. The favorite subjects for these illustrations were the fall of Satan, the Expulsion, the temptation and fall of Eve, and the war in heaven, in that descending order of popularity. Conspicuously absent from this list of favorite subjects is the Son's offer, an indication of the degree to which editors and illustrators (and presumably *readers*) of these volumes were missing Milton's main point.

There is a certain classic irony, too, in the fact that Craig's conservative designs appeared at a time when Blake had already begun illustrating Milton's poetry and rescuing him in the mythology of *Milton*. That artists so vastly different should have been illustrating the same epic at practically the same time underscores the accuracy of a comment Anders Nygren makes in a somewhat different context:

> At the supremely important turning-points in the history of religion when something really new appears on the scene, it is curious to observe how the consciousness that the new is emerging is coupled with a conservative retention of the old. . . . It is merely a symptom of the fact that all the really great revolutions begin from within and the new life only gradually bursts asunder the old forms and creates new ones for itself.[29]

What Nygren says here of the history of religion is equally applicable to the history of critical response, not only to Milton's diffuse epic but also to the system of Christianity upon which it draws and which it was finally seen to subvert. Gradually, inevitably, revolutionary artists and thinkers were coming to recognize in Milton, in his life and his work, a fellow revolutionary. That discovery and its celebration were to lead inexorably toward a critical awakening and reassessment that was not to be obstructed by even the most tenacious impercipience of critics like Craig.

In summary, then, we may make several observations concerning the tradition of *Paradise Lost* illustration Blake inherited. First, and of greatest importance, illustrators had repeatedly shifted the focus of Milton's poem, minimizing the central significance of the Son's offer—made in book 3 and effectually fulfilled in the vision of book 12—to redeem man. This critical deviation led to a virtual replacement of the hero with the antihero, Satan, a demonic parody of the Father. His elevation owes in large degree to evaluations made by unperceptive critics who mistook—or deliberately substituted—his greater emotional, dramatic activity for heroism. Thus Pointon tells us: "Satan appears in the work of Barry, Fuseli and nineteenth-century artists with athletic form, handsome features and determined but suffering visage. Adam and Eve, Uriel, Raphael and Michael are all now minor characters in the drama. Satan is the embodiment of all that is of primary interest in *Paradise Lost*."[30] While perhaps overstating the case, Pointon identifies a shift in attention that was in many ways the logical result of the trend that began with Renaissance art of transforming Satan from a grotesque, gothicized monster into a physically attractive humanoid figure. The critical error of heroizing Satan was starkly apparent to Blake, who attributed this mistaken and self-perpetuating shift of focus and value largely to the misdirected efforts of the impercipient verbal and visual commentators who preceded him and, to a considerable extent, to Milton himself.

It is further worth noting in this context that critical opinion has generally accounted the fascination with—the elevation of—Satan a distinctively *Romantic* phenomenon. Yet study of the eighteenth-century illustrations to *Paradise Lost* makes it quite clear that such an interest was well established before the Romantic period. The reasons for which the two periods esteemed Satan differed, to be sure: the Romantics seized upon his rebelliousness, the eighteenth century his theatricality. Yet both these are essential parts of Satan's character, the latter particularly illustrative of his vain concern with show, with superficiality, with self. It is important that we reevaluate our own conceptions (or misconceptions) about the centrality of Satan to eighteenth-century thinking about *Paradise Lost*.

Second, in light of the evolving tendency during the period to regard Satan as a dramatic, heroic figure—indeed, a Romantic, Promethean hero—*Paradise Lost* had come to be reduced in illustration to a series of emotionally charged episodic designs that further emphasized the figure of Satan. Rather than summarizing individual books as the synoptic designs had, or epitomizing them as the mixed designs generally attempt to do, these customarily dramatic designs isolated single incidents, sacrificing the perspective and contextual significance provided them by the poem as a whole and generally diminishing both the stature of man and the role of the Son in the process.

Third, and closely related to this tendency, scenes came frequently to be treated in theatrical terms, with incidents represented in variously terraced environments resembling stage settings and with characters costumed and choreographed as if for the stage. This tendency, combined with that toward the visual heroic, contributed to the selection for illustration of moments of greatest dramatic—or, in some of the poorer illustrations, melodramatic—action or potential, stageable moments that were not necessarily the most important. Illustrations of this sort increasingly and inevitably sacrificed and subordinated the interior content and unity not only of the particular scenes they depicted but also of the epic as an aesthetic whole to superficial, ephemeral components of its external narrative spectacle. While Blake clearly felt that some of the blame for this tendency had to be placed squarely on Milton for obscuring much of this interior design with an overabundance of narrative and doctrinal material, he felt even more strongly that it was the illustrator's duty to separate vision from mere detail—even when the poet himself had failed to do so—and to concentrate in his designs on the former, not the latter, on elucidation rather than decoration.

Finally, illustrators had paid ever less attention to Milton's textual details as the eighteenth century drew toward its close. Early deviations like Aldrich's book 2 *putti* gave way to gross departures in detail and in focus. As artists like Hogarth, Stothard, Barry, Fuseli, and others more frequently made *Paradise Lost* the titular basis for separate, independent works of art, infidelity to the text increased as individual scenes were presented out of context by artists and illustrators who carelessly indulged their audiences and highlighted their own technical specialties.

Together, these several factors helped shape a tradition of illustration, contributing significantly in the process to a critical attitude toward Milton's poem that seemed to Blake perverted and chaotic, a situation Blake set out in his designs to remedy. If we accept Eric Newton's view that the classic in art concerns itself essentially with the *exterior* of a work, while the romantic seeks to draw the reader-viewer into the *interior* of its subject, then we can better understand the Romantic view of *Paradise Lost* Blake's criticism articulates.[31] Judged by this standard of interiority, the epic is clearly romantic in its exploration of the internal, psychological ramifications of the Fall myth and its place in Christian thought. The epic's essentially romantic nature is further suggested by the Augustan critics' frequent grumbling about the "roughness," "wildness," or "irregularity" of Milton's verse, his seeming disregard for the conventions governing the technical and mechanical exterior of his poem, as well as his apparent willingness to tamper with traditionally inviolable matters of received religion and orthodox theology.[32]

It was perhaps inevitable that illustrators before Blake had often so nearly approximated in their designs the sort of critical response that typified the verbal criticism of the eighteenth century. They worked, after all, for editors who frequently subjoined critical essays to the volumes the artists adorned. But Blake's emphatic contention that the Son is the real hero of the epic is in sharp contrast to the conventional position advocated by influential critics from Dryden and Blackmore to Voltaire—and including both Richardson and Johnson—that Adam is more the hero; it disagrees as well with the critical cult that argued Satan as the hero. Influenced as it doubtlessly was by Cowper's notes and Hayley's equally romantic understanding of Milton, Blake's own reading resembles most nearly the sort of clear-sighted opinion voiced a century earlier by Joseph Addison, whose aesthetic sense is often so romantic itself:

The Paradise Lost is an Epic, or a Narrative Poem, and he that looks for an Hero in it, searches for that which *Milton* never intended; but if he will needs fix the Name of an Hero upon any Person in it, 'tis certainly the *Messiah* who is the Hero, both in the Principal Action, and in the chief Episodes. [*Spectator*, no. 297]

Blake, of course, came in his later years to believe Milton did intend the Son as his hero, consciously elevating him above the traditionally superior Father by demonstrating his heroism in his love-motivated offer to die for man, an offer whose completion demands that he sacrifice in the process what he shares with his fellow man—his human life—in order to appease his fellow God who demands such a retributive act of total reparation as the price of man's redemption.

While that human life—the vegetable body—is, of course, of no value to the Son except as an "incrustation," "an Obstruction to the Soul or Spiritual Body" (Annotation to Berkeley's *Siris;* E, p. 653), it serves to fallen man as an indication of shared experience *as men.* Recognizing this aspect of their mutual relationship, man may then—like Adam, Milton, and Albion—proceed to the corollary recognition that "God becomes as we are, that we may be as he is": that man is, like the Son, divine. Blake tells us that "Jesus considered Imagination to be the Real Man" (Annot. Berkeley; E, p. 635), and the sooner man recognizes this fact as the ultimate reality of his existence—which the Son's death as man illustrates for him—the sooner may he reject the puritanical notion of sensual repression and embrace the correct view of the body, not as an impediment, but as a gateway to his imaginative perfection, the key to regaining the paradise within. In the long view, the Son's offer involves a deliberate choice based upon his recognition that his experience *as man* will lend the most convincing credibility to the imaginative paradigm his crucifixion epitomizes for the race of Adam. Blake's designs anatomize the Son's offer, presenting its various aspects and effects in a series of designs that analyze the universal significance of this crucial act of choice about which the entire poem—indeed the whole history of man—ultimately revolves. Blake's mature awareness that the Old Testament God of vengeance has been eclipsed in Milton's poem by the benevolent, humanistic forgiver of Sins in a paradigmatic act of self-realization underlies his entire visual interpretation. That interpretation constitutes the most radical rupture with conventional, conservative interpretation in the entire history of *Paradise Lost* criticism.

Chapter 5: Blake's *Paradise Lost* Illustrations

Blake completed two sets of designs for *Paradise Lost*, the first for the Reverend Joseph Thomas in 1807, the second for Thomas Butts in 1808, after having executed a number of separate but related drawings and paintings over the previous fifteen years. In addition, three more designs, from a set begun for John Linnell, date from 1822. The earliest set (HH, now at the Henry E. Huntington Library and Art Gallery), contains twelve designs. The second set (BM, at the Boston Museum of Fine Arts) also originally contained twelve designs, though the set was at some time broken and three designs were dispersed: *Satan Arousing the Rebel Angels* (Victoria and Albert Museum), *Satan, Sin, and Death* (a separate version at the Huntington Library), and *The Judgment of Adam and Eve* (Houghton Library, Harvard University).[1]

The only other Milton designs of which Blake made multiple sets are those to the *Nativity Ode* and *Comus;* in both cases each design in the first set is repeated in the second set. It is uncharacteristic of Blake to delete a design from an early set and replace it with a new and previously unseen design in a later set. Yet *Satan's and Raphael's Entries into Paradise* (HH 4) disappears from the BM set, while *Adam and Eve Sleeping* (BM 5) does not appear in the earlier set. It is equally uncharacteristic of Blake to *introduce* into a second set of designs visual inconsistencies not originally present in the initial set; his practice, as we note in the *Nativity Ode* and *Comus* designs, is just the reverse. Yet in the separate *Satan, Sin, and Death* at the Huntington Library the appearances of both Sin and Death are inconsistent with their subsequent appearances in *Michael Foretells the Crucifixion*. In the former, Sin's hair, for instance, is dark, and Death is beardless; in the latter, Sin's hair is lighter, and Death is bearded. These inconsistencies may be the result of a lapse of time during the preparation of the designs. While most designs in the second set are signed and dated "W Blake 1808," two designs, *Satan, Sin, and Death* and *Michael Foretells the Crucifixion*, deviate from this pattern. *Satan, Sin, and Death* is signed "inv W B.," without a date, and *Michael Foretells the Crucifixion* is neither signed nor dated. The signatures on the other BM designs are so located that we may reasonably conclude that nothing of any possible signature has been trimmed from the latter design (as has happened, for instance, in the sixth design of the *Nativity Ode* set at the Whitworth Art Gallery, Manchester). This visual inconsistency suggests that these two designs may not have been executed at the same time as the others, even though they ultimately became part of the same set.[2]

Of more immediate importance is the manner in which Blake deals with inherited materials, in this case material deriving both from Milton and from his previous illustrators. By the time Blake came to make his designs, the iconography of *Paradise Lost* illustration was beginning to solidify. Yet even as Blake selectively quotes that iconography in the conventional designs with which he begins his sets, he modifies and—especially in his portrayal of Death—*corrects* it. We need only recall the un-Miltonic Death figures of Cheron or Barry to prove the point. Invoking the entire critical and illustrative tradition at the outset is a subtle and entirely intentional maneuver on Blake's part, for in doing so he identifies the tradition of interpretation—or misinterpretation—he is about to overturn. Expecting first to encounter Satan in hell and, next, Satan, Sin, and Death together in the first designs for the epic, and finding that Blake does indeed deliver just these scenes, viewers instinctively recall the entire series of conventional designs to which they are accustomed, anticipating new versions of all the other established set pieces as well. Marcia Pointon's pejorative remark that Blake's designs follow the iconographical patterns of earlier illustrations "very closely" and portray moments well established in *Paradise Lost* illustration betrays a misunderstanding of the artist's subversive intentions,[3] for Blake surely *wants* his reader-viewer to anticipate the conventional. Thus manipulated, the viewer is subsequently the more struck by Blake's obvious departures from both the form and the content of conventional illustration and, if alert and sensitive, can be drawn into a critical act of comparison involving at once Milton's text, previous verbal and visual commentary, and Blake's designs. Such is consistently the methodology of Blake's visual criticism.

Acutely aware of artistic and interpretive traditions surrounding the epic, but fundamentally revolutionary in his approach to his primary and secondary materials, Blake does not "enter into the forms of his art like an indwelling spirit, but approaches them analytically and externally, tearing them to pieces and putting them together again." First, Blake saw a poetry that had to be dismantled in order to liberate the vision it appeared determined to conceal, much in the manner that Milton's dis-mantling on plate 16 of *Milton* frees the natural, naked man concealed beneath the "rotten rags." This liberation involved an effort to "soften, humanize, and, by his standards, Christianize his Puritan mentor." Hence his designs involve, to a far greater extent than has generally been recognized, direct correction of points Blake took as indicators both of Milton's self-imposed enslavement and of his externally engineered critical misinterpretation.[4] Second, Blake is even more anxious to identify and annihilate deficiencies of vision in previous commentary. He hoped once and for all to rid Milton's poem of the visual incrustations that seemed increasingly bent on imposing upon *Paradise*

Lost a set of values and meanings the poem clearly resisted and to return the poem to its proper perspective.

Blake's wish to have his own reading of the poem clearly differentiated from the readings of his predecessors explains his brilliant manipulation of the iconographic tradition of *Paradise Lost* illustration. Though we discern elements of this traditional iconography in every design, they are consistently presented in a new light and generally in symbolic fashion. This symbolic conception, in fact, most clearly marks what is new and different in Blake's designs; his is a unified vision unlike anything previously attempted on a large scale in *Paradise Lost* illustration and criticism. Even Fuseli, whose Milton Gallery pictures frequently involve a symbolic reading of the poetry, nowhere approaches the sort of unified conception Blake's designs reveal. This symbolic orientation is immediately suggested by the artist's rejection of "plausible visualization" and overtly "heroic" depiction of scenes and by his choice instead of a stylized, symmetrical representation of the "ideas" embodied in the scenes depicted.[5] More than any other set of his Milton illustrations, the *Paradise Lost* designs exhibit an insistent visual symmetry that discourages perception on any purely realistic plane. Blake's designs likewise inherently confute the strict narrative sequence of Milton's poem. Adhering closely to the details of the text, the designs are still concerned with idea rather than narrative, with internal vision rather than with external detail. Hence it is a mistake to criticize Blake's performance in these designs, as Pointon does, for his rejection of narrative, his "eclecticism" in figure drawing, and his tendency toward "abstract pattern-making" on the grounds that these tendencies result in a repetition of basic types of composition.[6] Not a flaw at all, this visual repetition is an indication of Blake's own use of the structural and stylistic pattern of "parallel with difference" he learned from Milton.

While Blake may repeat postures, settings, and even entire visual structures within sets of designs, there is no instance of useless literal repetition, even in massive sets like the *Night Thoughts* illustrations. Visual echoes are deliberately employed to recall specific contexts as stimuli to mental activity; we are constantly urged forward into an increasingly complex comparative perspective upon an individual incident. As is his practice in every set of Milton illustrations, Blake takes in his *Paradise Lost* designs a single incident and fragments it into its component parts, illustrating it from a variety of perspectives. Every design in the *Paradise Lost* series elucidates some aspect of the Son's offer to redeem man, rediscovering and reemphasizing its significance by exploring its various aspects. We observe the full range of activities and motivations leading up to the Fall that necessitates the Son's offer; we see, too, the offer itself and a vision of its fulfillment. Thus Blake subtly returns our attention to the symbolic significance of the Son's experience as imaginative paradigm of love and creative energy for man, a point implicit—though "mantled"—in Milton's poem as well. Showing the Son first in his divine nature, asserting in heaven his bond of love with man, Blake returns us in the penultimate design to the figure of the Son, shown this time in his human and corporeal frame, as he completes the physical aspect of his offer, dying on the cross and presenting man thereby with a visual symbol, not of death, but of life transcendant and eternal. Viewing Blake's designs, we gradually build a dominant impression of the Son less as God than as man, and of man as less man than god, which is Blake's point if not Milton's.

In showing both the Son's offer and its fulfillment Blake affirms the simultaneity of both parts of that offer, uniting them in visionary time. Refining the epic procedure of Milton's poem, Blake orders the various scenes less in the chronological narrative time of the Bible and the epic than in the instantaneous visionary time in which all aspects of the central event recede spatially from it. Blake wishes his viewer to participate in this radical reorganization of time, this discovery of internal simultaneity, the prophetic moment of in-sight in which man beholds "a World in a Grain of Sand": the world within his own imaginative being. Leslie Brisman's comment that the prophetic poet's business is to open up a shadowy world into new imaginative space and time, "more than on earth was previously understood," applies to the Blake who declares in *Jerusalem* that it is his "great task" to open man's eyes inward to eternity and the imagination (*J* 5.17–20; E, p. 146).[7]

In a world containing infinite numbers of imaginatively liberating grains of sand for us to peer into, we do well to follow Blake's advice in seeing the true moment of vision within what we have termed "visionary time," that period "Within a Moment: a Pulsation of the Artery" in which "all the Great / Events of Time start forth & are conceivd" (*M* 29.1–3; E, p. 126). This is the moment within the imagination "that Satan cannot find" but that, "when it is once found . . . renovates every Moment of the Day if rightly placed" (*M* 35.42–45: E, p. 135). The key to visionary in-sight, as Milton learns in *Milton*, is, not narrative expansion, but narrative contraction. All history is condensed within the visionary instant "Ever expanding in . . . the Human Imagination." Blake did not bind his Milton designs, nor did he generally attach numbers or line citations to them;[8] the designs thus encourage the reader-viewer to discover in them, not so much a chronological *sequence* of individual visions, as interrelated simultaneous facets of a single unified vision that augments, clarifies, and finally corrects the vision embedded in Milton's poem. Blake invites his viewer to observe the incident celebrated from a continually shifting and expanding imaginative perspective by constantly reintegrating the designs as new echoes and elaborations are introduced visually.

Blake's first HH design, *Satan Calling His Legions*, (pl. 2), initiates the visual symmetry of the designs even as it depicts the scene in hell. Blake's careful execution of the background and figure arrangement here call attention also to the V structure we will see repeatedly in the designs, its sides curving (as here) or straight, the whole inverted (as here) or upright. Satan here is decidedly unlike the Satan most previous illustrators have given us. He is muscular, but rather heavily built (like Barry's figures) and not strikingly athletic. Gone is the antique military clothing and headgear. Gone also are his wings; neither Satan nor any of his rebels is winged, nor is Satan in the second design showing him at the gate of hell. Indeed, Blake abandons this traditional iconographic reference to the rebels' angelic origins, showing them in hell as troubled, imprisoned figures without wings. Blake implies that Satan and the rebels are wingless in hell, that in their own element their appearance differs from that in which they are customarily perceived in heaven and on earth. Blake's treatment of the rebels is an improvement over traditional depictions; eliminating the conventional mass of wings enables Blake to present more figures without creating the customary visual clutter. A shield and several spears are visible here, but these and the structural details of the setting are all Blake quotes of the traditional iconography of this standard opening scene.

In depicting Satan frontally Blake resolves a question previous illustrators had avoided by clothing their figures in some manner: that of whether an angel—even a fallen angel—would have genitals. Blake solves the problem brilliantly, replacing Satan's genitals in this and succeeding designs with an expanse of scales that suggests Satan's alter ego the Serpent, the only offspring he could hope to engender, the perverse projection of his own narcissistic nature.[9]

Already in this design Satan's distress is obvious. His consistently troubled expression throughout the designs reflects his mental distress and his inability to control situations in which he finds himself. We get no sense in this design that Satan is actually *rallying* his fallen comrades, but that he is, rather, merely attempting to gain their attention, asserting himself for the first time in hell. His companions—and not even all of them, at that—are only just turning to him. Four figures at lower center and left are still in chains, one evidently unconscious. The resting figure behind Satan has his face averted. Satan is scarcely in control of the situation, as his hand gestures attest.[10] His raised hands, palms outward, suggest that he is, not rousing his rebels, but *silencing* them. This detail is most important, for it reveals Blake's intention here of showing, *not* the traditional rally, but instead the first act of Satan's demonic parody of the Father in heaven, his first attempt to impose order on the chaos that surrounds him. His lack of success in this attempt should immediately serve to confute those who would argue that Blake champions and heroizes Satan. In Blake's separate paintings of this scene (1795–1805; B, pls. 888, 889), Satan's posture is more commanding; his body is arched actively with his hands raised, palms upward, as he exhorts his rebels.[11]

Satan is obviously modeled upon the figure of Fire Blake created for the seventh plate of *The Gates of Paradise*, which figure Blake consistently associates with man's psychological energy, his desires and aspirations, indeed both with Orc and with the Devil of *The Marriage of Heaven and Hell*.[12] In the forms of the latter two, the figure is clearly fallible, as he certainly is as Satan. Yet, as we know from the mythology of Orc, he is likewise an emblem of apocalyptic purification. His modified cruciform posture here recalls *The Dance of Albion* (fig. 3) as well as *that* picture's relation to *The Ancient of Days* (fig. 19). Put most simply, Satan's posture is an emblem of "contrary possibilities."[13] It points us at once toward the apocalyptic self-sacrifice of the Crucifixion—the ultimate instance of creative energy—and toward the Satanic parody of prideful self-centeredness.

Here, as in Blake's own poetry, Satan represents contrary possibilities in that energy is always *potentially* liberating. But Satan is himself a contrary: humanity must evaluate and act upon (and ultimately reject as error) what he represents. To understand and applaud Satan's resistance to the Father's impositions is potentially liberating; to reproduce that resistance blindly and for selfish purposes (as Eve does) is, of course, retrogressive. Satan is as good—or as evil—as the Father against whom he rebels. Energy in resistance to reason is creative and constructive—the dialectic always is; energy perverted to repression of creativity, however, is destructive. Recognizing this, man must rediscover with Blake the correct alternative: the liberating imaginative creativity epitomized in the Son as Blake finally came to apprehend him.

Satan's rebellion initiates a process by which he sets up in hell a parodic counterpart to the repressive hierarchical system of heaven. As Frye notes, Satan's rebellion is based upon a sense of rivalry—or attempted rivalry—with God.[14] Such rivalry assumes a mutually unflattering quality that itself warns us against overly championing the Father. As the Old Testament demonstrates, the characteristic effect of both Satan and the Father upon the world of mankind—as far as the great majority are concerned—is harsh destructiveness. Against this destructive standard is eventually placed the alternative epitomized in the New Testament by the Son and individually recreated in everyone.

Blake's second version of *Satan Calling His Legions* (*Satan Arousing the Rebel Angels;* BM 1, pl. 3) is significantly altered. All the ascending figures have been eliminated; those that remain are drawn larger. Satan is still appealing for silence, but his facial expression is more severe now, and his left foot—not his right as before—is extended. This foot alteration would seem to suggest Satan is advancing now in the material (or "Reason"-dominated) world, rather than in the spiritual,[15] a conclusion apropos of Satan's first essays in hell. The striking old figure in the lower foreground, lying unconscious in near-cruciform posture, prefigures the outstretched figure of Death at the foot of the cross in *Michael Foretells the Crucifixion*. Blake's altered design suggests a moment slightly earlier than the other, a moment at which Satan's crew has not yet begun to rise at all. The second design is the more dramatically effective, with Satan, the only erect figure, towering above the rebels he hopes to arouse.

Indeed, the second set of designs differs substantially from the first in both size and style. The later pictures are considerably larger and more highly finished, their figures more carefully modeled.[16] Their dimensions approximate those of the two tempera versions of *Satan Calling up His Legions* (each about 55cm x 41cm), the earlier of which (about 1795–1800) appears to underlie the first design to *Paradise Lost*. Blake had in this period also produced *The Fall of Man* (fig. 51) and at least one version of *The Last Judgment* (fig. 49) in approximately the same size, and it is not at all unreasonable to see in the "rhythmic and monumental solemnity" of the designs for Butts a conscious decision of Blake's part to endow these second pictures with the grander scale and style of such encyclopedic visions.[17] Furthermore, the illustrations from the Bible Blake had produced for Butts by this time had moved gradually toward a more flatly colored linear style that defies conventions of space and perspective in its presentation of multiple flat planes. The later *Paradise Lost* designs exhibit this visual style. The three pictures executed in 1822, incidentally, follow the Butts pictures in size and conception,[18] though their style is typical of Blake's later work in terms of both color and handling of visual effects.

The tradition of theatrical staging inherited by Blake and perhaps responsible for his overt use of levels in HH 1 (pl. 2) is carried over into HH 2 (pl. 4), *Satan, Sin, and Death*, along with a rather uncomfortable, melodramatic positioning of the figures. The scene is set on a stagelike dais, with a properly fiery backdrop. Blake suggests the portcullis of hell by a heavy grid at the right, rejecting the doors of Aldrich's scene and the variations thereon of most of his successors.[19] Blake constructs this design effectively, superimposing an upright V (upraised arms and striding legs of Satan and Death) upon an inverted V (with Satan's shield at its apex), creating a symmetrical visual tension that also frames and emphasizes the figure of Sin. Within this symmetrical arrangement Blake's figures are strongly active, with both Satan and Death striding forward. Each seems ready to hurl his spear, grimly determined as he glares into his opponent's face. For the first time in *Paradise Lost* illustration, we are given a Death faithful to Milton's description. Blake discards the skeletal figure borrowed by his predecessors from the old dance-of-death illustrations and variously metamorphosed for over a century, replacing him with a powerful, transparent figure with "dreadful Dart" and "Kingly crown" (2.672–73).

Death's crown prefigures both the crowns of amaranth the angels bring the Son in the next design and the Urizenic crown worn by Death in *The Judgment of Adam and Eve* (pls. 18, 19) and *Michael Foretells the Crucifixion* (pls. 20, 21). The crown will figure again in *L'Allegro*, plate 4 (*The Sunshine Holiday;* B, pl. 675) in the large spirits of materialism at the center of the design. Milton's handling of the confrontation scene conveyed clearly to Blake the point Roland Frye has also recognized:

The image of Death shaking his dreadful dart against a frightened human soul is here transposed to represent the return of evil upon itself, to imply the self-destructive, self-defeating qualities of Sin and Satan's kingdom. . . . by at once invoking and revising the visual tradition [Milton] introduces a strong note of Christian hope in the very presence of the demonic trinity.[20]

What is most horrible in the heavenly order is parodied here: the brutal and intolerant struggle for supreme power that turns one against his own progeny, a power struggle we see repeatedly in Blake's early prophetic poems. It is only a short step to the Romantic notion of the Father sacrificing his own Son in his desire to demonstrate (to whom but himself, we might ask?) that he will have his way at all costs.

Blake depicts Sin attempting to separate Satan and Death, her snaky coils spiraling out symmetrically to the edges of the dais. Sin's torso is rather clumsily joined to her coils, but Blake's was not the first design to fail to a considerable extent in this regard. Previous illustrations of this very popular scene attempted various solutions to the problem, none of them entirely successful. Blake's solution was that of most of his predecessors: extending Sin's hips down in outline allowed the joint to be covered by the upreared heads of her hounds, a passable—if not entirely satisfactory—solution.

Satan, Sin, and Death (pl. 4) identifies unmistakably the contrary, parodic trinity that both Milton and Blake are presenting to an audience already familiar with the customary heavenly trinity of orthodoxy. By its clear visual reference to previous illustrations, this design serves further to identify the visual tradition—a tradition steeped in distracting theatricality—Blake is in the process of rejecting. Here, for instance, previous illustrators had settled, not upon the most significant aspect of book 2, the mutual recognition and subsequent leaguing of the demonic trinity for man's destruction as part of Satan's scheme to spoil the Father's designs for man, but rather upon the aspect with the greatest visually dramatic potential: the fierce initial confrontation. In again quoting early on the tradition of *Paradise Lost* illustration—even as he already begins to transform and redirect that tradition—Blake establishes his critical authority, demonstrating his familiarity with the conventional response and appealing to the perceptive reader-viewer to heed his counterargument.

The second version of *Satan, Sin, and Death* (pl. 5) is more effective than the first. Employing the larger figures and arrested action that characterize all the designs of the second set, Blake depicts his three figures in different positions, with Satan again extending his left foot rather than his right. The stances of Satan and Death are shortened in such a way that each seems now not to advance, but rather to lean backward as if recoiling in horror from his adversary, unable to thrust his spear. Indeed, each looks not into the other's eyes as before, but down, perhaps already recognizing his kin by the similar absence of genitals (note Satan in pl. 5, Death in pl. 4). Sin is also altered here, made more immediately sensual through Blake's careful delineation of her thrusting bosom, her facial features, her almost caressing gestures,

and her flamelike hair. Her left hand is raised further now, as if to stay Death's flaming dart. Milton tells us that Sin is

> foul in many a scaly fold
> Voluminous and vast, a serpent arm'd
> With mortal sting. [2.651–53]

Interestingly, though, Milton's "foul" figure is given much that is visually attractive. As in *The Ancient of Days* (fig. 19), Blake combines in a single image aspects of apparent attractiveness and dynamism with those of real evil, positing in such figures the difficult ambivalences man faces at every turn. Blake conflates images in BM 2 (pl. 5), having each of Sin's coils end in a serpent's head, while maintaining the Cerberus image of the hellhounds issuing from her womb.[21] This first appearance of the Serpent likewise deftly foreshadows the form Satan is soon to adopt and further cements the mutual and incestuous kinship of the demonic trinity.

A preliminary sketch for this second version (fig. 45) shows Death leaning more actively toward Satan. Blake has particularly worked up the figure of Satan here, even adding watercolor washes to it and some to Death as well. More interesting, though, is the figure of Sin. Though sketched only roughly, she is depicted frontally, her arms raised symmetrically to hold Satan and Death apart. In this respect she is like Barry's Sin (fig. 27), suggesting that Blake may have had some version of Barry's picture in mind when he made the sketch.

The third design, *The Son Offers to Redeem Man* (pls. 6, 7), focuses our attention on the initial aspect of the poem's central act. Blake's picture is unlike anything his predecessors had attempted, presenting in visual counterpoint the symmetrical, integrated heavenly scene with its curved, encompassing, upright V lines, and the asymmetrical, solitary Satan, angular and troubled, outside heaven. The juxtaposition works to brilliant effect: on visual grounds alone one recognizes harmony and closure in the former, dissonance and incompletion in the latter. The upper section of Blake's design is related to an early sketch of the Trinity,[22] in which we observe much the same configuration of Father and Son, except that the Son's legs extend off to the right, as if he were literally flying to the Father's embrace. The Father's arms are draped over the Son's shoulders and down his back in the sketch, while overhead the Holy Spirit (depicted only as a hovering head and wings, perhaps with arms) extends his wings to cover the figures below. This sketch, which dates from about 1793, provides us with an indication of how early Blake had begun thinking about the nature of the Trinity—and perhaps about the situation in heaven in book 3—and certainly relates to Blake's work at the time on *The Marriage of Heaven and Hell*, with its pejorative comments on Milton's Trinity and its expression of surprise at the Holy Spirit's absence from that Trinity.

The Son Offers to Redeem Man is a most effective design, both aesthetically and critically. Unlike previous illustrators like Medina and

Cheron who had found it necessary to include in their designs for this scene some overt physical representation of the cross in order to allude to the Crucifixion (P, pls. 8, 18), Blake accomplishes the reference by depicting the Son in cruciform posture, though seen from the rear. The result is a more aesthetically pleasing and symbolically pregnant picture that effectively points to the Son's offer. In addition, the Son's posture is identical to that of the resurrected Christ in *The Ascension* (B, pl. 574), a painting Blake made at about the same time as the *Paradise Lost* designs. But it also resembles the *Dance of Albion* (fig. 3) posture indicative throughout Blake's visual canon of visionary energy, suggesting the positive, joyous aspect of the Crucifixion as imaginative liberation and redemption. Both Milton and Blake—the latter in particular—were acutely aware of the metaphorical implications of the Crucifixion, which emblem carries with it in Western art connotations not of death and self-sacrifice only but also of brotherhood, redemption, and creativity.[23]

For Milton the Crucifixion was the physical emblem of the Son's death on the human level and of man's rebirth on the spiritual, the emblem of an act both tragic and joyous. Blake took the point further still, seeing the Crucifixion as the emblem of the conscious annihilation of the selfhood in an act of love and integration effected *from within*, by conscious choice. Blake celebrates, not Christ's passion and death, but rather the archetypal imaginative redemption and reintegration of mankind it represents, the mental act by which man transcends his mortality—his vegetable body—and enters the paradise of fourfold vision. By fusing the various aspects of the Son's offer through the visual device of the cruciform posture that permeates the designs and epitomizes the messianic identity of the Son, Blake weighs the implications of that act and discovers in it a metaphorical paradigm for the necessary eradication of error in the individual, the act of repudiation and annihilation by which full visionary perception is to be attained. The gesture is doubly appropriate in its invocation of Blake's early visual symbol, *The Dance of Albion* (fig. 3). Created originally in 1780, as Blake tells us (E, p. 660), and metamorphosed verbally and visually for some forty-five years, the figure represents the union of all "the Nations," all the members of Albion—by extension, all mankind—in the One Man "Giving Himself for the Nations" (E, p. 660), whose prototype is the crucified Christ and whose descendants are all who reject error and embrace truth in individual last judgments. The gesture, particularly as explicitly manifested in the Crucifixion, is the "enacted exhortation to brotherhood" that opens the way back into eternity for man,[24] as we see in the empathetic relationship of Albion to the Jesus who is crucified on the tree of materialism on plate 76 of *Jerusalem* (fig. 50). Blake's telescoping of these traditional and iconoclastic symbolic referents for the Son's cruciform posture alerts the reader-viewer to the imaginative act of community the Crucifixion presages, the psychological liberation from the separate and Satanic selfhood and the resultant immersion in the "One Man Jesus the Savior" (*M* 42.11; E, p. 142) that reveals to every man the eternal and continually redemptive truth: "God is Jesus" (*Laocoön;* E, p. 271). The "Divine Body of the Lord Jesus" that is liberated through the passage of the inferior, vegetable body to "Eternal Death" is, in fact, "the Human Imagination" (*M* 3.3–4; E, p. 96) in which all men share. Hence the figure of the Son in this third design suggests all the connotations Blake associates with the figure of Christ as the creative principle, the "Human Form Divine."

Further, the Son's posture in this design places his heart against the Father's forehead, which rests on the Son's breast, his face thus hidden. This positioning emphasizes the difference between their two natures, juxtaposing the Son's humane and loving motivation with the Father's impersonal rationalism. Denied the guidance of facial expressions, we must read the body language of the gestures, which quickly suggests the expansive energy of the Son and the enclosing, confining pressure of the Father.[25] Yet the very fact that Blake arranges his figures as he does indicates the degree to which his understanding of their relationship had modulated from that articulated by the Devil in *The Marriage*. Rather than dwelling on the Father and pursuing the analogy with Urizen, Blake here merely suggests his age and nature and conceals his face behind the Son's body, preferring to keep our attention on the Son, whom he now fully acknowledges as hero.

Separated from the Father and the Son, and from the angels who cast down their crowns of gold (crowns which, by the way, lack the flowers of amarant with which Milton says they are interwoven [3.352–55]), is Satan, his estrangement physically reinforced by the bounding rim of clouds with which Blake frequently separates different spiritual or imaginative states. He hovers in the airy void, his sinister wings flowing behind him, armed with shield and spear pointed downward, perhaps at earth.[26] His facial expression still discontented, Satan is an isolated spirit, the embodiment of a vain separation and disintegration, and a troubling presence in this third design where he is forced downward by the visually dominant scene in heaven. While the visual arrangement in heaven is, as noted, orderly and self-enclosing, with all its lines and gestures gracefully suggesting circularity and integration, Satan's appearance in the design offers a series of open and incomplete visual gestures expressed in lines moving outward without completion—without integration—into the lonely void.

Another painting, *Christ the Mediator* (B, pl. 497), done between 1795 and 1800 for Butts, is of special interest here. At the center of this painting Blake portrays Christ in frontal view and in cruciform posture interceding for man (represented by the female figure, who may be the Magdalen) with the elderly Father seated at the right holding his sceptre. On the left, young and old angels alike express their approbation. Blake's painting sheds additional light upon HH 3 (pl. 6), for it illustrates Paul's statement that "there is one God, and one mediator between God and men, the man Jesus Christ" (1 Tim. 2:15), a statement that underlies Blake's later, revised view of the Son's role early in book 11. Blake was, of course, firmly committed to the concept of the mutual divinity of God and man, as his earliest aphoristic manifestos demonstrate. Moreover, the interpretation that informs his *Paradise Lost* designs, taken together with the implications of *Christ the Mediator*, indicates an alteration in Blake's thinking regarding Milton's Son as he turned his thoughts away from the worldly effects of the Fall, with which he had seemingly been preoccupied in the 1790s (as the prophecies of the 1790s attest), to its most significant psychological and spiritual consequence: the promise of imaginative and spiritual salvation epitomized in the various aspects of the Son's offer (a shift likewise discernible in Blake's three epics).[27] Blake's deliberate employment of the cruciform posture in *Christ the Mediator* and *The Son Offers to Redeem Man* indicates the artist's insistence that we recognize the mediatorial function of the Crucifixion within a framework far broader than that of the insignificant vegetable world of materiality.

In the second version of *The Son Offers to Redeem Man* (pl. 7) Blake presents the Son's face in side view and extends his legs off more to the right, alterations that suggest Blake's return to his earlier conception of the Son "flying" to the Father. In keeping with Milton's text, Blake here adds the flowers to the crowns offered by the angels. The angels themselves, in both designs, represent an interesting development from those customarily included in scenes of the Son in heaven. Previous illustrations were frequently crowded with a distracting and cluttered mass of adoring cherubs often popping incongruously from clouds, as well as with elaborate celestial machinery (P, pls. 8, 18, 38). Blake's symmetrical composition infuses the scene with a beauty and a calm serenity appropriate to heaven and totally absent from previous illustrations. Blake also changes the figure of Satan in the later design, showing him now glancing, not up at the heavenly scene, but rather vacantly down and toward the dark void at the lower right. His expression in this later design has modulated from his previous jealous discontent to one of troubled confusion, a more accurate reflection of Milton's comment that "the hot Hell . . . always in him burns, / Though in mid Heaven" (9.467–68). Finally, perhaps anticipating the rise of Satan as phallic power in man's world, his spear is now turned point upwards.

Blake employs the symmetrical V composition again in his next design, *Satan's and Raphael's Entries into Paradise* (pl. 1), to merge in a single design passages drawn from books 4 and 5. At the right Adam and Eve walk hand in hand in a visual foreshadowing of the manner in which Milton has them leaving Eden at the conclusion. They are contented, compatible figures; the similarity of their postures and facial expressions as they gaze at one another indicates their fully integrated prelapsarian unity, a unity further reinforced by their joined hands (to which Milton makes recurrent references in the poem). The representation of this ancient symbol for plighting and keeping faith is itself a rare gesture in pre-Miltonic depictions of Adam and Eve.[28] The Edenic setting is a bright, open one with lush vegetation of bountiful nature in the background.

Satan occupies the left third of the design. His body, with its folded wings, is enwrapped by the coils of the Serpent, whose head rises above him and who looks with an expression remarkably like Satan's toward the couple at whom Satan stares with his customary troubled expression. This area of the design is dark and closed, with trees surrounding Satan. Blake has carefully drawn the bare branches of the tree at the far left, externalizing Satan's mental state and demonstrating through physical nature its cold, dark barrenness that blights the very environment with which it comes into contact. In this design, for the first time in the series, Satan and his alter ego the Serpent are physically united. Developing the visual suggestions of the first three designs, Blake shows the Serpent's body coiled across Satan's genital area. Reinforcing the perverse and narcissistic sexual association of Satan and his phallic alter ego, this arrangement of the Serpent's coils recurs in subsequent depictions of Satan, and it makes a surprising and significant appearance in *The Temptation and Fall of Eve* (pls. 16, 17).

Satan's sexuality is, of course, the perverted and isolationist sexuality of jealousy and paranoia that seeks to condemn, to deny, and to destroy what it cannot possess, understand, or appreciate. Satan represents the sour grapes mentality of Aesop's fox pushed to an impossible extreme and perhaps best epitomized in the self-serving stance Blake's Pebble describes:

> Love seeketh only Self to please,
> To bind another to its delight;
> Joys in anothers loss of ease,
> And builds a Hell in Heavens despite.
> ["The Clod & the Pebble"; E, p. 19]

This travesty is love turned inside out. Satan is himself the ultimate inversion. In turning his original angelic nature (see *Satan in His Original Glory;* B, pl. 554) inside out, Lucifer becomes the horrible parody of the Father we see in *Paradise Lost.* In addition, as the figurehead for "Every Religion That Preaches Vengeance for Sin" (*J,* pl. 52; E, p. 199), Satan is "The Accuser who is The God of This World" (*Gates of Paradise;* E, p. 266).

So wrapped up in self-worship and declarations of his own supposed divinity ("I am God alone / There is no other!" [*M* 9.25–26; E, p. 102]) that he cannot—indeed *will* not—distinguish truth from error, he is incapable of recognizing the terrible irony at the center of his existence:

> Truly My Satan thou art but a Dunce
> And dost not know the Garment from the Man
> [*Gates of Paradise;* E, p. 266]

Like his heavenly counterpart, the Father, Satan surrounds himself with a hierarchical support group to feed his ego at the expense of humanity. Damon has remarked that Satan is eternal death, "the inability to receive the divine light."[29] As eternal death, "the Limit of Opacity" (*FZ* 56.19; E, p. 331), Satan is himself limited, though he realizes his limitations no more than the Father recognizes his own. The mental triumph the Crucifixion symbolizes is victory over the inverted vision that regards mortal death as the worst of all evils: *eternal* death. Hence it is appropriate that in depicting the Crucifixion later in the designs Blake has the nail in the Son's foot pierce the Serpent's head, for the Crucifixion represents the ultimate act of love and community, an integrative gesture totally beyond the capacity of the self-centered prince of pride.

Separating the two areas of earthly experience in *Satan's and Raphael's Entries into Paradise* (pl. 1) is the figure of Raphael, descending in the arrow of clouds that comprises the central third of the design and that presents an extension of the heavenly realm to earth in the form of Raphael's mission at the Father's command. Raphael's placement indicates his function at this point: sent to warn Adam and Eve of their danger, he separates them from Satan until they can arm themselves against his psychological warfare. Raphael is an incongruous figure, given awkward hand and facial gestures. Looking directly above himself toward the Father leaves him rather precariously positioned, seemingly about to fall out of his cloud. As indicators of his perfect submission to the Father's will, Raphael's posture and gestures seem visually unsuccessful. But this apparent failure should alert us to the subtle humor of Blake's design: here we see clearly the incongruities that result from unquestioning obeisance. In modestly covering his paps (just as his wings cover his genitals) he folds his arms inward, collapsing what might otherwise be a cruciform gesture into a closed and unintegrating one. Are we to surmise this is the consequence of his absolute submission to the Father, as opposed to the Son's free and willful act of choice? Perhaps so, for Raphael stands here in danger of taking a fall himself, much as Adam and Eve do in a less literal and certainly less humorous sense. Yet Blake's point about the necessity of thinking and choosing for oneself is implicit in both situations.

Raphael finds a visual precedent in the piper from the frontispiece to the *Songs of Innocence*. Blake's piper likewise steps forward (though with his left foot, not his right, suggesting a preponderance of materiality rather than spirituality) while looking directly up at the child on the cloud ("Introduction"). The closed background of the frontispiece, its figures framed and backed by trees, anticipates the background in *Satan's and Raphael's Entries into Paradise*, where, of course, the physical innocence of the Edenic landscape reflects the spiritual innocence of Adam and Eve. Prelapsarian Eden has not yet admitted the bifurcation of sensibility Blake will call innocence and experience: Adam and Eve are growing spiritually and intellectually, moving in mutually reflective visual unison, as yet untouched by the perverse influence of Satan, although as viewers we see the bifurcation has already begun, as the left side of the picture demonstrates. Thus this fourth design alludes visually to Blake's *Songs* and by extension to "the Two Contrary States of the Human Soul."[30] That the superior visionary perspective is already implicit in the *Songs of Innocence* (the *Songs of Experience* merely throwing the point into higher relief) points to the Edenic parallel, where Adam and Eve are already provided, *before* the Fall, with the means of overcoming the Fall and reconciling the dialectical conflict of contraries through enlightened choice: the active imagination that Blake never tires of reminding us is "the Bosom of God" (*M* 5.20; E, p. 146). The incongruity of Raphael's figure points us back to the lesson Jesus learns in *Paradise Regained* and Milton learns in *Milton:* like the piper of innocence who is also intuitively correct in his apprehensions, Raphael needs to substitute for his dependence upon external guidance (the cherub on the cloud, the Father, respectively) the frank sense of self-sufficiency attained by those heroes. The analogy with the *Songs* also serves to explain the dark barrenness of the Satanic third of Blake's design: such is the condition of the world we encounter repeatedly in the *Songs of Experience*. Satan's lament, "Myself am Hell" (*PL* 4.75), clearly reflects his view of his own experiential fall (as well as the falls of all those trapped in the self-made hell of experience who build "a Hell in Heavens despite," and helps to explain the blighted, darkened condition of the environment in which Blake places him in this design.

Hovering at the top of the design, presiding like some celestial puppeteer, is the Father. The attribution of wings to the Father is iconographically unusual, but Blake employs the image repeatedly, as in *The Lazar House* (B, pls. 397–99) and *The Tempter Inspiring Jesus's Ugly Dreams* (*Paradise Regained*, pl. 8; B, pl. 691).[31] Consistently associated in its other appearances with the negative influence of Urizen, who often hovers with outstretched, waving wings over the scene of his cruelties, the figure of the Father here, as in the previous illustration, points to Blake's revision of the orthodox Trinity and its significance. There is no escaping the suggestion that the Father is here directing and manipulating the scene below, even if only by allowing it to be played out to mankind's detriment. The Father's unusual wings and his gesturing arms anticipate their eventual metamorphosis into God, Satan, *and* Job in Blake's *Job* illustrations. The serpent-wrapped figure of Job's dreams (*Job*, pl. 11), God in the whirlwind and in Job's vision of the universe (*Job*, pls. 13, 14), and Job himself (*Job*, pl. 20) all echo the Satanic dispenser of afflictions (*Job*, pls. 3, 6). The convergence of Father and Satan, engineered visually through the association of wings, gestures, and physical appearance in *Satan's and Raphael's Entries* further alerts the reader-viewer sensitive to Blake's iconography to the parodic parallels inherent in the two figures throughout Milton's epic.

When Blake made his second set of designs, however, he eliminated this design entirely, perhaps feeling it was too obviously synoptic, perhaps fearing the inherent humor of the Raphael figure brought his design too near the comic inappropriateness of the Satan-Uriel episode that had appeared so often in the illustrations to book 3. Perhaps, more simply, he felt visual and symbolic continuity would be best served by transposing the floating figure of Satan from *The Son Offers to Redeem Man* (pls. 6, 7) directly into *Satan Watching Adam and Eve* (pls. 8, 9), where it provides a dramatic echo of the former. *Satan Watching Adam and Eve* had been a popular scene since Hayman introduced it. The scene's obvious dramatic potential undoubtedly had influenced Hayman's selection of the episode in the first place. Blake's elaborately stylized design, however, replaces the outward dramatic context with symbolic content of universal significance and elaborates on the visual terminology with which he will explain the Fall.[32]

Satan's parodic relationship to the Father has already been suggested; now we see also his relation to Adam and Eve. Just as Adam embraces Eve, kissing her with his right hand cradling her head, so too does Satan embrace the Serpent in a gesture of phallic autoeroticism, cradling its head with its mouth near his own in a Satanic kiss. Their eyes meet as do Adam and Eve's below them, but the couple's contented expressions are replaced in Satan by that characteristically troubled one. Satan points to Adam and Eve as if indicating to the Serpent the goad to his "jealous leer malign" (*PL* 4.503).

This design contrasts the mental conditions of Adam and Eve on one hand and Satan on the other, as well as the quality of the love those conditions produce. Satan's essential characteristics, as revealed both in the context of these designs and in the wider context of Blake's entire verbal and visual canon, are simultaneously the causes and the effects of his own fall. His character is shaped by the inordinate pride manifested in his vain and self-deceiving assumption that he could yet be the Father's opponent, though in ruin, and be free after his fall. His pride leads him to a self-centered and narcissistic doctrine of separatism: hence his repeated appearances within the coils of the Serpent he so lovingly regards. This is the dead-end emotion of lust, the depersonalized bestial pursuit of physical pleasure divorced from the liberating spiritual regeneration produced by the sensual act of community— or commingling—the sexual act implies. This is all Satan is capable of, which further explains the nature of his fall. Milton has him declare himself in book 4 in a firm dedication to evil ("Evil be thou my Good" [4.110–13]). After this declaration of inverted values, Satan appears in Milton's text as a grimly determined though constantly degenerating figure, though in book 9 he is still enough himself to declare that "only in destroying I find ease" (9.129) and to bring about the Fall.

Blake felt that Milton had erred significantly in diminishing Satan's dynamism in the poem, reducing him to a hopeless fatalist and effectively precluding further serious consideration of the persistent mental torment Blake considers implicit in his character and which he surely noted in Satan's remark in book 9 about feeling "torment within me, as from the hateful siege / Of contraries" (9.121–22), a remark Milton himself seemed to Blake to have ignored. Blake's idea is not that Satan is heroic or even attractive within the context of *Paradise Lost;* like Shelley, Blake recognizes the repugnance of Satan's enormous, selfish

Plate 1. William Blake. *Satan's and
Raphael's Entries into Paradise*. HH 4.
25.1 cm by 20.4 cm. *Reproduced by permission of the Huntington Library, San
Marino, California*

Plate 2. William Blake. *Satan Calling His Legions*. HH 1. 25 cm by 21.1 cm. *Reproduced by permission of the Huntington Library, San Marino, California*

Plate 3. William Blake. *Satan Calling His Legions (Satan Arousing the Rebel Angels).* BM 1. 51.8 cm by 39.3 cm. *Victoria and Albert Museum, London*

Plate 4. William Blake. *Satan, Sin, and Death*. HM 2. 24.8 cm by 20.8 cm. *Reproduced by permission of the Huntington Library, San Marino, California*

Plate 5. William Blake. *Satan, Sin, and Death.* BM 2. 49.5 cm by 40.3 cm. *Reproduced by permission of the Huntington Library, San Marino, California*

Plate 6. William Blake. *The Son Offers to
Redeem Man.* HH 3. 25.7 cm by 21 cm.
*Reproduced by permission of the Hunt-
ington Library, San Marino, California*

Plate 7. William Blake. *The Son Offers to Redeem Man.* BM 3. 49.6 cm by 39.3 cm. *Subscription of 1890. Courtesy, Fine Arts Museum, Boston*

Plate 8. William Blake. *Satan Watching Adam and Eve.* HH 5. 25.8 cm by 21.3 cm. *Reproduced by permission of the Huntington Library, San Marino, California*

Plate 9. William Blake. *Satan Watch-ing Adam and Eve.* BM 4. 50.7 cm by 38.2 cm. *Courtesy, Museum of Fine Arts, Boston*

Plate 10. William Blake. *Raphael Warns
Adam and Eve.* HH 6. 25.7 cm by 20.9
cm. *Reproduced by permission of the
Huntington Library, San Marino,
California*

Plate 11. William Blake. *Raphael Warns Adam and Eve*. BM 6. 49.7 cm by 39.7 cm. *Courtesy, Museum of Fine Arts, Boston*

Plate 12. William Blake. *The Rout of the
Rebel Angels.* HH 7. 25.7 cm by 20.8 cm.
*Reproduced by permission of the Hunt-
ington Library, San Marino, California*

Plate 13. William Blake. *The Rout of the Rebel Angels.* BM 7. 49.1 cm by 38.2 cm. *Courtesy, Museum of Fine Arts, Boston*

Plate 14. William Blake. *The Creation of Eve*. HH 8. 25.3 cm. by 20.8 cm. *Reproduced by permission of the Huntington Library, San Marino, California*

Plate 15. William Blake. *The Creation of
Eve*. BM 8. 49.9 cm by 40 cm. *Courtesy,
Museum of Fine Arts, Boston*

Plate 16. William Blake. *The Temptation and Fall of Eve.* HH 9. 25.4 cm by 20.9 cm. *Reproduced by permission of the Huntington Library, San Marino, California*

Plate 17. William Blake. *The Temptation and Fall of Eve.* BM 9. 49.7 cm by 38.7 cm. *Courtesy, Museum of Fine Arts, Boston*

Plate 18. William Blake. *The Judgment
of Adam and Eve.* HH 10. 25.1 cm by
20.2 cm. *Reproduced by permission
of the Huntington Library, San Marino,
California*

Plate 19. William Blake. *The Judgment
of Adam and Eve.* BM 10. 49.6 cm by
39 cm. *The Department of Printing
and Graphic Arts, Houghton Library,
Harvard University, Cambridge, Massachusetts*

Plate 20. William Blake. *Michael Foretells the Crucifixion.* HH 11. 25.2 cm by 20.4 cm. *Reproduced by permission of the Huntington Library, San Marino, California*

Plate 21. William Blake. *Michael Foretells the Crucifixion*. BM 11. 50.1 cm by
38.1 cm. *Courtesy, Museum of Fine Arts,
Boston*

Plate 22. William Blake. *The Expulsion.*
HH 12. 24.9 cm by 20.5 cm. *Reproduced
by permission of the Huntington Library,
San Marino, California*

Plate 23. William Blake. *The Expulsion.*
BM 12. 50 cm by 38.8 cm. *Courtesy, Museum of Fine Arts, Boston*

Plate 24. William Blake. *Adam and Eve
Sleeping.* BM 5. 49.2 cm by 38.8 cm. *Courtesy, Museum of Fine Arts, Boston*

pride. But in order even to be a credible villain he must be a worthy adversary, else where is the value in battling him? Even Milton's remark about "virtue untried" in the *Areopagitica* says as much. To see Satan in the simplistic orthodox manner, branding him in stereotypical, absolute terms of moral evil, is to ignore the paradox that makes informed choice always so difficult: the fact that real evil so often appeals to man in the guise of apparent good. In developing the Satanic dynamism Milton eschews, Blake attempts to alert us, through the contrast that results, to one of the crucial instances of cloudy thinking—of vision obscured— brought on by Milton's overimmersion in dogmatic orthodoxy.

Satan's psychological condition in *Satan Watching Adam and Eve* is the converse of Adam and Eve's. Their state in Eden at this point, in fact, represents precisely the qualities of Satan in their *unfallen* state, a point that is demonstrated by the nature of the temptation Satan subsequently offers Eve, by the temptation she in turn offers Adam, and by the couple's behavior toward one another after their fall. Their characters are summed up in HH 5 (pl. 8) in the unfallen counterpart to pride: humility and integration. Just as Satan's pride turns his attention inward upon himself, so does the humility of Adam and Eve turn theirs outward, not in exaltation of self, but in love and service to one another. Theirs is the state of benevolent selflessness recommended by the "Proverb of Hell" that states that "the most sublime act is to set another before you" (*MHH*, pl. 7; E, pl. 35). In their unfallen state Adam and Eve are united and unified, their correct love manifested outwardly in their mental contentment and physical pleasure. Their relationship comes as near the androgynous state Blake described to Crabb Robinson as possible in the physical world.

As a *mental* construct, this design alludes to the Eden of Blake's mythology, the state of the fully integrated personality. In terms of the *physical* metaphor of Eden, the design represents the state of Beulah, in which even though man is divided from his emanation they still exist in perfect marriage. The former basks in the sun of eternity, the latter is illuminated by the moon, both of which Blake includes in his design. Blake's design points toward the Fall, citing its origins in the division of identities that grows increasingly pronounced as the drama unfolds. Adam and Eve have not yet reached Ulro and the separation of the female will, a mental division that will find its physical counterpart later in Eve's insistence on working alone. But as subsequent designs—and indeed the second version of *this* design—make clear, the Fall has already begun, as Eve's thrusting *left* foot in both versions suggests by its contrast to Adam's right, and as is further indicated in both versions by the facts that Adam wears a wreath of roses (foreshadowing the Son's crown of thorns) and that both Adam and Eve are seen to pluck iconographically significant flowers—he a lily, she a rose.

The physical and spiritual integration of Adam and Eve at this early moment is underscored by the gracefully self-contained visual arrangement of their bower. Like the heavenly scene in *The Son Offers to Redeem Man*, to which this design provides the earthly counterpart, the bower scene is concave and symmetrical, its lines circular and turning inward but with the curving V now inverted. Satan's excluded position—now above the scene, signaling his ascendancy of influence, rather than below it[33]—leaves him once again inscribing angular, asymmetrical lines that lead off toward the void whose darkness Blake had intensified in the later version of *The Son Offers to Redeem Man*. The integration and unity of the unfallen couple serves to remind Satan of what from his own fallen perspective he would regard as the similar primal integration of Father and Son in heaven, both of which situations are alike intolerable to Satan, the proud outcast to whom such interpersonal integrative unity is now eternally denied and who prostitutes the concept in his narcissistic infatuation with his own alter ego, the Serpent, and in his incestuous relations with the self-generated members of his trinity. The striking repetitions of the inverted V structure, the symmetrical and asymmetrical areas, and the arrangement and gestures of Satan's body serve further to link this scene and that in heaven.

The evolution of this design interestingly reveals how Blake went about perfecting his conceptions of given scenes. The first evidence we can consult is a rough pencil sketch for a separate painting of this scene (B, pl. 723). The sketch merely suggests the blocking of the figures, with Adam and Eve drawn in their bower. The figure of Satan, the part of the design that changed most in its evolution, hovers above with arms indistinctly positioned. His left hand seems to point to the bower, and there may be a suggestion of the Serpent drawn in at his right hand, though it is difficult to tell for sure. The sketch reveals Blake's early indecision concerning the nature of Satan's condition in this episode. Blake must have known Rigaud's design for this scene (fig. 46), published in 1801, for already in the sketch the postures of Adam and Eve are remarkably like those of the Rigaud illustration, though Rigaud treats the bower in a more representational fashion and handles Satan much differently.

The separate painting that evolved from the sketch (B, pl. 644) gives us a Satan quite different from that in HH 5 (pl. 8), BM5 (pl. 24), and even the pencil sketch.[34] Here he hovers actively over the bower, wingless but in flames, perhaps in consequence of his declaration that "which way I fly is Hell; myself am Hell" (*PL* 4.75). His face is contorted, and his hands clutch at his head, as if tearing his hair in rage or despair. The Serpent is separated from him, winding beneath the feet of Adam and Eve at the bottom of the design. Lacking the symbolic universality of its counterparts in the *Paradise Lost* sets, this picture is less effective than those two designs, despite its inherent drama.

Blake made several significant alterations in the second version of *Satan Watching Adam and Eve* (pl. 9). The most obvious of these involved reversing Satan's position so that he now drifts off to the right rather than to the left, which permits his descending gaze to meet the ascending gaze of Eve; even though she is apparently looking specifically at Adam, and Satan at the Serpent, the design implies multiple eye

Figure 46. After Stephen Rigaud. *Adam and Eve in Their Bower.* 1801. *By permission of the British Library, London*

contact. In this way Blake suggests the beginnings of Satan's infiltration of Eve's mind preparatory to her temptation.

To support his suggestion Blake has made another alteration that, while seemingly slight, proves of considerable importance. He reversed the original positions of the sun and moon here, placing the sun now on the right where the moon had been in HH 5 (pl. 8), and he removed the morning star, replacing it with a generally starry sky.[35] By the standards of traditional iconography, this celestial rearrangement changes the moment represented from sunrise to sunset, which in terms of Milton's poem places the new design at a point more immediately previous to Eve's troubled dream. Though the HH design is not incorrect in locating the moment at sunrise, the BM design more effectively suggests the

relationship of the moment to the nature and significance of the temptation sequence to come, especially since the next design in the BM set (pl.
24) shows the Satanic toad at the ear of the sleeping Eve.

When Blake made his second set of designs, he chose to eliminate
Satan's and Raphael's Entries into Paradise and to insert a new scene,
Adam and Eve Sleeping (pl. 24), after *Satan Watching Adam and Eve*.[36]
Blake interestingly commemorates the irony of Eve's troubled dream,
showing us the toad at her ear at the moment she is dreaming of the
tempter as a beautiful angel. That dream image merges in Blake's design
with the figures of Ithuriel and Zephon, who are searching for Satan
(4.788–800). While one worried angel points to the toad, the other,
though his face reflects obvious concern, gestures as if to calm or silence
him. Adam is drawn, interestingly, in the posture of supposedly postcoital repose we see again in the male figure in *Milton*, plate 42 (fig. 6).
This design takes us a step beyond the mutualism of the embrace in the
previous design and toward the further separation we see in the design
that follows. Here the sun has vanished, its light replaced by the crescent moon of generation and the star of reason that mark the further
progress of the Fall. That Eve's face is turned away from both Adam and
the angels and toward Satan-toad indicates her decline and prefigures
her physical and psychological separation in the subsequent designs.

Though we do not see the content of Eve's dream, its nature is ade-
quately suggested through the design's iconography. We may relate this
illustration to *The Tempter Inspiring Jesus's Ugly Dreams* (*PR* pl. 8; B,
pl. 691), which further reflects the persistent fondness for illustrating
dream situations we see in Blake's designs for Young, Gray, Bunyan, and
Dante as well as in his *L'Allegro* and *Il Penseroso* designs. In illustrating
the dream of any character, Blake isolates—even prefigures—the psychological aspects of the temptations that are to follow, asserting with
Milton that while the dreamer cannot consciously control the nature or
the substance of his dreams, he *is* responsible for the reception and
informed utilization in his waking hours of the vision the dream contains. Eve subsequently fails in her crisis of temptation, where Jesus
succeeds in his (as they fail and succeed in responding to their dreams),
because she is unable to recognize the diabolical origin and content of
her dream and to employ that recognition in her own defense. The customary illustrative reference to this scene was *Satan Starting at the
Touch of Ithuriel's Spear*. Blake's decision to depart from this tradition
again suggests his desire to avoid heroizing or even dramatizing Satan.
He clearly wishes to suggest Satan's more insidious function in this
scene, which proves both psychologically and symbolically the more
productive approach.

Blake's next design, *Raphael Warns Adam and Eve* (pls. 10, 11), conflates several moments in Milton's narrative, particularly Raphael's actual warnings (*PL* 5.520–43, 8.633–43). Raphael, the guardian angel
par excellence, points with his right hand to the already heavily thorned
tree prominent in the center background and with his left up along the

right margin, perhaps indicating heaven, perhaps simply the world out-side Eden where he suspects Satan may be lurking.[37] In either case, his right hand points directly at the Serpent winding about the tree, a deft touch of ironic foreshadowing on Blake's part.

Adam and Eve, seated here at the left, listen attentively to Raphael, both seeming—if their unison gestures of left hands raised to their breasts is any indication—to react to Raphael's suggestions of their immediate personal danger. When Blake revised this scene for the BM set, he depicted Eve standing at the center, with the tree still visible over her left shoulder. This change breaks that original near-unison, separat-ing Adam and Eve in both form and function to emphasize their in-creasing separateness. The revision is also truer to Milton's narrative in removing Eve from the discussion, whose substance Milton tells us she prefers to hear later from Adam. Whereas in the original design she looks with Adam at Raphael, she now stands apart, looking only at Adam, and serving the meal. In thus occupying Eve with the emblems of domesticity, Blake likewise stresses the *physical*, sensual nature of Eve's role, in contrast to the mental abstraction of Adam's discourse with Raphael. The fruit in her hand, of course, anticipates the fatal fruit she is soon to accept at Satan's urging.

The revisions in Blake's later design produce a decided visual im-provement as well, setting up a symmetrical pyramidal structure within the graceful upright V arch that is itself a logical development of the vegetative bower in *Satan Watching Adam and Eve*. The increased styl-ization of both the gestures and the visual details heightens the calm balance of the design; Raphael's less insistent pointing, for instance, and the visual stasis of Adam's gesture reflect this change. The increased lushness of the vegetation here recalls the tendency in this direction in previous illustrations like Stothard's and Burney's, but the natural abun-dance here possesses none of the distracting quality we see in such designs.

Blake's use of the animals, as well as his placement of the tree on a hill, deviates interestingly from Milton's conception of the scene. Mil-ton has his tree on *flat* ground, beside a fountain and a row of myrtles (*PL* 9.627–28), none of which details Blake includes, probably feeling rightly that their inclusion would distract us from the tree he has placed on a rise in the ground in HH 6 (pl. 10)—a hill in BM 6 (pl. 11)—in anticipation particularly of the hill upon which Michael shows Adam the crucified Christ. Likewise, Blake has conveniently ignored Satan's description of the background for this scene:

> About the mossy Trunk I wound me soon,
> For high from ground the branches would require
> Thy utmost reach or Adam's: Round the Tree
> All other Beasts that saw, with like desire
> Longing and envying stood, but could not reach.
> [*PL* 9.589–93]

Blake apparently decided Satan was flattering himself here, for he shows only one animal—the horse—paying any attention to him. This is itself an indication of the insinuation of Blake's symbolism into Milton's garden, for Blake habitually associates the horse with both empirical reason ("the horses of instruction" [*MHH*, pl. 9]) and Urizen.[38] In front of the tree in HH 6 a lion lies beside the sheep, a visual reference not only to prelapsarian harmony but also to the condition forecast in Revelation. The cluster of animals Blake depicts about the base of the tree provides an interesting anticipation in the subhuman world of the clustered human figures at the foot of the cross in *Michael Foretells the Crucifixion* (pls. 20,21) and in separate paintings like *Soldiers Casting Lots for Christ's Garments* (B, pl. 571). All these designs illustrate Blake's facility at adapting and transforming traditional iconographical materials, suiting them to frequently radical new applications.

Finally, the BM design is symbolically superior; by placing the standing Eve and the Serpent-entwined tree in such visual proximity, Blake effectively suggests the Fall itself within the very scene in which Adam and Eve are presumably receiving Raphael's warning. The tree is, of course, a traditional iconographic representation of the cross and is used as such by Blake himself on plate 76 of *Jerusalem* (fig. 50), where Albion looks up at Christ crucified on the tree.[39] The tree symbolizes for Blake the vegetable body of generation; in the later design it represents the material world of the natural body upon which the Son is crucified. As a symbol of the generated universe, the tree typically figures in scenes representing the creation of Eve as well, as it does in fact in Blake's depiction of that scene. In *Raphael Warns Adam and Eve* (pls. 10, 11) the tree prefigures not only the tree of the Fall but also the cross of the Crucifixion, suggesting aspects of the Fall which the Son's death as man is to overthrow.

The two birds flying at the left of the tree may simply—and legitimately—be accounted a part of the harmonious state of nature in unfallen Eden; they may also constitute an example of the artist's reworking of that inherited iconography. Following the precedent established by Medina's design (P, pl. 10), Hayman's illustration for book 11, (P, pl. 43) displays the moment in which the eagle first becomes a predator (*PL* 11.182–86), depicting the eagle swooping down upon a large-billed bird that is upside-down beneath it in the air, perhaps defending itself but more likely falling. While these long-necked, wide-winged birds-of-paradise recur regularly in Blake's visual work prior to 1808, we may still reasonably speculate that the two birds in HH 6 (pl. 10) visually anticipate the moment Hayman had depicted, just as the *thorned* tree anticipates the Fall, chronological time being collapsed as Blake draws together sequentially separated details in a single design.

The Rout of the Rebel Angels (pls. 12, 13) is at once among the most active of the *Paradise Lost* designs and one of the most statically stylized and symmetrical, a visual ambivalence not unlike that created by *The Ancient of Days* (fig. 19). Blake's design is a remarkable reworking of the visual tradition associated with the Son's defeat of the rebellious angels. With the exception of Hayman's design and, to a lesser extent, Westall's and Fuseli's, all the major illustrations of this scene had been executed in terms of elaborate antique military conflicts, usually employing dated martial costumes and weaponry, as though the supernatural conflict had been waged with decidedly human implements of havoc. It appears not to have occurred to any illustrator of *Paradise Lost* seriously to attempt a depiction of the contending armies hurling mountains at one another, for which we should probably be grateful, although something of the sort had been attempted for illustrations of the Book of Revelation.

Medina's design for book 6 showed the heavenly army above and to the left, driving out the rebels on the right, who fall or leap off the clouds into hell below. At the upper center, highlighted in a break in the clouds, is the tiny figure of the Son, mounted on a clumsy cartlike chariot and brandishing a whip (P, pl. 7). Cheron's headpiece to book 6 depicts the conflict between the winged angels and the wingless rebels (P, pl. 20), reserving for the tailpiece the figure of the Son in his chariot. Hayman's more energetic design shows the Son rather incongruously holding up the hem of his garment and surrounded by angelic figures that seem to pop out of the clouds; he wields thunderbolts as he drives out the rebels who fall headlong and disoriented into hell (P, pl. 45). Satan alone of the rebels sees the Son and shakes his fist wrathfully at him. Westall's design expands upon Hayman's conception, depicting centrally the heroic figure of the Son wielding a handful of thunderbolts. He is the focus of the design, the rebels being reduced to a pair of shadowy, incomplete figures at the lower right and the loyal angels to a single determined face at the lower left. Burney's design returns the focus to Satan and his crew, depicting them centrally as they tumble into the dark abyss of hell, driven by the thunderbolts the Son hurls from his chariot in the upper right background. Nearest of all to Blake's symbolic conception of the scene—though still far from it—is Fuseli's 1802 illustration (fig. 47),[40] which also focuses upon the figure of Satan as he is driven from heaven. In two breaks in the clouds, at lower left and right, we see members of his rebel band plunging downward. Satan himself, though, is not falling, but is simply fleeing the presence of the Son, visible in the upper center background with his left arm extended. The significance of Fuseli's illustration lies in its portrayal of the rout as the result not so much of an external military action as of a verbal (perhaps even mental) command by the Son. Not armed for battle, the Son merely extends his arm, and the issue is resolved: Satan flees. Fuseli seems to have recognized that the traditional military conception of the scene distracted from the abstract, symbolic act that underlies the overthrow, even though his own *Paradise Lost* illustrations retain, to a great extent, that military metaphor.

Blake, of course, also recognized the symbolic nature of the overthrow and stressed it in his own design. The military metaphor is rejected entirely: we do not see in HH 7 (pl. 12) even a token spear or

Figure 47. After Henry Fuseli. *Rout of the Rebel Angels.* 1802. *By permission of the British Library, London*

shield as we had in *Satan Calling His Legions.* The bow drawn by the Son is a detail introduced into *Paradise Lost* illustration by Blake, a textually justified symbol of divine energy (6.712–14). Blake invites us to draw a number of symbolic inferences from this design, the first of which involves the thematically related picture, *The Ancient of Days* (fig. 19). Against the rationalistic old figure of that design, at work with his compasses in misdirected (and consequently "aged") energy, Blake offers for comparison in *The Rout of the Rebel Angels* (pls. 12, 13) the similarly positioned youthful, energetic figure of the Son in a flaming orb that radiates arrows symmetrically in a parallel of the arrow drawn by the Son. These are the arrows of imaginative energy and of true love (the "Arrows of desire" from plate 1 of *Milton*), the perfection of desire that forms the basis of the Son's character as Blake now apprehends it. This design shows us the positive use of the same essential energy that is employed negatively in *The Ancient of Days*. The Son turns those arrows here against the powers of pride, the perverted and narcissistic form of desire, in an assertion of the creative force by which physical and intellectual-imaginative life is to be lived and the unnatural tyranny of the selfhood overthrown. The Son is not quashing a justifiable rebellion here, but quashing instead the faulty *motives* for revolution epitomized in Satan. Satan represents the reasoning world of prideful materialism, the opacity that admits no light of humane and imaginative vision. Hence it is appropriate to invoke, as Blake does, the longstanding *Son-Sun* pun and to portray graphically the intolerance of Satan and his crew to imaginative light. In HH 7 (pl. 12) the arrowshaft is visible, outlined along the Son's left arm. In the corresponding BM design (pl. 13) that arrowshaft disappears, however, the Son's *arm* becoming the shaft and his whole person thus the arrow, as Blake clarifies and sophisticates his symbol.

The most important visual precedent in Blake's work for this design is his sixth illustration for Gray's "The Progress of Poesy" (fig. 48),[41] which portrays Hyperion in a brilliant sun-sphere, notching a golden arrow on a golden bow. From the sphere radiate dozens of other arrows. Beneath the sphere appear the contorted heads of Night's "spectres wan," put to rout by Hyperion's appearance. Blake's Gray design presents within the context of classical mythology the same sort of statement made in a Christian context by *The Rout of the Rebel Angels*. We may apply to both designs Sir Geoffrey Keynes's observation on the former that "Blake's conception of the Sun, symbol of imagination and poetry, dispelling the gloom and terrors of night would also suggest victory over the evils of materialism."[42] The Son's symbolic rout of the Satanic spectres of reason (and the religious orthodoxy associated with it) is synonymous with his narrative rout of the rebel angels. That Blake repeats the image of the bow—and indeed the entire visual configuration of the Gray design where his metaphor deals explicitly with poetic activity—indicates the importance he attached to the creative, imaginative aspect of the Son's action.

Also relevant is Blake's *Christ Trampling upon Urizen* (B, pl. 526),[43] showing Christ standing with his left foot upon the breast of the aged Urizen, who lies outstretched on the ground. The old, bearded figure of Urizen is very like the Death of *The Judgment of Adam and Eve* (pls. 18, 19), *Michael Foretells the Crucifixion* (pls. 20, 21), and the HH version of *Satan, Sin, and Death* (pl. 4), but without the crown. He is also much like the Ancient of Days and the Father of the *Paradise Lost* designs, all of which associations coalesce in the visual emblem of the arch-reasoner who appears so frequently as well in Blake's illuminated poetry. Urizen's left arm reaches vainly upward, his fingers barely able to touch the bow like Hyperion's that Christ holds in his left hand; in his right hand Christ holds a single arrow. The temporal proximity of the heavily symbolic *Christ Trampling upon Urizen* suggests its close connection to the *Paradise Lost* designs, and, more importantly, to the

85 THE PROGRESS OF POESY.

O'er her warm cheek, and rising bofom, move
The bloom of young defire, and purple light
    of Love.

II. 1.

Man's feeble race what ills await!
Labour, and Penury, the racks of Pain,
Difeafe, and Sorrow's weeping train,
And Death, fad refuge from the ftorms of Fate!
The fond complaint, my fong, difprove,
And juftify the laws of Jove.
Say, has he given in vain the heav'nly Mufe?
Night, and all her fickly dews,
Her fpectres wan, and birds of boding cry,
He gives to range the dreary fky:
Till down the eaftern cliffs afar
Hyperion's march they fpy, and glitt'ring
    fhafts of war.

                     II. 2.

Figure 48. William Blake. Illustration for Thomas Gray's "The Progress of Poesy," p. 6. About 1797–98. 42 cm by 32.5 cm. *From the Collection of Paul Mellon, Upperville, Virginia*

relationship of the God figures of the Old and New Testaments. In showing the imaginative triumph of Christ over the Urizenic selfhood, Blake is also giving us the ascendancy of the Son over the Father, an emblem not only of Milton's poem but also of the millennial reorientation of religious thinking Blake had announced prophetically as early as *The Marriage*.

The symbolism of Christ's exaltation has its strongest roots in Rev. 4:3, where the throne of God is described as surrounded by a rainbow. Visual art had combined the references, often showing the Revelation throne as a rainbow throne. When Milton has the Son mount a throne within his chariot in book 6, and when he specifies that it is the sapphire throne of Revelation, "inlaid with pure / Amber, and colors of the show'ry Arch" (6.758–59), there is no doubt it is the throne of his apocalyptic ascendancy. As Roland Frye points out, the Son mounts his throne at the numerical center of the epic, further alerting us to the epic's Christocentrism (even in the sense the pun suggests). Thus in his triumphant act the Son "assumes a familiar iconographic pose which emphasizes his supremacy not only in this one combat with the powers of darkness, but also alludes graphically to him as the All-Ruler throughout history and as the ultimate consummation at the end of time."[44] Blake would not have missed the implications of the moment, for in taking the throne the Son becomes an obvious alternative to the enthroned Father whom he thus effectually surpasses. The defeat of Satan—the Father's parodic counterpart—carries with it the point Milton seems so clearly to imply: the assumption of absolute centrality, as the Revelation references suggest, by the Son, "the Christ" who is the fulfilled God and messiah.[45]

The more carefully delineated details, particularly evident in the facial features of all the characters, give the BM version of *The Rout of the Rebel Angels* (pl. 13) a proportionally greater dramatic effect than its predecessor. The Son's expression is made more sublime, more detached than before, in keeping with the visual tradition of calm and unimpassioned victory over Satan by Michael figures we have already considered. The faces of the six angels surrounding the Son's sphere are carefully drawn to express, in conjunction with their open-handed gestures, a general sense of wonder, of "mingled fear and admiration."[46] The faces of Satan and his crew are grotesquely contorted, with the positions of a number of the rebels altered in this design for greater visual impact.

Attempting to read both versions of *The Rout of the Rebel Angels* from too narrowly representational a standpoint has led at least one critic to conclude that Blake's demonic figures are far more successful than those of the Son and the angels.[47] But such a conclusion reflects too great a dependence upon Blake's pejorative comments in *The Marriage* and seems almost to assume them as a gloss on designs made over a dozen years later, by which time Blake's opinions had changed drastically. Satan and his crew appear more successful visually only if one is looking for contorted and obviously *moving*, theatrically conceived forms rather than calm, stylized, and suspended symbolic figures. To judge Blake's design on the basis of external dramatic activity is to miss its interiority—its symbolic significance—and impose upon it the premises of narrative visualization we see in the theatrical illustrations of an artist like Hayman, an imposition Blake's entire series stubbornly resists. The point is not that the Son and the angels are artistically unsuccessful, but that they conform to different artistic rules from those by which one routinely judges a picture. Like Fuseli, Blake asserts in his design that the Son functions less by conventional physical exertion than by *idea embodied in gesture* (as we see again in *The Creation of Eve*) and articulated in "the Lineaments of the Countenance" which are the "forms and features that are capable of being the receptacles of intellect" (*VLJ*; E, p. 550; *Descriptive Catalogue*; E, p. 535). In all his appearances, Blake's Son manifests precisely the characteristic facial expression Milton assigns him already in book 3:

> In his face
> Divine compassion visible appear'd,
> Love without end, and without measure Grace.
> [3.140–42]

Blake intends for us to make a qualitative distinction between the two visual areas of the design as we do in *The Son Offers to Redeem Man* (pls. 6, 7) and *Satan Watching Adam and Eve* (pls. 8, 9), being guided in our choices once again by his visual cues. His alteration of facial details in the BM design is only one such visual indicator. As in the previous designs, Blake again juxtaposes the graceful and integrated symmetry of the one scene with the violent and visually chaotic arrangement of the other decisively to convey his own qualitative judgment, a judgment in which he invites us to concur.

Blake follows Milton's lead in asserting that it is the intervention of the Son as creative, redemptive imagination that determines the outcome of the war in heaven. Woodhouse's contention that the Son *as victor* sets the standard of heroism misses the point, at least from the Blakean perspective, since he stresses the wrong aspect of the Son's epic predecessors Achilles and Aeneas. The Son's power stems not from "the Father's irresistible might," brought increasingly "under the control of morality and religion" and ultimately combined with these two influences in a "sustained and exalted" condition.[48] Blake clearly wishes to overturn just such misconceptions of the Son's integrity, which even Milton himself appeared frequently to have adopted. Ascendancy by force is, not victory, but tyranny. As Christian visionary and prophet Blake could no more abandon his fellow man than the Son was willing to abandon *his*. Corrective criticism is itself an act of love and "Forgiveness of Sins," and we should not overlook the implications of Blake's conviction that he and Christ looked much alike (E, p. 673).

Without the Son's participation the battle in heaven remains in doubt, particularly as the Father eschews active involvement. Both

Blake and his prophetic predecessor appear to question the Father's motives in remaining a spectator and using his Son. Milton's explanation is that the Father wants to appoint his Son his surrogate avenger,

> That his great purpose he might so fulfil,
> To honor his Annointed Son aveng'd
> Upon his enemies, and to declare
> All power on him transferr'd.
> [6.675–78]

Blake's implication, however, is that only the Son, motivated as he is by the divine vision of love and imaginative energy, is *capable* of overcoming Satan's threat. The Father and Satan, Blake suggests, are both too caught up in artificial and rationalistic hierarchies and self-aggrandizing operations to meet each other on any but a stalemate basis. That the Son's victory is temporary (at least as far as man is concerned, since Satan does reappear, as we know all too well), not permanent, assures the continuation on earth and in the mind of man of that salutary conflict of contraries that forms the basis for human choice and progress. As in *Paradise Regained*, there is neither absolute victory nor absolute defeat, but, rather, a temporary ascendancy of visionary insight in a miraculous act of self-sufficiency until the conflict is transferred to another arena.

Blake's design does, of course, prefigure the Day of Judgment, the definitive and apocalyptic rout of Satan. We should note, for instance, the similarity of the falling rebels to their counterparts in the several versions of *The Last Judgment* (fig. 49, and B, pls. 868–73), all of which show falling figures clutching at their heads "in various attitudes of Despair & Horror (to Ozias Humphrey, February 1808; K, p. 131). In this sense the design is related also to *Michael and Satan* (B, pl. 585), which shows Michael's struggle to bind the dragon-formed Satan. We discover in Blake's design a form of the act Los recounts in *Milton:* the millennial rout by Christ-Los at the end of the six-thousand-year period of history. In the visionary time of the *Paradise Lost* designs this definitive conclusion is proleptically implied in its beginning (*The Rout of the Rebel Angels*, pls. 12, 13) as well as in its related forms (*The Son Offers to Redeem Man*, pls. 6, 7; and *Michael Foretells the Crucifixion*, pls. 20, 21). For Blake, then, the Son's action in book 6 stood finally as paradigm for liberation from the isolating forces of pride and materialism, both a symbol and an instance of the imaginative Last Judgment the poet describes in *A Vision of the Last Judgment*.

The Creation of Eve (pls. 14, 15) depicts the event Adam recounts in book 8. But Blake alters Adam's account in the interest of symbolism. Whereas Adam recalls that in creating Eve the figure "of shape Divine" had opened his side, withdrawn a rib and flesh, and formed it with his hands, Blake shows Eve's creation in far more aesthetically and symbolically successful fashion, depicting it as a commanding gesture by the Son,[49] who is iconographically related to the elderly Father figure who creates Eve with much the same gesture in both Michelangelo's

Figure 49. William Blake. *The Last Judgment.* 1808. 51 cm by 39.5 cm. *Petworth House, Sussex. By permission of Courtauld Institute of Art, London*

and Raphael's versions of the creation. Eve rises, fully formed and with hands nearly clasped, from the side of the sleeping Adam. She appears to be drawn out of him by the ascending outstretched hand of the Son, rising toward the crescent moon, symbol of the generated world.[50] Blake's preliminary sketch for this design (B, pl. 727) anticipates the final version in all respects but one: in the sketch it is the Son's *left* hand that is extended. Though Blake may have altered this detail for purely aesthetic purposes—for the visual improvement—he regularly associates creative energy with the right hand and distorted energy or reason with the left (*The Rout of the Rebel Angels*, right; *The Ancient of Days*, left).[51] Hence it would seem inappropriate to Blake to derogate Eve as Milton had seemed to do by representing her as a creation of perverse rational energy and materialism. She is Adam's emanation, as Ololon is Milton's, and to picture her creation in entirely pejorative fashion would prejudice the case against her and make it unwise for Adam even to redeem her. Besides, in showing the Son as Eve's creator in the physical world of Eden, Blake both emphasizes the Son's compassionate concern for man's welfare and more clearly defines Eve's vital place in the scheme of man's redemption. She is man's sexual counterpart, and her presence in prelapsarian Eden—indeed from the hand of the Son—counters in advance the error Milton had supposedly asked Blake to correct: the mistaken notion that sexual activity and the Fall are causally related. Blake creates a visually lovely, robust Eve whose sexuality is never in doubt, especially in the second set of designs. Remembering Blake's comment in *The Marriage* about sensual enjoyment as key to the "Last Judgment," we should recognize here, with Blake's prodding, the creative and liberating nature of sensual-sexual activity.

This design represents the external division of the sexes, the previous scenes of Adam and Eve having been principally concerned with their increasing mental (or internal) distance within a still-unified consciousness. Eve's creation marks man's further descent from fourfold Eden into the material, generated universe. Hence it is historically performed under a tree (the symbol not only of the fateful tree and the cross, but also of the generative, sensual life) or with trees nearby, and in the midst of plants and flowers.[52] Blake includes these iconographic elements here and again, interestingly, in *Michael Foretells the Crucifixion*, which presages the Son's victory over material death-in-life in the generated universe. In psychological terms, Eve's creation represents the emanation's release from the subconscious, the rise of the female will that begins to operate in potentially creative conflict with the essential consciousness.[53] Her creation stands, in a sense, as the initiation of the "Mental Fight" that characterizes a healthy existence in the mortal (and spiritual) world and provides the vehicle for passage back to Eden or eternity, where they will return to the androgynous union Blake described to Robinson. But, as we see in all Blake's prophecies and perhaps most clearly in *Europe*, the emanation quickly verges into selfishness and separatism, a tendency the individual or male must constantly counteract lest the vegetable world lapse into the chaos that pervades *Europe* and leads so inexorably "to the strife of blood" (*Europe* 15.11; E, p. 65). This very impulse towards separatism underlies Eve's desire to work alone, her physical separation from Adam, and finally her Fall. Adam's decision to participate in the Fall—the result of an attempt to make matters right—only worsens the situation by provoking further mental and physical acrimony, as we discover in book 10.

The later versions of *The Creation of Eve* (pl. 15; B, pl. 658) are virtually the same as the first, though their details are once again more highly finished. One significant alteration does appear: in these two later designs Blake turned Eve's gaze away from the Son's face and upward toward his hand, more dramatically directing our attention to the mental or imaginative aspect of the creative act itself.

While it employs much of the traditional iconography of the Fall, Blake's *Temptation and Fall of Eve* (pls. 16, 17) is a visual statement unlike any of its predecessors. Rejecting the practice of artists like Cheron, Hayman, and Barry, all of whom had illustrated book 9 as the drama of Eve's temptation of Adam (P, pls. 21, 49; fig. 28), Blake isolates the fall of Eve, implying that Adam's fall is inherent in Eve's because she is his emanation and because of the disruption of his better judgment his attitude toward her in book 9 reveals. The circumstances of book 9 make it painfully clear that once Eve falls, Adam will fall as well. Blake's conception of the scene is more akin to that of Burney and Fuseli, whose illustrations represent Eve confronted by an extraordinary Serpent (P, pl. 85; fig. 29).

Blake locates the moment of Fall at Eve's tasting the forbidden fruit as it is held in the mouth of the Serpent coiled about her body. Here Blake again brilliantly employs posture repetition: Eve's posture as she cradles the Serpent's head is now almost exactly the same as that of the flying Satan who likewise cradles the Serpent's head in HH 5 (pl. 8), though rotated to an upright stance.[54] By this visual device Blake subtly identifies the nature of Eve's fall: she falls by erring in the direction of all the mistaken values epitomized by Satan in that earlier design. Eve responds to his appeals to her own narcissistic pride and vanity, her desire for both physical and mental separateness, and her deviously induced egotistical dissatisfaction with her own state. All these tendencies—latent in every individual—have grown disproportionate in her, becoming full-blown traits through Satan's deceptions. In her fall, Blake implies, Eve becomes a type of Satan.

As it had particularly in Renaissance art, the temptation scene carries strong sexual overtones, most obvious here in the suggestive manner in which the Serpent's coils pass over Eve's genital area just as they cover Satan's in previous designs. The phallic serpent represents the illicit sexual love of Satan—illicit, not because it is *sexual*, but because it is *selfish*. The horrible kiss Eve shares with the Serpent, barely mitigated by the intervening fruit, is a travesty upon the prelapsarian kiss with Adam, just as her new sexual relationship travesties her previous one.

We must treat Blake's sexual commentary in these designs carefully. For Blake, unlike many of Milton's eighteenth-century commentators, sex (and sexuality) is never inherently bad, as we recognize from the striking image of the three naked children riding the jovial serpent in *Thel*, plate 6, and *America*, plate 11. (*IB*, pp. 40, 149). On the contrary, as we have seen, sexuality and sexual activity liberates and regenerates. The convergence of innocent children and serpent (which conventional moral education *conditions* us to regard as innately sinister) points up the paradox and forces us to reassess our preconceptions of the serpent *as icon* just as "The Tyger" forces us to do with that animal.

The only real connection between sexuality and the Fall lies in assuming (as Eve does in this design) the selfish, introverted masturbatory sexuality of Satan—the single-minded, isolationist pursuit solely of self-delight—as the appropriate standard for interpersonal sexuality. This is more an *intellectual* sexuality than a physical one: a motive rather than a manifestation. In being dissuaded from her intuitive sense of right by the *semblance* of logic Satan advances, Eve demonstrates the degree to which she is falling victim to the limited rationalistic vision of the material universe that spawns the puritanical moralists who see in healthy sexuality the measure of man's depravity.

We can better understand Blake's intentions in this design if we look at two separate paintings that preceded it. The preliminary sketch for the first, *Satan Exulting over Eve* (1795), portrays only the flying Satan, wingless but with a spear, shown in the posture in which he appears in the painting. In the color print itself (B, pl. 389) Satan hovers at the center, naked, with great green bat wings, and armed as in the *Paradise Lost* designs with spear and shield. Across the bottom lies the outstretched figure of Eve, asleep or dead—either is symbolically appropriate, the latter perhaps more so. The fruit lies beneath the palm of her hand. The Serpent coils about her legs and thighs, its neck extending up beyond Eve's head and its head sensually placed directly upon her breast. Though Eve lies upon grassy ground, sheets of flame flare up behind her, a visual cue Blake had used just the year before in the general title page to *Songs of Innocence and of Experience*, where the deeply bent figures of Adam and Eve recall both the judgment within Eden and the Expulsion as typically rendered in eighteenth-century illustrations of *Paradise Lost*. Most important, Satan looks, not down at Eve as we might expect, but upward with an expression that is yet more troubled than exultant.[55] Blake's painting alerts us to the nature of the victory Satan claims: Satan enjoys the fall of Eve (and of man) in that it controverts the Father's intentions. Only in this perverse sense, Blake implies repeatedly, is the fall of man of any value to Satan; it is merely one event in an ongoing psychological warfare in which man is but a pawn.

Eve Tempted by the Serpent (B, pl. 402; about 1799) shows another aspect of Eve's fall. While Adam sleeps at the right, Eve stands at the center with her right arm raised, gesturing in acknowledgment of the

Serpent and reaching for the branch just above her. The entire left third of the painting is occupied by the massive trunk of the tree, twisted like the trees of experience. The enormous coiling Serpent rises up between Eve and the tree, its head directly over hers, its tail winding out around Adam. Eve stands within one of the Serpent's coils, but is not bound by it as in other pictures. Eve's figure is a remarkable visual anticipation of that of Mirth (*L'Allegro*, pl. 1; fig. 8), who is herself associated with the materialistic world of experience. Indeed, the convergence in this painting of river, waterfall, waning moon, and the particulars of the subject matter clearly suggests that very world of experience Eve is about to enter, taking mankind with her.

These two pictures and *The Temptation and Fall of Eve* (pls. 16, 17) all demonstrate Blake's location of man's fall in the archetypal act of Eve, in the mistaken choice by which she responds to the crisis posed by the Serpent's temptation. Blake stresses that the essential nature of Eve's error involves separation and disintegration. Beginning with the induced notion that she is being deprived of something that is rightfully hers, Eve comes to identify with and to assume in herself the psychological and imaginative imbalances of Satan. Adam's fall, to be sure, is critical, but his own vainly self-sacrificing offer to accept death (a darkly ironic parody of the Son's offer in book 3) by participating in what he *consciously recognizes* to be Eve's error is merely another manifestation of the inflated pride of selfhood that blinds man's better sensibilities, to which Adam now suddenly succumbs. Hence in Blake's design it is Eve's fall that triggers the disruption in nature at which Adam marvels in the two versions of the design. Blake includes in his designs Milton's own symbol for the rupture inherent in Eve's fall: the broken garland (in Adam's hand in HH, on the ground in BM), the Edenic counterpart to the amaranth-laden crowns borne to the Son by the angels in *The Son Offers to Redeem Man* (pls. 6, 7) and perhaps another proleptic reference to the crown of thorns we see in *Michael Foretells the Crucifixion* (pls. 20, 21). This detail provides yet another instance of the merging of separate moments in visionary time, for in Milton's text that garland is not dropped until Adam sees Eve again; indeed, it is not broken at all (9.892–93). Nor, for that matter, does the storm indicated by the lightning break in the epic until later. In depicting the breaking of the garland—symbolizing the rupture in the couple's primal unity—and placing this action previous to their physical reunion after Eve's fall, Blake underscores his contention that the Fall has already occurred before Adam ever tastes the fruit. The Fall is for Blake a mental phenomenon, an act of dis-integration and separation that occurs to each individual who "contracts his imaginative vision, denies his mortal body as sinful flesh, and represses or perverts Energy." It begins earlier in the designs with the increasing separation of Adam's emanation, Eve, into a distinct personality. By book 9, she is sufficiently separated from him to succumb to the Serpent's deception at a moment when Adam's back, ironically, is turned.[56]

If the first major consequence of the Fall is Eve's acceptance of the fruit, its second involves Adam's foolish response. He quickly and self-ishly rejects what he knows to be truth and right, vainly embracing Eve's own transgression. His participation in the Fall alienates him from God, from Eve, and from himself, thus both repressing and perverting his creative energy. Too often Adam's error is excused by an assertion that he acts emotionally here, rather than rationally. But his error is, like Eve's, one of subscribing to the *semblance* of logic. He convinces himself that the selfish and pseudo-chivalric ideas of self-sacrifice for Eve he mouths are *reasonable* justification for overthrowing his intuitive knowledge of right and wrong. The love he declares and Eve praises repeatedly (Milton's mastery of subtle irony coming to the fore) is, not love, but idolatrous adoration of Eve (and himself), against which Raphael had specifically warned him.[57] The mental disintegration of Adam and Eve is further demonstrated by the regression and deterioration of their physical relationship.

The profusion of roots emanating from the base of the tree in *The Temptation and Fall of Eve* signal that in the moment of the Fall the tree becomes the tree of error,[58] sending out its roots into the now-fallen world. That Eden becomes in this moment the world of experience is proved by the ominous thorns Blake adds to the tree in the BM version of the design (pl. 19). The tree itself is an iconographic reference to the cross, the symbol of the act by which the Fall is reversed and eternal reintegration accomplished. The tree also appears, as noted earlier, in *Jerusalem*, plate 76 (fig. 50), adorned with the same sort of fruit and providing the rough cross upon which Jesus is crucified there. The scene in *Jerusalem* is summed up by the ailing and selfhood-dominated Albion, who stands before the tree, arms outstretched in mutual crucifixion with Jesus:

> O Human Imagination O Divine Body I have Crucified
> I have turned my back upon thee into the Wastes of Moral Law.
> [*J* 24.23–24; E, p. 168]

Blake's tree, in both cases, is the tree of error, the tree of simplistic ideas of moral good and moral evil promulgated by the narrow-minded empiricist codifiers of materialism—"those who restrain desire" (*MHH*, pl. 5; E, pl. 34)—to rationalize the presence of apparent evil in the world. On this tree the imagination is mistakenly sacrificed through the incorrect choices by which man falls into the original sin of selfhood, which sacrifices can yet be turned to good in exposing the error so it may be recognized and repudiated, as we see in the examples of Milton in *Milton* and Albion in *Jerusalem*. In much the same manner, Blake suggests, Christ's death on the cross for man exposes the fallacy of the tree of the Fall—the divisive doctrine of retribution and atonement—enabling man to repudiate *it* and its negative influence and espouse instead the principle of divine integration epitomized in Jesus Christ, the "forgiver of Sins."

In 1807 Blake completed a related painting, *The Fall of Man* (fig. 51), a complex and encyclopedic vision of man's fall *and* salvation that

provides a useful contextual perspective for the *Paradise Lost* illustrations. Unlike the latter, *The Fall of Man* is synoptic, assembling in a single picture the entire spectrum of causes and consequences of the Fall as Blake derived them from both Milton and the Bible.

The picture is divided into five main areas: three levels flanked by a pair of marginal columns. The central level portrays Christ leading Adam and Eve gently from Eden, grasping each calmly by the hand. Christ here anticipates the gentle gesture Michael employs in Blake's version the Expulsion.[59] To the right, Adam turns to look at Christ, his left arm raised, while at Christ's right Eve places her cheek sadly upon her right palm. Behind the three figures is a series of horizontal lines that most likely echo the curious set of steps customarily included in illustrations of the Expulsion. On either side of the group stands a symmetrical cluster of sorrowful angels, all burying their faces in their hands. Above them, toward the background, we see two aspects of the fatal tree. The prelapsarian tree at the left is smooth and fruitful, the tree at the right heavily thorned and enfolded within the Serpent's coils, though its branches are still laden with fruit. Grasping the Serpent's neck is a flying (but wingless) figure with an upraised sword in his right hand; this is presumably the archangel Michael. At the base of this central tableau are arranged in partial view a horse, a tiger, a lion, a bull or ox, and a reclining sheep flanked by two angry eagles.[60] The upper and lower levels of Blake's painting are parodic counterparts whose visual relationship again suggests the parallels between the Father and Satan. At the top the elderly, bearded Father leans forward from his throne, arms extended (like the figure in *Satan's and Raphael's Entries into Paradise* and *The Lazar House*), his right leg drawn up and his left extending down. Around him in a flaming cloud circle angels, a dozen making hand gestures of admiration or adoration, others bearing various emblematic objects (three swords, a chalice, a plate with a sphere, a spear, a death's dart, and a scroll inscribed "INRI"). From the outer edges of the cloud thunderbolts flash downward, accompanying the militant angels who drive Satan's rebels down the symmetrical marginal columns.

The lower scene depicts an elderly bearded, dragon-winged Satan beneath the cramping roof of his hellish cave. He appears to be seated upon a rock and leans forward from this seat, arms extended, right leg drawn up and left extended down a bit. The visual parallel with the Father above is immediately obvious, and the similar arrangement in the rest of the hell tableau reinforces the parallel. At Satan's right is Sin, much as she appears in *Satan, Sin, and Death*, the worm of generation draped across her midriff; at Satan's right a female figure with an overturned chalice in her left hand and a sword in her right faints backward from a kneeling position. Beneath the three a myriad of spear points projects as from a pit, accompanied by some helmeted heads (presumably Satan's legions) and by a crowned figure with a sceptre (probably emblematic of tyrannical empire). At the lower left of the painting a

Figure 51. William Blake. *The Fall of Man.* 1807. 48.3 cm by 38.7 cm. *Victoria and Albert Museum, London*

standing young figure, strongly reminiscent of the younger Satan Blake shows us elsewhere, apes the old man's extended left hand while indicating with his right the heavenly scene, a visual configuration not unlike that in the Whitworth Art Gallery version of *Nativity Ode*, plate 5 (B, pl. 662). His gesture suggests recognition of equation—perhaps he perceives that the lower scene is but a mirror of the upper. Finally, we see at the lower right an outstretched, beardless figure whose posture is that of the unconscious bearded figure at the base of *Satan Calling His Legions.*[61]

The Fall of Man draws our attention insistently to the central figure of Christ. More importantly, Blake's painting symbolically separates and insulates Adam, Eve, and Christ from the complicated supernatural activity that surrounds them. The painting clearly demonstrates the interrelation of the aspects of the Fall, but it just as clearly advances a reading of the Fall myth directly related to the sort of opinions Blake was expressing as early as *The Marriage*. Blake sets out here overtly to distinguish the figures of Adam, Eve, and Christ from the convoluted retributive mythology of a punitive Father and a tormenting Satan attached in conventional orthodox thought *and iconography* to the Fall. Just as man falls through his own will—a point agreed upon by all parties—so is he to redeem himself through another assertion of will by participating in the vigorous mental and imaginative process of choice for which Christ (particularly the Jesus we encounter in *Paradise Regained*) provides the paradigm. That this reading of the Fall informs Blake's *Paradise Lost* becomes increasingly and inescapably obvious.

Between the two designs representing the Fall and its prophesied reversal Blake interposes *The Judgment of Adam and Eve* (pls. 18, 19), in which he reassembles the principal figures of the epic. This scene had been depicted in rather harsh terms before Burney's illustration of 1799. Previous illustrators generally represented the chastisement of Adam and Eve or a scene of the pair either cowering in anguished supplication or futilely attempting to evade the agent of their judgment. Cheron's headpiece to book 10, an interesting early version (P, pl. 22), shows the angels leaving Eden, moving off to the left while Adam and Eve look forlornly after them. Meanwhile Death, a skeleton with a scythe, leads Eve toward the right, grasping her wrist.[62] Cheron's design poignantly captures the mood of the moment. Other illustrators, particularly those who furnished only a single design for book 10, tended generally to distort this part of the poem. Hayman, for instance, shows a crestfallen and homely couple being judged by a rather passive Son accompanied by angels, while a small Serpent creeps away. The other tendencies may be seen in Hamilton's 1802 design showing a penitent Adam and Eve at night, kneeling in supplication, and in Richter's 1794 design showing the apprehensive couple as they hear God's voice.

The really significant break with the tradition of severity comes with Burney's design,[63] which shows Adam and Eve kneeling in supplication, Eve with her face averted, as the Son descends from heaven. In Burney's illustration the Son is not berating them, however, but is instead looking back up to heaven with his own left hand raised, interceding with the Father on their behalf. This new, more hopeful note is directly related to Blake's treatment of the judgment scene and recalls the tone of his *Christ the Mediator* (B, pl. 497).

Blake sums up in the figures of Adam and Eve the whole spectrum of emotional states in which he has depicted them previously. At the right Eve buries her face in her hands in a gesture of mingled sorrow, shame, and penitence, while at the left Adam stands with head bowed and hands folded as if in prayer, his posture expressing reverence and total submission to the Son's judgment. For the only time in the designs, the couple's bodies are shown exactly in side view, a technique Blake sometimes uses to indicate figures who are somehow incomplete or whose integrated insight is either disrupted or not yet accomplished.[64] Depicted frontally between them is the Son, his hands raised in a conciliatory gesture almost of blessing. His posture here recalls the gestures (made in different contexts) of both Adam in the previous design and in *Raphael Warns Adam and Eve* (pls. 10, 11), and Satan in *Satan's and Raphael's Entries into Paradise* (pl. 1), a similarity further reinforcing the visual unity and the sense of simultaneity of the entire series as well as the increasingly apparent symbolic interrelation of all the characters. The Son has a traditional halo in this scene, the only one Blake employs in the entire set.

The demonic trinity reappears here as well, beginning its joint incursion into Eden. Satan, seen now and hereafter only as the Serpent, creeps across the bottom of the design behind the three central figures; Sin and Death reappear at the top. Death, still wearing his crown from the second design but grown now to resemble the Father, aims his darts down unemotionally on the left. Sin pours out the flaming contents of two vials on the right in an act reminiscent of that of Disease in Blake's design to Young's *Night Thoughts*, "Night the First", page 10.[65]

We should note the canopy of clouds separating the Son, Adam, and Eve from Sin and Death, by which device Blake suggests that, as in *The Fall of Man*, though the couple has fallen, the Son's loving nature prompts him not only to deal compassionately with them but also to afford them a measure of protection from the direct onslaught of Sin and Death. As Martin Butlin correctly notes, in doing so he also deflects the full wrath of the Father above.[66] Blake thus returns the focus of book 10 to Milton's own description of the Son: "mild Judge and Intercessor both" (*PL* 10.96), correcting the tradition of illustration that had wandered away from the presentation of the loving Son Milton had himself intended. Blake says in *A Vision of the Last Judgment*, "First God Almighty comes with a Thump on the Head Then Jesus Christ comes with a balm to heal it" (E, p. 555). Most obviously a reference to the Son's part in man's *redemption*, Blake's point is not inappropriate to *The Judgment of Adam and Eve*.

Blake made several changes in the second version of this design. The Son was made to look directly at the viewer, and Adam's head was raised so that he looks now with a peaceful expression directly at the Son. Sin and Death are now more carefully detailed, with Sin's hounds and coils made more ominous. Her face, more distinct now, expresses demonic glee as she empties her vials. Her right arm is now positioned, not above the cloud canopy, but directly upon it; the same holds true for Death's left arm. Death too wears an expression far more actively sinister than before. Blake apparently made these changes to suggest the pair's aggressive intrusion into Eden more emphatically, even in the salutary presence of the Son, indicating the artist's deepening understanding of the irrevocability of the Fall.

J. B. Trapp has observed that in any work of art made by or for a Christian portraying the Fall "there must always be a more or less explicit proleptic reference to Redemption and / or Judgment."[67] Milton satisfies this requirement in *Paradise Lost* in several ways. First, his subject itself implicitly suggests the corresponding redemption of man forecast in the Bible. Second, already at the fourth line of the poem Milton alludes to that redemption. Third, in book 3 he presents the Son's offer to redeem man, well before he has presented the Fall. Fourth, when the Son judges Adam and Eve in book 10, Milton has him refer to his promise. Finally, in book 12 Milton details, through the vision Michael unfolds to Adam, the fulfilment of that promise of redemption. Once introduced at the fourth line of the poem, the "proleptic reference" to redemption is never wholly absent from the poem. Blake likewise maintains his designs' focus upon the redemption through his insistent visual emphasis upon its various aspects. His penultimate illustration to *Paradise Lost* constitutes his most explicit rendering of the act all the other designs suggest in one way or another.

Blake was the first artist to treat the Crucifixion explicitly in a set of *Paradise Lost* illustrations. Most had dealt with it through iconographic suggestion, including in their designs for books 3 or 6, for instance, some visual suggestion in the form of a cross or crown of thorns carried in heaven by the Son or one of his attendants. Blake employed such iconographic suggestion himself in at least one painting. *The Christ Child Asleep on the Cross* (B, pl. 496; around 1799), which shows the young Jesus asleep in cruciform posture on a heavy cross while a female figure (presumably Mary) looks on with clasped hands.[68] Behind him is a gabled structure, perhaps an unfinished shed of some sort, perhaps a visual echo of the stable where he was born. Of major significance in terms of Blake's own iconography is the compasslike instrument resting against a post of this structure, just at the top of the cross. Much like those employed by the Ancient of Days and Newton (fig. 19; B, pls. 394, 408), it intimates Blake's view of the dual nature of the Crucifixion as both physical death *in* the vegetable world and eternal, imaginative triumph *over* that world. Seen from the clouded perspective of orthodoxy, both compass and Crucifixion allude to the apparent subduing of creative energy by mechanistic reason; seen correctly from the clear visionary perspective, however, both imply the annihilation of such hopelessly blind orthodox notions. The compass, like so many of Blake's icons, points both ways, and it remains for the viewer to cleanse his doors of perception sufficiently to enable him to recognize which is the correct signification in any given instance.

Michael Foretells the Crucifixion (pls. 20, 21) renders the Crucifixion somewhat differently than Milton presents it. The poem suggests that Michael shows Adam his vision from atop a hill, almost in the manner of a prospect poem, and this was the sense in which most illustrators dealt with the illustration for Michael's prophecy. Medina placed Adam and Michael on a precipice (P, pl. 10), and Cheron, dispensing with the precipice, still placed the prophesied scene at a visual distance (P, pl. 23). Hayman returned the pair to the precipice in his design (P, pl. 43), displaying prominently Cain's murder of Abel below, a scene that had been popular with Genesis illustrators. The most popular scenes illustrators placed in the distance in their designs for Michael's prophecy were, in fact, Cain and Abel or the Deluge. Particularly in the latter case, it became imperative to set the prophesied scene at some visual distance to avoid incongruity. In fact, before Blake's design every portrayal of Michael foretelling the future introduces some specific distancing device, however minor, between the representation of the prophecy and the figures of the pair who behold it.

Blake breaks entirely with this practice, dramatically portraying the Son crucified atop the very hill on which Adam and Michael stand, the base of the cross being only a step or two uphill from them and not at all recessed into the distance. All the major figures of the poem except the Father (it would *seem*) are reunited in this powerful design. Michael, winged and attired in the military garb of the cherubim,[69] stands at the left with his face and left arm lifted, both presenting and indicating the crucified Son. Adam stands at the right, seen now from the left rear but in a posture similar to that of the previous design. There are, however, significant differences. First, Adam's head is now raised, not bowed, as he looks up at the Son. Second, his right foot is forward here, indicating an improvement over the error-stricken condition—typified by his extended left foot—in which the previous design had shown him. Further to denote the special, purified state in which he receives the vision, and in which Eve will subsequently receive it from him, both Adam and Eve are again depicted naked, after having been girded with vines in the previous design. We should assume that this special condition is directly related to the prophetic nature of the vision, for when Adam and Eve return to the physical reality of their fallen condition in *The Expulsion* (pls. 22, 23), they once again wear their vines. Vines are, we recall from Blake's illuminated poems, symptomatic of the world of experience, a world clearly incompatible with the momentary visionary revelation of *Michael Foretells the Crucifixion*. The special nature of this visionary moment is still further underscored by James Holly Hanford, who reminds us that in Milton's poem, after their fall, Adam and Eve lapse into a deep despair, "from which they must be rescued by the angelic vision, with its promise of redemption."[70]

The overthrow of the demonic trinity through the Crucifixion is represented in the figures of Death and Sin outstretched at the base of the cross. Death's appearance recalls the Father's here, for the Son's death and apotheosis effectively end the tyranny of the retributive Old Testament Father even as they accomplish the overthrow of Satan, replacing their joint reign of terror with the system of love and divine integration in which we are invited to participate. The Serpent is coiled about the base of the cross here, his head between the Son's feet, pierced by the nail that holds them to the cross. The death of Satan-Serpent fulfills the prophecy in Genesis that the seed of Adam would bruise his head, a prophecy to which Satan refers light-heartedly in the poem. In seeing in these figures "the Orcan sexual serpent" and both Urizen and "Vala-Rahab, fallen sexual nature," Hagstrum properly suggests the sexual implications of the design.[71] For the Son's death in the world of generation and materialism over which Satan presides (as "The Accuser who is The God of This World") is also the death of that Satan. Satan-Serpent's death demonstrates for the viewer that the "wages of sin is death." But what is sinful is, not sex itself, but rather the incomplete and self-destructive nature of the selfish phallic sexuality Satan epitomizes. At the same time, his death emphatically marks the demise of the puritanical view of sexuality as evil, a perverse dogma that likewise takes its toll on creative energy, crucifying the human imagination on the cross of moral evil. Nor should we forget that Blake's design also comments on the doctrine of the Atonement, removing the Son's act from the context of ransom paid the Father and Satan and locating it instead in the context of the ultimate humanistic act of self-sacrifice and creative vision.[72]

Michael Foretells the Crucifixion clearly invites the viewer to recall traditional depictions of the Crucifixion for comparison. For one thing, the Son is shown in the calm tranquillity of death, with none of the sense of agony invoked, for instance, by Reformation crucifixions. Most often in traditional versions, the base of the cross is surrounded by sorrowing friends of Jesus, generally including his mother and Mary Magdalen and often the centurion who pierced his side with the spear. Indeed, Blake invokes this tradition in *The Crucifixion: Behold Thy Mother* (B, pl. 600) and *Soldiers Casting Lots for Christ's Garments* (B, pl. 571), both done about 1800. But in *Michael Foretells the Crucifixion* the customary surrounding figures are gone, replaced by Adam and Michael, the latter interestingly replacing the centurion. Likewise, the usual sense of anguish is replaced by calm reverence.

When Blake made his second version of this design, he increased the size of all the figures considerably, making the design still more striking. Finally, in the third version (B, pl. 659), done about 1822, Blake significantly added bright shafts of light that radiate out from behind the Son's head in a sort of elaborately stylized glory rather like that with which Milton appears in *Milton*, plate 16 (Copy D; fig. 4).[73] In this way Blake both reinforces the symbolic significance of the Crucifixion and stresses that this design does indeed present a miraculous vision.

Michael Foretells the Crucifixion represents the fulfillment of the Son's offer to redeem humanity. Blake purposely portrays him here, as

Milton had done, in his human form, having given his mortal life for man. Michael goes on in book 12 to forecast his resurrection, which Blake had painted in 1805 (B, pl. 573),[74] but in writing his epic Milton would naturally have expected his readers to assume the Resurrection. The point Milton wished specifically to make, was not that the Son rose as God, *but that he died as man.* Milton repeatedly emphasizes the Son's humanness. Recognizing Milton's intention, Blake likewise avoids directly representing the Resurrection, showing in his design the death of the man Jesus. For Blake, of course, the Crucifixion represents metaphorically the annihilation of the selfhood, the abasement of the rationalistic intellect and aesthetic, the act by which the Son passes "the limits of possibility" (*J* 62.19; E, p. 211), showing as he does so the way in which others may follow him into resurrection and reintegration of visionary insight.

The singular convergence of Blake's symbolism and Milton's epic becomes particularly apparent with the Crucifixion, whose overwhelming lesson is forgiveness through creative self-sacrifice—what Blake regards as the repudiation of the spectre and the redemption of the emanation. Adam must *forgive* Eve, rather than blaming her for his problems as he does in book 10. He must recognize that her errors are *his* errors and that they are natural because they are those of the female principle, the five senses, the materialistic error of supposing the physical, vegetable world is the only world there is.[75] Under the domination of the female will Adam reproduces Eve's faulty logic and chooses unwisely, looking to selfish earthly desires (lust, for instance, rather than properly integrated love) rather than to eternal, spiritual, and imaginative realities. Adam must redeem her though, as Milton redeems Ololon in *Milton,* because she holds his whole potential for love, aspiration, and self-sacrifice: in short, all that is good in him.[76]

Jesus explains to Albion why he must die:

> Unless I die thou canst not live
> But if I die I shall arise again & thou with me
> This is Friendship & Brotherhood without it Man Is Not
> . . . .
> . . . Thus do Men in Eternity
> One for another to put off by forgiveness, every sin
>
> Albion replyd. Cannot Man exist without Mysterious
> Offering of Self for Another, is this Friendship & Brotherhood
> I see thee in the likeness & similitude of Los My Friend
>
> Jesus said. Wouldest thou love one who never died
> For thee or ever die for one who had not died for thee
> And if God dieth not for Man & giveth not himself
> Eternally for Man Man could not exist! for Man is Love:
> As God is Love: every kindness to another is a little Death
> In the Divine Image nor can Man exist but by Brotherhood[.]
> [*J* 96:14–28; E, p. 253]

As Jesus dies for man, so man must die—sacrifice his self-centeredness, or spectre—in order to redeem his emanation in an act of "Friendship

& Brotherhood" that reintegrates his psyche and thus *regains paradise*. This, then, is the Blakean import of the Crucifixion as symbol. On a sensual level, imagination (Adam) must free the senses (Eve) because the senses themselves cannot discover infinity, being empirical and mortal.[77] The marriage must be preserved. Or, as Damon puts it, "forgiveness judges nothing, but accepts. Therefore accusation, judgments and punishments are to be replaced by understanding, sympathy, and toleration. When every one understands every one else completely, the original harmony will be restored."[78]

With Adam's vision completed and the viewer's attention redirected to the significance of the Crucifixion, Blake concludes his *Paradise Lost* illustrations with a reworking of the traditional illustration to book 12, *The Expulsion* (pls. 22, 23). As we have seen, Aldrich's illustration for the 1688 edition (fig. 20) initiated a tradition of infidelity to Milton's description of the Expulsion. Copying from Chapron's engraving of Raphael's Expulsion picture (P, pl. 31), Aldrich shows Adam with his face buried in his hands and Eve attempting to hide her near-nakedness as Michael, his left hand on Adam's shoulder and a twisted sword in his right, expels them from Eden. But for some reason Aldrich copies Raphael's setting as well, curiously placing the group of figures at the base of a severely angular stairway. Aldrich may have known the Genesis illustration for the Expulsion from a 1682 Bible (P, pl. 30) in which Michael's sword, straight in Raphael's picture and Chapron's engraving, is twisted in the manner Aldrich shows it. But if Aldrich did know this latter version, his elimination of the natural setting of Eden is all the more inexplicable. Aldrich's pessimistic depiction of this despairing couple's departure must surely have confused or undermined the interpretation any sensitive reader might have drawn from a close reading of Milton's text. The effect of such a thoroughly inappropriate final visual cue to the reader could only have been a debilitating and misleading one.

Aldrich's negativism was reinforced by Cheron's headpiece to book 12 in the next illustrated edition of the epic (P, pl. 24). Cheron's design is clearly indebted to Aldrich's, and, though it is considerably reworked and made to include some of the scene in Eden, it still presents Adam and Eve driven from the foot of the stairs, here with even greater violence than before. Cheron's tailpiece to book 12 (fig. 21) does attempt to furnish an optimistic, prophetic ending, showing "Christ Risen," but the design thus shifts attention at the end away from the departure of Adam and Eve and toward the miraculous resurrection Milton had so carefully deemphasized.

The first real shift in the tone of an illustration of the Expulsion came with Hayman's design (P, pl. 52). Recalling Milton's statement that

> In either hand the hast'ning Angel caught
> Our ling'ring Parents, and to th' Eastern Gate
> Led them direct,
> [*PL* 12.637–39]

Hayman shows Michael now *leading* the pair, not driving them, holding each by a wrist. This alteration completely eliminates the sense of violent, wrathful eviction with which the scene had been endowed previously. Yet despite this change, Hayman retains much of the conventional iconography. Adam's face-in-hand pose recalls his previous appearances; the same holds for Eve. And despite the design's predominantly natural setting, the angular stairs are still visible behind the group. Finally, perhaps to compensate for his less violent action, Hayman dresses Michael, not in angelic robes like his predecessors, but rather, as in his previous design, in a theatrical antique military costume.

The design most like Hayman's is Burney's (fig. 43), in which Adam and Eve look back longingly at Eden as they are led out, held at the wrists by a Michael very similar to Hayman's. The stairs have been virtually eliminated in Burney's design; they are suggested only in the sloping ground down which Adam and Eve are led. Burney infuses his design with greater dramatic impact by depicting the group frontally, with Michael pulling the couple forward directly at the viewer. The sense of despair employed by most previous illustrators is moderated here to reflect more faithfully the wistful reluctance to leave Milton had described.

But while Burney's Expulsion scene moved in the direction of moderation, other artists' depictions, in accordance with the Burkean concept of the sublime nature of the Expulsion, perpetuated the violent, melodramatic conception of the scene, as in Fuseli's 1802 version (fig. 52), for instance. Typically, Romney's sketches also reflect the violent view (P, pls. 114, 115). Only the Richter design (fig. 36) offers any real suggestion that Adam and Eve depart by their own power and without considerable prodding.

Blake himself sketched a scene, *Adam and Eve Leaving Paradise* (B, pl. 1026), that is in this tradition, though he seems never to have worked it up into a picture.[79] The sketch shows a pair of angels departing to the right while Adam and Eve, moving and gesturing in perfect unison, step toward the center, their heads turned back over their shoulders and their left arms raised in a parting salute. At the left Satan gestures excitedly toward a contorted group of followers, perhaps exhorting them to rise and assume their places in the fallen world. Of greatest importance in the sketch is Blake's use of unison movement for Adam and Eve, a visual device we have seen in *Satan's and Raphael's Entries into Paradise* (pl. 1), suggesting here their reintegration following the divisive activities that had led to their fall.

Blake's *Expulsion* (pls. 22, 23) provides a brilliant culmination to his series of designs that again invokes established iconography to provide an interpretive context for his own critical statement. Like Burney, Blake presents his figures in direct frontal view, suggesting their imaginative reintegration. He softens the tone of the scene even more than other artists had done, showing for the first time an unarmed Michael and an Adam and Eve who reflect a discernible sense of hope. In Blake's

Figure 52. After Henry Fuseli. *The Expulsion.* 1802. *By permission of the British Library, London*

design Michael holds them, not by the wrists, but more personally by the hands, as Jesus does in *The Fall of Man*. A much earlier precedent for this gesture is the manner in which Lot leads his daughters from Sodom and Gomorrah—particularly the hand gestures and the extended left foot—in *Lot's Escape* (based on a Rubens original), which Blake engraved around 1781 for *The Protestant's Family Bible*.[80] In an odd echo of earlier illustrations and of *The Fall of Man*, done the previous year, Blake adds behind the group and between the outer streaks of lightning some horizontal shadings that once again suggest the steps from which the couple had so often descended in previous illustrations of the Expulsion. Moving between Michael's feet, the Serpent crawls out with them, among the thorns and thistles into which they all move. This harsh wilderness of experience is further indicated by the fact that Michael's *left* foot is extended in both versions of the design, suggesting the advent of the material world of generation into which Adam and Eve have fallen. This suggestion is, however, countered by the hopeful note struck by Adam's slightly advanced right foot. Eve is still very much in the physical world of the senses, though, as her extended left foot indicates. The shortened strides of both alert us to their gradual return to a more moderate behavior. Both Adam and Eve—and, to a certain extent, Michael as well—look up and back at the great plume of the flaming brand left at the gate of Eden to remind them all that there can be no going back.

By depicting the four horsemen of the Apocalypse at the top of the design, Blake effectively foreshadows the Last Judgment, the return of Christ prophesied in Revelation, the event that will end mortal time and reestablish the eternal Eden for the redeemed. Though Milton does not mention the horsemen specifically in this scene, he does allude in book 12 to Revelation, in his reference to the wiping of Adam and Eve's tears (12.645). Blake probably included the horsemen here as part of his consistent plan to explore all aspects of the Son's offer to redeem man, an exploration that would have required some allusion to the ultimate aspect of the offer, the Day of Judgment already tentatively introduced through the iconography of *The Rout of the Rebel Angels* (pls. 12, 13).

Wittreich has remarked that Blake's final design provides both an epilogue to the poem and an epitome of its action: "The Serpent recalls the fall (its cause), the thunderbolt the action that immediately ensues (the judgment); and the fall and judgment together point to the ultimate consequence of transgression (man's expulsion from Eden)." Butlin suggests another unifying scheme for poem and designs, though his arrangement is based only on the reassembled BM set and takes no account of the original HH series. In this latter arrangement, Butlin argues, Blake devoted three pictures to "preliminaries," three to Adam and Eve before the Fall, three to the ultimate causes of the Fall, and three to its consequences.[81] The relationship is still more complex, for each design sets up new, shifting resonances in relation to all the other designs and to the series as a whole. The repetition of figures, gestures, and details in the final four designs suggests, for instance, Blake's desire that we see cause, enactment, and consequences of the Fall (including the vision Michael presents, which shows after all the most important consequence) as a single unified event that is at once sequential and simultaneous. In like manner, Blake would have us join to this action all that has happened previously in hell, in heaven, and in Eden. This prior action that leads inexorably to the Fall is likewise indivisible, in Blake's view, from the Fall itself. Like so many of the critics who have commented on Milton's poem over three centuries, while we might be tempted to consider the whole series of Blake's designs a depiction less of the Son's offer than of man's fall (being taken in by the epic's title), we must remember that both Milton and Blake emphasize that the Son's offer is made *before* the temptation and Fall occur: the Fall when it occurs simply assures the completion of the act the Son's offer promises. Viewed in proper perspective, both poem and illustrations suggest that the Fall itself is an integral component of that larger act, the Son's offer; it is an inversion that necessitates the physical assertion of his bond with man.

Blake's second version of *The Expulsion* (pl. 23) involves several significant alterations. Wittreich rightly points out that the original design (pl. 22) is perhaps *too* optimistic in terms of Milton's text; Adam and Eve seem to be leaving Eden rather too willingly.[82] In the second version Blake has them looking, not up, but toward the ground, apparently at the threatening Serpent. And he has made the thistles and thorns more ominous. In fact, Adam's left foot is directly upon one of the thorns. Even the appearance of the thistle here underscores the fusion of separate moments Blake intends for us to recognize. The traditional symbol of "earthy sorrow and sin because of the curse pronounced against Adam by God" (Gen. 3:17–18), the thistle is often associated because of its thorns with the crown of thorns that figures in the Son's passion and death.[83] Blake had included the crown of thorns, of course, in *Michael Foretells the Crucifixion*. Michael's expression is more stoic in the later design, though it is still somewhat troubled, and he seems to lead the couple less reluctantly. In addition, his grip on the two is slightly altered. Here he holds Adam more loosely and grasps Eve more compellingly, holding her now by the wrist. Even this seemingly minor change reflects Blake's conscious fidelity to the nuances of Milton's text; Blake recognizes that at this point Adam has at least received the consolation of his vision, a vision he has not yet had an opportunity to share with Eve, who is thus understandably the more reluctant to leave.

It is worth noting here, at the end of our consideration of the *Paradise Lost* designs, Blake's separate portraits of Adam and Eve. *Eve Naming the Birds* (fig. 53) was probably done first. Not among Blake's best works to begin with, the painting has "suffered from repainting in oil colours."[84] It is a full-bust representation of Eve done in a vaguely Raphaelesque style, with Eve's hands raised from the elbows, her head surrounded by ornate and unidentifiable winged figures bearing little or no representational similarity to real birds, with the possible exception of a vaguely dovelike bird at the upper right. Eve's tightly curled hair tumbles down behind her, while from her curiously severe face her narrowed eyes gaze intently at the viewer. This is not at all the graceful, even delicate Eve we see in the *Paradise Lost* designs, but rather a much harsher sort of eighteenth-century matron placed in an Edenic setting.

Adam Naming the Beasts (fig. 54) is more visually successful. Its similar full-bust format suggests, along with its subject, that the painting is contemporary with *Eve Naming the Birds* and only just after the *Paradise Lost* series.[85] Adam looks calmly, almost passively, directly at the viewer, his right forearm raised from the elbow with the index finger erect, as if pointing either to heaven or to the bough of the tree behind

him. That tree is an oak, as Blake makes sure we recognize by including an oversize acorn exactly at the point to which Adam's erect finger directs our attention. Since the oak is Blake's icon for stubborn, rooted error, the artist likely wished further to emphasize the ominous presence of the crested bluish Serpent coiled about Adam's left arm and caressed by his left hand,[86] a serpent clearly resembling that in the *Paradise Lost* designs. In the open background we see a variety of animals: cattle, sheep, a horse, a lion, a stag—all familiar elements of traditional Genesis iconography—and the rolling hills of Eden, along with a river. Blake's inclusion of the Serpent here with Adam is interesting, since we more naturally associate it with Eve; if Eve's duties involve the naming only of birds, however, as the other picture suggests, we should then scarcely expect the Serpent there.

Blake had, of course, previously depicted Adam naming the beasts in his frontispiece to *Designs to a Series of Ballads* by William Hayley (1802),[87] where Adam sits before a heavy tree, an eagle perched with extended wings in the tree above him. To his left we see a horse and a ram: to his right an ox, a peacock, a rooster, and some small bird (perhaps a dove). A lion lies beside Adam's right foot, licking his toes; Adam's right hand rests on the lion's mane. In the foreground, beneath Adam's seat, a long, coiling serpent looks with apparent relish at a pair of posturing doves in the immediate foreground whose bill-to-bill positions suggest a squabble is taking place. These two doves, separated from Adam as they are by the Serpent, probably foreshadow the disruption of paradise—in both the human and the natural contexts—we know comes all too soon.[88]

Though included in neither set of *Paradise Lost* designs, Blake's picture of *The Lazar House* derives obviously from Milton's description in book 11 (ll. 477–93). Blake's conception of the scene may have been influenced in general by the eighteenth century's growing interest in sickbed and deathbed pictures and in particular by Fuseli's version of this same subject, but except for the coldly ominous figure that hovers over Fuseli's scene, there is little similarity between the two artists' pictures.[89] Blake's early drawing (B, pl. 307), from the early 1790s, shows a group of recumbent afflicted figures lying with heads to the right, while an upright figure enters from the left carrying a dagger. He points to a ghostly figure hovering at the upper right, an elderly figure of Death brandishing his dart. The scene is much improved in the stylized color print of 1795 (B, pl. 397–99), where the recumbent figures are reversed and the standing figure, now thoroughly altered, naked and with bowed head, stands at the right with the dagger held limply at his side. The blind, extravagantly bearded figure of Death hovers over the scene with arms extended, a ribbon of death darts between them with points descending from each hand. This ominous figure resembles Blake's depictions both of the Father and of Urizen. He may well have originated with Fuseli's sketch for *The Fertilization of the Nile*,[90] which Blake engraved for the 1791 edition of Erasmus Darwin's *Botanic Garden*. In

Figure 54. William Blake. *Adam Naming the Beasts.* 1810. 75 cm by 62.2 cm. *Glasgow Museums and Art Galleries, Stirling Maxwell Collection, Pollok House*

that engraving, importantly, Blake modified Fuseli's original figure to produce the hovering Urizenic figure we see repeatedly in Blake's pictures and illuminations.

Blake's 1805 watercolor, *Michael and Satan* (B, pl. 585), is at least tangentially related to the *Paradise Lost* designs. This striking painting shows the powerful, wingless Michael wrapping and locking the dragon-formed Satan in an elaborate chain. Satan is now represented as a scaly serpent whose body flares into short, bat-winged projections; he is a fusion of Satan, the Serpent, and the old dragon of Revelation. His contorted body trails off to the upper right behind the powerfully arching figure of Michael, who appears to be attaching the length of chain to Satan's neck.

These several paintings, like those pictures discussed above in connection with particular *Paradise Lost* designs, offer useful insights on Blake's reading of Milton. But, as separate works, they are generally freer interpretations, less strictly focused upon Milton's text, than the designs themselves. Like the works in Fuseli's Milton Gallery, they are essays upon Miltonic subjects that often draw freely upon other sources and traditions as well: Bible illustration, historical and genre painting, Blake's own poetry, and of course the Romantic artistic sensibility itself. Some are, for instance, illustrations of the Bible painted for Butts before the Milton pictures; these, while they may invoke Miltonic contexts, reflect substructures governing form and content within the internal logic of biblical sequences. *The Angel of the Divine Presence Bringing Eve to Adam* (B, pl. 512), for instance, while it treats an episode often associated with *Paradise Lost*, belongs in fact rather to a sequence of Bible pictures beginning with *God Blessing the Seventh Day* (B, pl. 511) and presenting a differently oriented interpretive commentary.

One point becomes clear, however: Blake's separate pictures suggest that he came to perceive with increasing clarity the nature of Milton's often daring departures from orthodoxy in his epics, even when the weight of that burden significantly damaged his production in Blake's eyes. Blake does not read Genesis as he reads Milton's Genesis in *Paradise Lost;* visual evidence proves that. We see in Blake's *Paradise Lost* designs an attempt to liberate the vision he saw embedded in Milton's epic, to correct its errors in order to align its essence with his own radical reading of human history, his own "Bible of Hell." In this sense, Blake's separate pictures can frequently serve us as helpful indicators of what that liberated view of *Paradise Lost* is *not*.

Several points about Blake's illustrations for *Paradise Lost* must be emphasized in conclusion. First, as is the case in every instance in which he made multiple sets of designs to a particular poem, Blake's second set attends even more rigorously to details and suggestions of Milton's text than does the first. At the same time, though, the second set always moves steadily toward a fuller symbolic representation of the *ideas* the poem embodies. Blake accomplishes this latter feat by a number of methods. First, he enlarges the figures in the second set so that they literally fill up the designs. Second, he departs from the practice of most previous illustrators and consistently shows us the least physically active moment of each situation. In every case, he illustrates an instant of suspended action: a dramatic pause or freeze, a contemplative moment, or the externalization of a mental condition. And, as we see in the case of *Satan, Sin, and Death* (pls. 4, 5), the second design consistently heightens any sense of arrested action that may have existed in the first version, drawing from it more fully realized insights into the psychological and symbolic significance of the moment depicted and forbidding the viewer to be distracted by purely narrative details. In this way Blake acknowledges the poem's external narrative without disproportionately emphasizing its physical activity as previous illustrators were all too ready to do, choosing instead to represent its unified *interior* vision. Hence he virtually abandons strict narrative time and proceeds in visionary time, combining incidents and iconographic references from various points in the poem within single designs. This sense of simultaneity is further enhanced by the symmetrical composition Blake employs, a stylistic device that consistently subverts naturalistic interpretation and reinforces the reader-viewer's gathering insight into the symbolic nature of the designs. Blake's decision neither to number nor to bind his designs further adds to their independence from the narrative, as does the artist's refusal to attach line citations to them (*L'Allegro* and *Il Penseroso* excepted), even though we tend naturally to arrange them in an order approximating that of the poem each set illuminates.

Another important technique Blake employs is the repetition of gestures. Such repetition expands the context of individual designs and produces a strong, unifying effect on the series, as we recognize through their constant repetition their symbolic universality.[91] In the BM set, for example, we see it not only in the person of the Son (pls. 7, 13, 21) but in Satan (pls. 3, 5), Sin (pl. 5), Death (pls. 5, 21), Adam (pls. 23, 24), and Raphael (pl. 11). The cradling gesture, with one hand raised and the other near the side, is employed by Satan (pls. 7, 9), Adam (pl. 9), and Eve (pls. 9, 17). And the blessing gesture, with arms raised from the elbows, palms outward, is used by the Son (pl. 19), the angels (pl. 13), and Adam (pls. 11, 17). These and other obvious similarities of gesture imply that Blake wished us to recognize in the characters a continual interchange not just of characteristics but, indeed, of roles. (Recall, for instance, the obvious repetitions of bodily gestures paralleling the mental conditions of the characters in *The Son Offers to Redeem Man* [pls. 6, 7], *Satan Watching Adam and Eve* [pls. 8, 9], and *The Temptation and Fall of Eve* [pls. 16, 17].) This implication is akin to the one presented by plate 76 of *Jerusalem* (fig. 50), which informs us visually that Albion and Jesus are types of one another, the point Jesus makes to Albion in the text on plate 96. If we apply the appropriate parallel in the case of the *Paradise Lost* designs, wherein the various characters come to symbolize constantly shifting mental states or attitudes, we can see that the same sort of chiasmus occurs throughout. Clearly, Blake treats Milton's characters, not as flat, static entities, but rather as complex figures in states of continual flux.

The frequent recurrence of visual imagery in Blake's canon suggests a flexibility and adaptability we customarily deny iconography. For us, a cross atop a church generally communicates the same essential message, thus lending that cross a meaning not inherent in it merely as *physical object*. We respond automatically (as a result of cultural conditioning) to countless stimuli, including cruciform postures, snakes, and colors of wedding gowns. Blake, however, wants to educate us out of this intellectual automatism and into the sort of informed analysis by which we interpret gesture and image, not by convention, but by contemplation. Hence gestures and images used in one design may be repeated in an entirely different context in another to encourage the viewer not just to observe but to enter into the figures, to participate actively in the act of comparative evaluation.

A third point, best approached in retrospect, involves what Blake might regard as the correct relationship of the forces of reason and desire. The point can tell us much about why Blake reacted to *Paradise Lost* as he did. At the risk of oversimplification, we may briefly characterize their ideal married state as that of perfect love and liberty Blake elsewhere calls "Jerusalem." In this state both love and liberty exist free and open in a mutual reciprocal relationship among the characters, grounded in repeated correct and informed choices among perceived alternatives of thought or action. Liberty is represented in a real, intrinsic order whose perfect integration is maintained naturally and by free choice because no element threatens the integrity of any other element. This is an order unlike that of the fallen world in which liberty becomes the slave of law, love is seen as weakness, and those who thrive are the devourers who triumph, like Satan and the Father, at the price of the death and suffering of others, as in the strict doctrine of the Atonement or in the Puritan moral and sensual ethic.[92] In the mutual Eden love is characterized by a sense of equality and a mutual sharing of experience like that Jesus explains to Albion on plate 96 of *Jerusalem*. This is the integrated state of unfallen Eden. It is the constant and eternal state, according to Blake's final interpretation of *Paradise Lost*, of the Son alone, though it is always open and available to every individual. Most correctly, it is the state of Jesus in *Paradise Regained* and the figure of Jesus Christ in Blake's personal mythology. Adam and Eve, by definition, cannot maintain their prelapsarian condition permanently, though through the agency of the Son they are enabled to approximate a general accord after their fall and reintegration and are assured of an eventual restoration of their primal unity.

The condition of imbalance is that of selfish excess, characterized consistently on the level of reason by a tyranny and imposed order manifested in a struggling, dissatisfied system held together only by force and violence, by threats and curses; Blake's *Tiriel* is an early analysis of such a system and its consequences. On the level of desire this flawed condition is characterized by lust and greed.[93] It is a mental imbalance that is manifested in the physical, and it is the condition that precipitates the falls of Adam and Eve, Satan and his crew, and, indeed, the Father. Those who act under the influence of this imbalance at its extreme are clearly identifiable by their intensely narcissistic pride, their desire for adulation, and their obsessive need to have their way at all costs, to dominate no matter what the cost to others.

The struggle between agents representing various degrees of imbalance, along with the balancing example of the Son as Blake idealizes him in Jesus Christ, underlies Blake's entire interpretation of Milton's diffuse epic. At every moment of physical or mental action one or more of the characters is faced with a critical choice of some sort. The ability to choose correctly is predicated upon each character's insight into himself, his ability to know who and what he is and therefore to know what is truly right. But to the extent that any character slips from the proper tension between reason and desire and into a condition of excess, to that extent will his choice be incorrect. To that extent will he fall and continue to fall until he recognizes and repudiates his error and rectifies the imbalance. Only the Son maintains the proper balance, for reasons of self-awareness and self-sufficiency that *Paradise Regained* makes clear. Hence only he can make the choice upon which man's salvation depends, the choice to die for man, a choice motivated by his true, humble, and selfless love and his fully integrated, creative sense of divine humanity.

To the extent that we can deal with *Paradise Lost* as innocence and experience, we can draw one further conclusion regarding Blake's reading of the epic. It is not inaccurate to see the unfallen Eden as a type of the world of innocence, with the unfallen couple essentially sheltered and untested. To Milton, as to Blake, the state is unsatisfactory so long as it remains safe for its inhabitants, for as Milton himself states in the *Areopagitica*, there is scant value in virtue untested. Milton's statement underlies his emphasis of the matter of will and choice in *Paradise Lost*. Hence Adam and Eve are tested, and, because they are human and therefore particularly susceptible to imbalance and deception, they fall. The penalty for their mistaken choices is their expulsion into the world of experience. But as the last two books of the poem and Blake's last two designs to each set of illustrations clearly demonstrate, the poem concludes with the pair's fortunes improving. They are now advancing, though they have fallen, into the insight of what is sometimes loosely termed the higher, "organized" Innocence. They comprehend, through the vision Adam has received from Michael, the prophecy of their redemption and regeneration. More particularly, Adam has begun to redeem his emanation, overcoming his selfish complaining in book 10. That both Adam and Eve have recognized and repudiated their divisive error—or are in the process of doing so—is made clear by the combination of integrative details Blake incorporates into his final designs. Adam and Eve are indeed cast out into the wilderness, but it is in this wilderness of the mind as well as of the physical world that their subsequent trials and temptations will be played out.[94] The wilderness of experience is analogous to the dark forest of *Comus:* it is a testing ground. But unlike Milton's Lady, Adam and Eve are now armed for the psychological testing. Having been tried and found wanting, they have been penalized but also educated, provided with the increased insight that will enable them to choose more judiciously among the tempting alternatives that coming crises will present. Not in Eden, but in the wilderness, then, the wilderness that is both psychological and imaginative, lies the opportunity for the recreation of the lost Edenic integration by means of acts of conscious, informed choice.

Thus the Fall proves necessary to the couple's progress. Though inherently unfortunate, the Fall is not strictly tragic, for it is an integral part of a scheme of ultimately fortunate consequences. The Fall results from incorrect choices, from trials not passed, but without the trials and the resultant Fall Eden could have become a place of imaginative and experiential stasis like the vales of Har in which Thel mistakenly hides. It is, then, necessary for Adam and Eve to fall—to enter experience—in order for them to reject the Fall and attain the integrated and balanced condition. Yet the Fall certainly does not automatically usher in organized innocence. Adam and Eve must work consciously—often painfully—to resolve the conflict of contraries implicit in the two states. Once they understand the interrelation of the two and the salutary nature of "Mental Fight," they can achieve the insight characterizing organized innocence and can proceed accordingly to build Jerusalem "In Englands green & pleasant Land" (*M*, pl. 1; E, p. 95) or in any other mental landscape. If Satan can claim in book 4 that "myself am Hell," then man must learn that *he* can eventually claim, as Blake would have him do, "myself am heaven."

We need to remember above all that for Blake, perhaps even more so than for Milton, the Son is finally the absolute hero of *Paradise Lost.* Blake came at last to reject the tradition of interpretation that had elevated Satan to heroic eminence by its failure to perceive the symbolic significance of the Son's offer to die for man within the total vision of Milton's epic. Through his designs Blake determinedly focuses the reader-viewer's attention, for the first time in the history of the poem's illustration, upon the event he felt Milton had himself obscured and his earlier critics had neglected: the offer of "one greater Man" to die for all humanity—for Albion—in order both to effect and to provide the paradigm for eternal spiritual and imaginative resurrection.

Notes

Figure 55. William Blake. *Satan in Council* (*Paradise Regained*, plate 5). About 1816–20. 17.2 cm by 13.2 cm. *Reproduced by permission of the Syndics of the Fitzwilliam Museum, Cambridge*

Introduction

1. Henry Crabb Robinson, *Reminiscences* (1852), in *Blake Records*, ed. G. E. Bentley, Jr. (Oxford: Oxford University Press, Clarendon Press, 1969), p. 544.

2. Ralph Cohen, *The Art of Discrimination: Thomson's "The Seasons" and the Language of Criticism* (London: Routledge and Kegan Paul, 1964), pp. 2, 279. I have also discussed Blake's illustrations briefly in relation to the tradition and practice of imitative criticism in "The Polished Artifact: Some Observations on Imitative Criticism," *Genre* 10 (Spring 1977): 47–62.

3. Preliminary and instructive essays on individual poems have appeared in recent years. On *L'Allegro* and *Il Penseroso*, see John E. Grant's "Blake's Designs for *L'Allegro* and *Il Penseroso*," *Blake Newsletter* 4 (1971): 117–34, and 5 (1971–72): 190–202; and Stephen C. Behrendt, "Bright Pilgrimage: William Blake's Designs for *L'Allegro* and *Il Penseroso*," *Milton Studies*, 8 (1975): 123–47. On *Comus*, see Irene Tayler, "Say First! What mov'd Blake? Blake's *Comus* Designs and *Milton*," in *Blake's Sublime Allegory: Essays on "The Four Zoas," "Milton," and "Jerusalem,"* ed. Stuart Curran and Joseph Anthony Wittreich, Jr., pp. 233–58 (an expanded version of a study that first appeared in *Blake Studies* 4 [Spring 1972]: 45–80; and Stephen C. Behrendt, "The Mental Contest: Blake's *Comus* Designs," *Blake Studies* 8 (1978): 65–88. On the *Nativity Ode*, see Stephen C. Behrendt, "Blake's Illustrations to Milton's *Nativity Ode*," *Philological Quarterly* 55 (Winter 1976): 65–95.

On *Paradise Regained*, see Joseph Anthony Wittreich, Jr., "William Blake: Illustrator-Interpreter of *Paradise Regained*," in *Calm of Mind: Tercentenary Essays on "Paradise Regained" and "Samson Agonistes" in Honor of John S. Diekhoff*, ed. Joseph Anthony Wittreich, Jr., pp. 93–132; John Karl Franson, "Christ on the Pinnacle: Interpretive Illustrations of the Crisis in *Paradise Regained*," *Milton Quarterly* 10 (May 1976): 48–53; J. M. Q. Dvies, "'Embraces and Comminglings': Passion and Apocalypse in Blake's *Paradise Regained* Designs," *Durham University Journal*, December 1981, pp. 75–96; and Stephen C. Behrendt, "*Comus* and *Paradise Regained*: Blake's View of Trial in the Wilderness," *Milton and the Romantics* 3 (1977): 8–13. See also Pamela Dunbar, *William Blake's Illustrations to the Poetry of Milton*, a descriptive survey of all the designs. Related studies are Edward J. Rose, "Blake's Illustrations for *Paradise Lost, L'Allegro*, and *Il Penseroso*: A Thematic Reading," *Hartford Studies in Literature* 2 (1970): 40–67; Marcia R. Pointon, *Milton and English Art*; and Joseph Anthony Wittreich, Jr., *Angel of Apocalypse: Blake's Idea of Milton*.

4. See Northrop Frye, *The Return of Eden: Five Essays on Milton's Epics*, p. 92.

5. George Saintsbury, *A History of English Criticism: Being the English Chapters of "A History of Criticism and Literary Taste in Europe,"* Revised, Adapted, and Supplemented (Edinburgh and London: W. Blackwood and Sons, 1911), pp. 130–31.

6. Saintsbury, *A History of Criticism and Literary Taste in Europe,* 3 vols. (Edinburgh and London: W. Blackwood and Sons, 1900–1904), 3:266–69. William Butler Yeats, "William Blake and the Imagination," and "William Blake and his Illustrations to the *Divine Comedy,*" in *Essays and Introductions* (New York: Macmillan, 1968), pp. 111–45; William Blake, *The Works of William Blake: Poetic, Symbolic, and Critical,* ed. William Butler Yeats, 3 vols. (London: Bernard Quaritch, 1893), 2:308–11.

John Milton, *On the Morning of Christ's Nativity: Milton's Hymn with Illustrations by William Blake,* ed. Geoffrey Keynes (Cambridge: Cambridge University Press, 1923), p. 32.

7. Leslie Brisman, *Milton's Poetry of Choice and Its Romantic Heirs,* p. 8. See also Harold Bloom, *The Anxiety of Influence: A Theory of Poetry* (New York: Oxford University Press, 1973).

8. In this light we might apply Jerome J. McGann's comment that Blake's art "is visionary not because it records but because it induces vision" ("The Aim of Blake's Prophecies and the Uses of Blake Criticism," in *Blake's Sublime Allegory,* p. 5). In the Milton designs, though, Blake does both.

Chapter 1

1. Kester Svendsen, "John Martin and the Expulsion Scene in *Paradise Lost,*" *Studies in English Literature, 1500–1900* 1 (1961): 72–73, uses much the same terminology, seeing the vocabulary of a painting as a set of semantic gestures much like those employed in verbal art and "dependent in their relation to the artist's total climate and independent in their nature as acts of imagination." These two aspects are, respectively, tradition (or "form" and convention) as apprehended by the artist, and vision (or "content"). See also the related studies by Janet Warner, "Blake's Use of Gesture," in *Blake's Visionary Forms Dramatic,* ed. David V. Erdman and John E. Grant, pp. 174–95; and "Blake and the Language of Art: From Copy to Vision," *Colby Library Quarterly* 13 (June 1977): 99–114; W. J. T. Mitchell, *Blake's Composite Art: A Study of the Illuminated Poetry;* and Stephen C. Behrendt, "A Vocabulary of Lineaments: Blake and the Language of Art," *Blake Studies,* in press.

2. On "the language of art," see Ralph Cohen, *The Art of Discrimination: Thomson's "The Seasons" and the Language of Criticism* (London: Routledge and Kegan Paul, 1964), p. 253; on "pictorial language," see Warner, "Blake's Use of Gesture," pp. 174–75 (my italics). On the matter of imitation, see also Stephen C. Behrendt, "The Polished Artifact: Some Observations on Imitative Criticism," *Genre* 10 (1977): 47–62, which examines the consequences of Blake's assertion in greater detail.

3. John Dryden, "A Parallel of Poetry and Painting," *Of Dramatic Poesy, and Other Critical Essays,* 2 vols. (London and New York: J. M. Dent and Sons, 1962), 2:195; Richard Hurd, *The Works of Richard Hurd, D.D., Lord Bishop of Worcester,* 8 vols. (London: T. Caldwell and W. Davies, 1811), 2:232–33; Samuel Taylor Coleridge, *Anima Poetae* (Boston and New York: Houghton, Mifflin and Co., 1895), pp. 142–43.

4. Cohen, *Art of Discrimination,* p. 249.

5. Mario Praz, *Mnemosyne: The Parallel between Literature and the Visual Arts* (Princeton, N.J.: Princeton University Press, 1970), p. 34. Indeed, Robert Halsband makes this very point regarding eighteenth-century illustrations in *"The Rape of the Lock" and Its Illustrations, 1714–1896* (Oxford: Oxford University Press, Clarendon Press, 1980), p. 24.

6. Irene Tayler, *Blake's Illustrations to the Poems of Gray,* p. 34.

7. Irene Langridge, *William Blake: A Study of His Life and Art Work* (London: G. Bell and Sons, 1904), p. 136.

8. See Harold Bloom, *The Anxiety of Influence: A Theory of Poetry* (New York: Oxford University Press, 1973), p. 30; and Praz, *Mnemosyne,* p. 34. John E. Grant agrees, arguing that Blake scarcely would have considered his independence as an artist and thinker threatened by the truth of Milton's vision, "nor did he feel a compulsion to misrepresent Milton." See "The Female Awakening at the End of Blake's *Milton:* A Picture Story, with Questions," in *Milton Reconsidered: Essays in Honor of Arthur E. Barker,* ed. John Karl Franson, Salzburg Studies in English Literature, no. 49 (Salzburg: University of Salzburg Press, 1976), p. 79.

9. Mitchell, *Blake's Composite Art,* pp. 18–19. See also Joseph Anthony Wittreich, Jr., "William Blake: Illustrator-Interpreter of *Paradise Regained,*" in *Calm of Mind: Tercentenary Essays on "Paradise Regained" and "Samson Agonistes" in Honor of John S. Diekhoff,* ed. Joseph Anthony Wittreich, Jr., p. 123.

10. See Joseph Anthony Wittreich, Jr., *The Romantics on Milton: Formal Essays and Critical Asides,* pp. 19–20; and Northrop Frye, "The Road of Excess," *The Stubborn Structure: Essays on Criticism and Society* (Ithaca and New York: Cornell University Press, 1970), pp. 160–74.

11. Although he does not actually use these terms, S. Foster Damon leans in this same direction, recognizing that Blake was the first clearly to see Milton as a symbolic poet. See "Blake and Milton," in *The Divine Vision: Studies in the Poetry and Art of William Blake,* ed. Vivian de Sola Pinto (London: Victor Gollancz, 1957), pp. 89–96. Northrop Frye also develops the point in *Fearful Symmetry: A Study of William Blake.* We should remember, after

all, that in its original context *revolution* was an astronomical term denoting the regular and orderly motion of the stars, a point apropos of the word's application to English political affairs in 1660 and 1688. See Minna Doskow, "William Blake's *America*: The Story of a Revolution Betrayed," *Blake Studies* 8 (1979): 168. The word is exquisitely Blakean, connoting both the destruction and the renovation of primal order.

12. John Walter Good, *Studies in the Milton Tradition* (Urbana: University of Illinois Press, 1913), p. 248. See also John T. Shawcross, ed., *Milton: The Critical Heritage* (London: Routledge and Kegan Paul, 1970), and *Milton, 1732–1801: The Critical Heritage* (London and Boston: Routledge and Kegan Paul, 1972).

13. See James Holly Hanford and James G. Taaffe, *A Milton Handbook*, 5th ed. (New York: Appleton, Century, Crofts, 1970), pp. 287–88. On the Romantic notion of Milton, see also Wittreich, *The Romantics on Milton*, especially the introduction.

14. Good, *Studies in the Milton Tradition*, pp. 24–50 (see especially the chart, p. 49); and Marcia R. Pointon, *Milton and English Art*, pp. xxxii–xlii.

15. Major discussions of the Blake-Milton affinity include Denis Saurat, *Blake and Milton* (London: Stanley Nott, 1935); Bernard Blackstone, *English Blake;* Damon, "Blake and Milton"; Northrop Frye, "Notes for a Commentary on *Milton*," in *The Divine Vision*, ed. de Sola Pinto, pp. 99–104; Leslie Brisman, *Milton's Poetry of Choice and Its Romantic Heirs;* Joseph Anthony Wittreich, Jr., "Opening the Seals: Blake's Epics and the Milton Tradition," in *Blake's Sublime Allegory: Essays on "The Four Zoas," "Milton," and "Jerusalem,"* ed. Stuart Curran and Joseph Anthony Wittreich, Jr., pp. 23–58;

and Joseph Anthony Wittreich, Jr., *Angel of Apocalypse: Blake's Idea of Milton.*

16. On the first Romantic life, see William Hayley, *The Life of Milton*, in *The Poetical Works of John Milton*, ed. William Hayley, 3 vols. (London: John and Josiah Boydell, George Nicol, 1794–97); I quote here Hayley's *Life of Milton, in Three Parts, to Which Are Added, Conjectures on the Origin of Paradise Lost: With an Appendix* (Dublin, 1797), p. 52. Hayley's portrait series is discussed in William Welles, ed., *William Blake's "Heads of the Poets,"* (Manchester: City of Manchester Art Galleries, 1971). William Michael Rossetti, "Descriptive Catalogue," in *Life of William Blake, with Selections from His Poems and Other Writings*, by Alexander Gilchrist, 2d ed., 2 vols. (London: Macmillan and Co., 1880), 2:212.

17. See John Rupert Martin, *The Portrait of John Milton at Princeton and Its Place in Milton Iconography* (Princeton, N.J.: Princeton University Press, 1961), and Joseph Anthony Wittreich, Jr., "'Divine Countenance': Blake's Portrait and Portrayals of Milton," *Huntington Library Quarterly* 11 (1974): 125–60.

18. Milton's references to song occur at *PL* 1.6, 13; 3.17–18, 29; 7.12, 21, 24, 30; 9.6, 25; *PR* 1.1, 2, 12, 17.

19. The leaves are identified by W. M. Rossetti in Gilchrist's *Life of Blake*, 2:212. For their significance, see S. Foster Damon, *A Blake Dictionary: The Ideas and Symbols of William Blake* (1965; rpt. New York: E. P. Dutton and Co., 1971), p. 305. See also Pamela Dunbar, *William Blake's Illustrations to the Poetry of Milton*, p. 2.

20. In the discussion of *Milton*, all verbal references are to the Erdman text (E). But because Erdman does not number seven of the pictorial plates in the order in which they appear in Copy D, I follow the plate numbers assigned in those plates in Copy D in discussion of the plates.

See William Blake, *Milton: A Poem in Twelve Books*, ed. Geoffrey Keynes (London: Trianon Press, 1967). Erdman suggests that Copy D, printed on paper watermarked 1815, is the latest copy Blake made (E, p. 727). As such, Copy D probably best represents Blake's final thoughts on the poem.

21. Frye, "Notes for a Commentary on Milton," p. 103. Indeed, we do well to recall that Blake modeled *Milton* on the brief epic form Milton had used in *Paradise Regained*, the poem to which *Milton* is so significantly related in its central mythic action.

John Beer, *Blake's Humanism* (Manchester and New York: University of Manchester Press, 1968), p. 142.

22. On the fusion of epic and prophecy, see also Joseph Anthony Wittreich, Jr., *Visionary Poetics: Milton's Tradition and His Legacy.*

23. Jean-Paul Sartre, *What Is Literature?*, trans. Bernard Frechtman (1949; rpt. New York: Washington Square Press, 1966), pp. 28, 29, 36.

24. Joseph Chiari, *Realism and Imagination* (London: Barrie and Rockliff, 1960), pp. 104–15.

25. Harold Bloom, *Blake's Apocalypse: A Study of Poetic Argument*, pp. 308, 359. On "unveiling the whore": Florence Sandler, "The Iconoclastic Enterprise: Blake's Critique of 'Milton's Religion,'" *Blake Studies* 5 (Fall 1972): 56.

26. See also Wittreich, *Angel of Apocalypse*, pp. 35–38.

27. Blackstone, *English Blake*, p. 140.

28. For the significance of Blake's use of crosshatching, see Robert N. Essick, "Blake and the Traditions of Reproductive Engraving," *Blake Studies* 5 (1972): 59–103; and Wittreich, "'Divine Countenance.'" Wittreich also discusses the four title pages in *Angel of Apocalypse*, chap. 1. Another useful study of the mechanics of Blake's engraving process

is Morris Eaves, "Blake and the Artistic Machine: An Essay in Decorum and Technology," *PMLA* 92 (October 1977); 903–27.

29. Frye, *Fearful Symmetry*, p. 343. This concept of "visionary time," as developed here and in succeeding chapters, is also the subject of Ronald L. Grimes's essay, "Time and Space in Blake's Major Prophecies," in *Blake's Sublime Allegory: Essays on "The Four Zoas," "Milton," and "Jerusalem,"* ed. Stuart Curran and Joseph Anthony Wittreich, Jr., pp. 59–82, where it is applied specifically to the context of Blake's own epics. It also figures in Susan Fox's *Poetic Form in Blake's "Milton"* (Princeton, N.J.: Princeton University Press, 1976), where it is dubbed the "principle of simultaneity, by which the duration of the entire action of the poem is defined as a single unmeasurable instant" (p. 6).

30. As Wittreich has noted ("William Blake: Illustrator-Interpreter," p. 105), by this method Blake moves away from the eighteenth-century practice of representing in a single picture a series of related events involving the same central characters who, in such pictures, may appear more than once. See, for instance, Medina's illustrations to *Paradise Lost: Satan in the Garden* (P, pl. 5), *Michael Comes to the Garden* (P, pl. 9), and *Raphael Descending* (P, pl. 11).

31. See also W. J. T. Mitchell's "Blake's Composite Art," in *Blake's Visionary Forms Dramatic*, ed. Erdman and Grant, p. 73.

32. Damon, *A Blake Dictionary*, p. 95.

33. See also Wittreich, *Angel of Apocalypse*, p. 24–25.

34. This establishes an interesting perspective on Blake's practice in the printing of the *Songs of Innocence and of Experience*. Although Blake printed *Innocence* separately, without *Experience*, he never issued *Ex-*

perience alone. Careful study reveals that *Experience* is not a totally independent work in the manner of *Innocence*, but is, rather, one that works more clearly to delineate what is in fact *already implicit* in *Innocence*. As with Milton the old-new man in *Milton*, the "new" is already implicit in the "old"; *Experience* merely assists in its discovery and definition.

35. Sandler, "The Iconoclastic Enterprise," pp. 30–31.

36. Northrop Frye, *A Study of English Romanticism* (New York: Random House, 1968), p. 37; my italics.

37. Wittreich, *Angel of Apocalypse*, p. 43.

38. See also John E. Grant, "The Female Awakening at the End of Blake's *Milton*."

39. See also Mark Schorer, *William Blake: The Politics of Vision* (1946; rpt. New York: Random House, 1959), pp. 295–96. Schorer discusses this alignment in terms of the devourers and the prolific. Milton is essentially, "without knowing it," of the party of the revolutionary prolific, and the essence of his vision involves the struggle of the prolific against the devourers, who exalt reason and law in order to deny energy and the impulsive life. This relationship sums up, in Blakean terms, the dynamic conflict operating in Milton between his "prolific" nature and his "devourer" Puritanism, each struggling for supremacy in his poetry.

40. We should recall Blake's impressive depiction, *Satan in His Original Glory* (B, pl. 554); this is anything but a condemnatory depiction on Blake's part.

41. John Beer, *Blake's Humanism*, p. 30.

42. Frye's *Fearful Symmetry*, p. 219.

43. Harold Bloom, "Commentary," in *The Poetry and Prose of William Blake* (E), p. 810.

44. I have pursued this matter in greater detail in "Bright Pilgrimage: William Blake's Designs for *L'Alle-*

gro and *Il Penseroso*," *Milton Studies* 8 (1975): 123–47, in a reading that differs substantially from that advanced by Dunbar. The present discussion is intended to shed further light on the particular critical commentary on Milton the man Blake's designs advance. For other extensive examinations of these designs, see Edward J. Rose, "Blake's Illustrations for *Paradise Lost, L'Allegro* and *Il Penseroso:* A Thematic Reading," *Hartford Studies in Literature* 2 (1970): 40–67; John E. Grant, "From Fable to Human Vision: A Note on the First Illustration," *Blake's Visionary Forms Dramatic*, ed. Erdman and Grant, pp. xi–xiv; and "Blake's Designs for *L'Allegro* and *Il Penseroso*," *Blake Newsletter* 4 (1971): 117–34, 5 (1971–72): 190–202; Karl Kiralis, "Blake's Criticism of Milton's *L'Allegro* and *Il Penseroso* and of Its Author," in *Milton Reconsidered*, ed. Franson, pp. 46–77; and Pamela Dunbar, *William Blake's Illustrations to the Poetry of Milton*, pp. 115–62.

45. Dunbar, *Blake's Illustrations*, p. 139. Dunbar goes so far, in fact, as to assert that the youthful poet, who she assumes is Milton, is here in a state of "divine inspiration" (p. 157).

46. Kiralis and Rose feel quite otherwise. Kiralis, in particular, asserts that "a work about Milton makes the most sense if Milton is in it, and if he is not, the picture still applies to him" ("Blake's Criticism," p. 55 n), and Dunbar assumes without question that the youthful poet is Milton. Still, this contention is more wishful thinking than fidelity to Blake's own verbal suggestions, by which we do well to guide our opinions. Blake's only mention of Milton in his descriptions of the *L'Allegro* pictures occurs in connection with *L'Allegro*, pl. 3 (B, pl. 674), where he tells us one of the tiny figures at the bottom represents

Milton. Yet the central, *large* figures in five of the six *Il Penseroso* pictures are specifically identified as Milton. Kiralis is on safer ground in continuing, "in one way or another Blake is addressing Milton throughout the designs" (p. 55 n). On this point we agree, but I remain convinced that the intent of Blake's designs is comparative, giving us two significantly different histories of intellectual and imaginative development.

47. Dunbar considers Milton in this design to be mired in "mortal error," with "both the vision and its mediator . . . contaminated" (*Blake's Illustrations*, p. 157) Yet the images here are far more intense, far less regimented, than those in *The Youthful Poet's Dream*. These are the figures of all ages, all situations, full of energy and epic potential, part of no orderly, prepackaged dream, but rather of a free-flowing, totally uninhibited imaginative vision.

48. Don Cameron Allen, *The Harmonious Vision: Studies in Milton's Poetry* (Baltimore, Md.: Johns Hopkins University Press, 1954), p. 21. See also David Bindman, *Blake as an Artist*, pp. 198–99.

49. Rose, "Blake's Illustrations," p. 65.

Chapter 2

1. Leslie Brisman, *Milton's Poetry of Choice and Its Romantic Heirs*, pp. 55–56.

2. Hazard Adams pursues this aspect of Blake's thought in "The Blakean Aesthetic" (1954), rpt. in *The Visionary Hand: Essays for the Study of William Blake's Art and Aesthetics*, ed. Robert N. Essick (Los Angeles: Hennessey and Ingalls, 1973), pp. 173–200. See also David Bindman, *Blake as an Artist*, pp. 150–62.

3. Northrop Frye, *Anatomy of Criticism: Four Essays* (1957: rpt. Princeton, N.J.: Princeton University Press, 1971), p. 4. On marginal notes, see for instance, Sir Joshua Reynolds, *Discourses on Art*, ed. Robert Wark (San Marino, Calif.: Henry E. Huntington Library, 1959), where Blake's marginalia are the subject of a number of acid comments by the editor. A perceptive discussion of Blake's disagreements with Reynolds is furnished by Hazard Adams in "Revisiting Reynolds' *Discourses* and Blake's Annotations," in *Blake in His Time*, ed. Robert N. Essick and Donald Pearce (Bloomington and London: Indiana University Press, 1978), pp. 128–44.

4. Though each of Reynolds's discourses was printed in limited editions for release during the year in which it was delivered, and though the first seven were published together in 1778, the first complete English edition was that prepared by Edward Malone and published in 1798. It is this edition in which Blake's notes were entered somewhere between 1798 and 1808. The poet's remarks thus date from the period in which Blake was reevaluating his conception of Milton's work.

5. Martin Price, *To the Palace of Wisdom: Studies in Order and Energy from Dryden to Blake* (1964; rpt. Garden City, N.Y.: Doubleday and Co., 1965), p. 442. See also Anne Kostelanetz Mellor, *Blake's Human Form Divine*, pp. 103–10.

6. The original claim was made by Bernard Blackstone in *English Blake*, p. 140. Apparently basing his claim on Blake's early reactions and overlooking the altered perspective on the epic embodied in his illustrations, Blackstone tells us that Milton "ranges himself with the forces of oppression and sins against his own understanding. Throughout *Paradise Lost* he supports tyranny, law, cruelty, chastity, and 'unorganized innocence'" (p. 142). A more correct perspective, however, is contained in Joseph Anthony Wittreich, Jr.'s assertion that "*Paradise Lost*, Blake understood, was written in part to criticize the very theology it postulated"; that is, it undermines the orthodox doctrines of inflexibility and retributive justice for which Blackstone (and, perhaps, the *younger* Blake) would consider Milton the apologist (*Angel of Apocalypse: Blake's Idea of Milton*, p. 93).

7. Henry Crabb Robinson attributes to Blake the remark that Milton was busied "about this world, . . . till in his old age he returned to God, whom he had had in his childhood." See *Diary, Reminiscences, and Correspondence of Henry Crabb Robinson*, ed. Thomas Sadler, 2 vols., (Boston: Houghton, Mifflin and Co., 1898), 2:28.

8. We are told by A. S. P. Woodhouse, for instance, that "Milton thinks of the *Nativity* [*Ode*] as the first essay of one pledged to heroic poetry and an earnest of what he will attempt" (A. S. P. Woodhouse and Douglas Bush, eds., *A Variorum Commentary on the Poems of John Milton*, [New York: Columbia University Press, 1972], 2.1.35). On Milton's choice, see William Kerrigan, *The Prophetic Milton* (Charlottesville: University Press of Virginia, 1974), p. 200.

9. For a fuller discussion of Blake's *Nativity Ode* designs, see Stephen C. Behrendt, "Blake's Illustrations to Milton's *Nativity Ode*," *Philological Quarterly* 55 (1976): 65–95. After restudying the originals of these designs and those to both *L'Allegro* and *Il Penseroso* and *Paradise Regained*, and after extensive discussions with Martin Butlin on the dating of Blake's pictures, I feel Butlin is probably correct in assigning to the Huntington set, previously regarded as around 1803, a much later date, perhaps around 1815. Their scale, style, and luminous, stippled coloring share much with these other two later sets of designs. In my article on the designs I originally argued that the Huntington set was the earlier, basing that contention particularly on the first design's strong resemblance to the separate

painting of *The Nativity* (around 1800; B, pl. 502). But as Butlin convincingly argues, other aspects of the HH set seem to indicate their later origin. As for the first design, apparently Blake simply tried a new conception in the set made for the Reverend Joseph Thomas (around 1808–1809; the Whitworth set), and then returned in the subsequent set for Butts to the basic conception we see in *The Nativity*, making the initial design now both an introduction to and an epitome of the series as a whole. I take some comfort, in thus reversing my earlier position, from Blake's remarks in *The Marriage* about "the man who never alters his opinion."

My ordering of the *Nativity Ode* designs differs, for reasons upon which my article elaborates, from those of C. H. Collins Baker in his *Catalogue of William Blake's Drawings and Paintings in the Huntington Library*, rev. and ed. Robert Wark, pp. 32–37; David Bindman, *Blake as an Artist*, pp. 193–95; and Pamela Dunbar, *William Blake's Illustrations to the Poetry of John Milton*, pp. 91–114.

10. See John Walter Good, *Studies in the Milton Tradition* (Urbana: University of Illinois Press, 1913); and John T. Shawcross, ed., *Milton: The Critical Heritage* (London: Routledge and Kegan Paul, 1970), and *Milton, 1732–1801: The Critical Heritage* (London and Boston: Routledge and Kegan Paul, 1972), on the critical reputation of the *Nativity Ode* in the eighteenth century.

11. Only in this sense can we put much stock in Dunbar's notion that the child seen at the furnace is a "mannikin Christ-child" (*Blake's Illustrations*, p. 107) who thus forms "a proleptic vision of the Christ-child breaking out of the house of mortality . . . through his death and atonement" (p. 109). Blake rejects the doctrine of the Atonement, as

we shall see. Furthermore, he portrays in the two stable scenes, not the "prison" Dunbar assumes when she sees in the increased quantity of manger straw in the final design proof of "the overwhelming of the soul by the forces of that [fallen or vegetative] world" (p. 113), but, rather, a peaceful world in which redemption is simultaneously both beginning and reaching its completion.

12. See the title page for "Night the Eighth" of Edward Young's *Night Thoughts*, reproduced in *Illustrations to Young's "Night Thoughts*," ed. Geoffrey Keynes (Cambridge, Mass.: Harvard University Press, 1927). See also S. Foster Damon, *A Blake Dictionary: The Ideas and Symbols of William Blake*, pp. 107–8.

13. Paul Fry, *The Poet's Calling in the English Ode* (New Haven, Conn., and London: Yale University Press, 1980), p. 47.

14. Irene Tayler finds in Blake's *Comus* designs a dissatisfaction with Milton's masque, which she refers to as "a kind of synopsis of Miltonic vision and error," a drama of "the bondage of sexual fears," "played in the theater of her [the Lady's] mind, where the error has been" ("Say First! What Mov'd Blake? Blake's *Comus* Designs and *Milton*," in *Blake's Sublime Allegory: Essays on "The Four Zoas," "Milton," and "Jerusalem*," ed. Stuart Curran and Joseph Anthony Wittreich, Jr., pp. 234–35). Tayler deflects attention from the Lady's failure and directs it instead toward the potentially crippling nature and consequences of the doctrine of chastity and virginity Milton's Lady articulates. Largely because she fails to consider Blake's second set of *Comus* designs, Tayler misses Blake's conscious effort visually to emphasize the Lady's paralysis and her consequent failure in her trial. A better reading is offered by Dunbar, *Blake's Illustrations*, pp. 9–34, though her comments are undermined by curious notions like the contention that "the terrors which

threaten the Lady are rendered as merely scarifying, or even comic" (p. 14), and the assertion that the Lady's parents clearly represent "fixity of outlook" and "uncompromising repressiveness" (p. 12). For a fuller discussion of the interpretation offered here, see Stephen C. Behrendt, "The Mental Contest: Blake's *Comus* Designs," *Blake Studies* 8 (1978): 65–88.

15. Angus Fletcher, *The Transcendental Masque: An Essay on Milton's "Comus"* (Ithaca, N.Y., and London: Cornell University Press, 1971), p. 210. Fletcher correctly reminds us that when we recall the youthfulness of the children who originally acted the roles of the Lady and her brothers, their speeches take on a heightened sense of ironic innocence and immaturity (p. 211).

16. [John Dalton,] *"Comus," a Mask: (Now Adapted to the Stage) As Alter'd from Milton's Mask at Ludlow-Castle, Which Was Never Represented but on Michaelmas-Day, 1634; before the Right Honble. the Earl of Bridgewater, Lord President of Wales* (London: R. Dodsley, 1738), pp. 62–63; [George Colman], *Comus: A Masque, Altered from Milton: As Performed at the Theatre-Royal in Covent Garden: The Musick Composed by Dr. Arne* (London, 1772).

The popularity of *Comus* as poem and stage-piece is reflected in the frequency and nature of its illustration prior to 1800. Designs were made by Francis Hayman (1752), Robert Smirke (about 1780), Joseph Wright of Derby (1785), Elias Martin (1788), Conrad Metz (1791), Richard Westall (1794–97), and Henry Fuseli (1799), along with others by A. Dighton, J. Roberts, S. Shelley, Edward Burney, Samuel De Wilde, and at least one anonymous artist. The designs most frequently depicted the Lady in some aspect of her central confrontation with Comus. Less frequently, they showed

Comus encountering or overhearing the Lady, the brothers driving out Comus, or the Lady's disenchantment by Sabrina. Some of the designs (Dighton's, Roberts's, Shelley's, and De Wilde's, for instance) portrayed contemporary actresses (Miss Storace or Miss Catley) in their roles, most notably as Euphrosyne—a character not even in Milton's original, but, rather, borrowed from *L'Allegro* and introduced by Dalton in his adaptation. Such illustrations contributed heavily to the increasing deflection of attention ever further away from the essence of Milton's masque.

17. In Blake's second set of *Comus* designs (the Boston set, about 1808–1809), this deliberate consistency of posture is made most explicit. In both sets the Lady's posture is identical in designs 5 and 6 within the same set, but in design 3 of the early set (the Huntington set, about 1801–1803) the Lady's posture before the temptation scene is slightly different (B, pl. 618).

18. Wittreich, *Angel of Apocalypse*, pp. 80–88.

19. Dunbar also points to the solemnity, even severity, of the final design (*Blake's Illustrations*, pp. 30–34).

20. These corrections sometimes produce significant new contextual suggestions, a point made effectively with respect to *Comus* by J. Karl Franson in "The Serpent-Driving Females in Blake's *Comus* 4," *Blake: An Illustrated Quarterly* 47 (Winter 1978–79): 164–77; and by Dunbar, *Blake's Illustrations*, in her comments on stylistic differences in the two sets of *Comus* designs.

21. Wittreich, *Angel of Apocalypse*, pp. 85–86. Dunbar assigns both sets of *Comus* designs to about 1801, which is clearly incorrect for the Boston set, and dates the Huntington *Nativity Ode* designs around 1808 (*Blake's Illustrations*).

22. The relationship between Blake's designs for these poems is discussed in greater detail in Stephen C. Behrendt, "*Comus* and *Paradise Regained:* Blake's View of Trial in the Wilderness," *Milton and the Romantics* 3 (1977): 8–13. Wittreich's perceptive discussion of the *Paradise Regained* designs furnishes an additional perspective on the following pages; see both "William Blake: Illustrator-Interpreter of *Paradise Regained*," in *Calm of Mind: Tercentenary Essays on "Paradise Regained" and "Samson Agonistes" in Honor of John S. Diekhoff*, ed. Joseph Anthony Wittreich, Jr.; and *Angel of Apocalypse*, pp. 103–44, an expanded version of the former.

Dunbar's discussion of the designs (*Blake's Illustrations*, pp. 163–86) contains an interesting consideration of Satan as Jesus' Spectre.

23. See also Kathleen Raine, *Blake and Tradition*, 2 vols. (Princeton, N.J.: Princeton University Press, 1968), 2:198.

24. Stuart Curran, "The Mental Pinnacle: *Paradise Regained* and the Romantic Four-Book Epic," in *Calm of Mind*, ed. Wittreich, p. 136.

25. Wittreich contends in *Angel of Apocalypse* that Jesus' gesture indicates he is *declining* the bread and wine, not blessing them. "In parody of the traditional symbol of benediction . . . Christ's gesture implies a rejection of not the offering but the doctrine, the mystery religion, that it signifies" (p. 113). Wittreich's assertion pushes the matter too far, I think, for we ought to notice that Christ's gesture is a calm, relaxed one like that Blake assigns him in *The Vision of the Last Judgment* (B, pl. 870), and is quite unlike that with which he declines Satan's banquet in the sixth design. Jesus' gesture in the eleventh design is quite properly that of sacramental *consecration*, an act which should be distinguished from that of *benediction*, typically conferred *upon people* by means of raised, outspread hands. Consecrating the bread and wine that symbolize his body and blood, Jesus effectively validates the sacramental reminder of his own experience in mortality. Introduced at the Last Supper, the symbolic bread and wine point to man's participation in the eternal *spiritual* body of Jesus; their symbolic force comes from their applicability to the *spiritual*—not the physical—banquet of the Eucharist.

26. On previous illustrations to the poem see Joseph Anthony Wittreich, Jr., "Appendix A: Illustrators of *Paradise Regained* and Their Subjects (1713–1816)," in *Calm of Mind*, ed. Wittreich, pp. 309–29; J. Karl Franson, "Christ on the Pinnacle: Interpretive Illustrations of the Crisis in *Paradise Regained*," *Milton Quarterly* 10 (1976): 48–53; and Robert F. Gleckner, "Blake's Illustration of the Third Temptation in *Paradise Regained*," *Blake: An Illustrated Quarterly* 11 (Fall 1977): 126–27.

27. Those who would contend that Blake's depiction of a mild and passive Jesus is an indication of the artist's implicit disapproval of Milton's character would do well to recall Roland Mushat Frye's point about Renaissance depictions of Michael defeating Satan. Frye notes that Michael generally appears passive and serene, even apathetic, at the moment of his victory precisely because "anger and pride are sinful passions, and as such are not within the emotional range of faithful angels" (*Milton's Imagery and the Visual Arts: Iconographic Tradition in the Epic Poems*, pp. 53–54. Blake's own familiarity with Renaissance iconographic traditions would have suggested that passions unbefitting an angel are, within the scope of *Paradise Regained*, likewise unbefitting Jesus. The point applies with equal force to Blake's *Paradise Lost* design, *The Rout of the Rebel Angels*.

28. John Karl Franson has demonstrated in an insightful essay

that Satan's "hunger temptations" and Christ's responses to them are central to Christ's growing self-awareness and self-sufficiency; see "Bread and Banquet as Food for Thought: Experiential Learning in *Paradise Regained*," *Milton Reconsidered: Essays in Honor of Arthur E. Barker*, ed. John Karl Franson, Salzburg Studies in English Literature, no. 49 (Salzburg: University of Salzburg Press, 1976). We might note too that while Satan had originally rejected Belial's suggestion that Christ be tempted with women (2.153–234), Milton—and Blake after him—includes women in the banquet temptation (2.353–61).

29. It is quite reasonable to assume that Blake knew the Trinity manuscript version of *Comus*, perhaps from Thomas Warton's edition of 1785 or Henry John Todd's of 1798. In Warton's *Poems upon Several Occasions, English, Italian, and Latin, with Translations, by John Milton* (London: James Dodsley, 1785), the Trinity MS variations are itemized in a supplementary appendix, "Original Various Readings," pp. 606, 608–15. In Todd's edition, *Comus, a Mask Presented at Ludlow Castle 1634, before the Earl of Bridgewater, then President of Wales: by John Milton, with Notes Critical and Explanatory by Various Commentators, and with Preliminary Illustrations; to which is added a Copy of the Mask from a Manuscript Belonging to His Grace the Duke of Bridgewater* (Canterbury: W. Bristow, 1798), the entire Trinity MS is included.

While the prominent figure in the dragon-drawn chariot above the trees in *Comus*, pl. 4 (B, pls. 614, 627), is not specifically mentioned in Milton's 1637 text, it is associated in the Trinity MS with the "Hesperian Gardens . . . on whose faire tree / The scalie-harnest dragon ever keeps / His uninchanted eye" (Todd, p. 153, ll. 1–6). Blake's use of this visual detail, along with other details

found only in the Trinity MS, suggests that he knew both versions of the masque before undertaking his illustrations. See also Franson, "The Serpent-Driving Females in Blake's *Comus* 4."

30. Barbara Kiefer Lewalski has remarked of the prelapsarian Eden that "for Adam and Eve the external paradise can be secure only so long as they cultivate and enhance the paradise within" ("Innocence and Experience in Milton's Eden," in *New Essays on "Paradise Lost*," ed. Thomas Kranidas [Berkeley, Los Angeles, and London: University of California Press, 1969], p. 96). The point clearly applies with equal force to postlapsarian existence as well.

31. See John Beer, *Blake's Humanism*, pp. 19–20. Beer points out that in any fall which occurs by process of division from within, *all* parties are consequently diminished. Thus Beer argues that in casting out Satan the Father is diminished as well, and "it will appear to Satan equally that God has been cast out" (p. 20), the very point made on plates 5 and 6 of *The Marriage of Heaven and Hell*.

32. Significantly, Erdman dates "To Tirzah" at 1802 or later (E, p. 722), which places it in what I regard as Blake's second period of Milton criticism, the period containing the more mature and systematic criticism of Milton and the *Milton* illustrations.

33. The phrase is Blake's, from the title page of his *Songs of Innocence and of Experience*. The reference is particularly appropriate, for the design with which this title page is illuminated represents a variation on the cowering figures of Adam and Eve at the moment of their clearest consciousness of their fallenness depicted by various illustrators of *Paradise Lost*, book 10.

34. Roland Frye, *Milton's Imagery and the Visual Arts*, p. 168.

35. Florence Sandler makes a related point about the implicit condescension of this arrangement in "The Iconoclastic Enterprise: Blake's Cri-

tique of 'Milton's Religion,'" *Blake Studies* 5 (1972); see especially p. 30.

36. This matter of justice has received perhaps its fullest attention in Desmond M. Hamlet's "Recalcitrance, Damnation, and the Justice of God in *Paradise Lost*," *Milton Studies* 8 (1975): 267–91, and in his *One Greater Man: Justice and Damnation in "Paradise Lost*." Hamlet argues forcefully that Milton takes God's (that is, the Father's) justice to be "the same as His *righteousness*," possessing "more of an essentially restorative and liberating quality than the erroneously overemphasized characteristic of distribution and retribution" (*One Greater Man*, pp. 34–35). Of the Son's offer to die for man, Hamlet asserts that this offer in fact "confirms" the Son's own person and function "as the best expression of that very justice which is demanding that very sacrifice for Man's restoration" (pp. 36–37). Needless to say, Blake does not regard the Father-Son relationship in this manner, and he would certainly reject Hamlet's contention that "there is not—and has, in fact, never been—the slightest disharmony between the Father's motives and the Son's intentions for Man" (p. 36), just as he would regard as hopelessly self-contradictory Hamlet's identification of Christ as "the merciful, loving, gracious, and wise Justice of God" (p. 84).

37. Henry Crabb Robinson, *Reminiscences* (1852), in *Blake Records*, ed. G. E. Bentley, Jr. (Oxford: Oxford University Press, Clarendon Press, 1969), p. 544.

38. See also Jackie DiSalvo, "Blake Encountering Milton: Politics and the Family in *Paradise Lost* and *The Four Zoas*," in *Milton and the Line of Vision*, ed. Joseph Anthony Wittreich, Jr., p. 148.

39. See Florence Sandler, "The Iconoclastic Enterprise," pp. 28–31.

Chapter 3

1. Gert Schiff, *Johann Heinrich Füsslis Milton-Gallerie*. For discussions of English paintings exhibited, see Marcia R. Pointon, *Milton and English Art*. An interesting related example is Boydell's Shakespeare Gallery, which is the subject of Winifred H. Friedman's study, *Boydell's Shakespeare Gallery*. This study and its illustrations suggest both the variety of subjects illustrated from Shakespeare and the enormous differences in style and *treatment* of subject characterizing the various illustrations.

2. Hayley's influence is discussed by Joseph Anthony Wittreich, Jr., in *Angel of Apocalypse: Blake's Idea of Milton*, especially pp. 229–36; and in "Domes of Mental Pleasure: Blake's Epics and Hayley's Epic Theory," *Studies in Philology* 69 (1971): 201–29.

3. Bernard Blackstone, *English Blake*, p. 140.

4. Robert N. Essick, "*Preludium*: Meditations on a Fiery Pegasus," *Blake in His Time*, ed. Robert N. Essick and Donald Pearce (Bloomington and London: Indiana University Press, 1978), p. 2. Essick rightly points to Northrop Frye's *Fearful Symmetry* as an example of such an approach.

5. S. Foster Damon, *A Blake Dictionary: The Ideas and Symbols of William Blake*, p. 275.

6. Northrop Frye discusses this aspect of *The Marriage* in *Fearful Symmetry: A Study of William Blake*. See also John Beer, *Blake's Humanism*, pp. 24–34, and Harold Bloom, *Blake's Apocalypse: A Study in Poetic Argument*, pp. 79–83. *The Marriage* has been regarded not only as satire but, more recently, as "a medley of genres—a poem, a proclamation, an argument, a critique, history, allegory, and philosophical statement" (Mary V. Jackson, "Pro-

lific and Devourer: From Nonmythic to Mythic Statement in *The Marriage of Heaven and Hell* and *A Song of Liberty*," *Journal of English and German Philology* 70 [1971]: 207). The nature of this work is perhaps best elucidated by Joseph Anthony Wittreich, Jr. (*Angel of Apocalypse: Blake's Idea of Milton*, pp. 188–219), who correctly regards *The Marriage* as *prophecy* carefully based upon the models of Isaiah and Revelation.

7. P. B. Shelley, *Shelley's Prose; or, The Trumpet of a Prophecy*, ed. David Lee Clark (Albuquerque: University of New Mexico Press, 1954), p. 257.

8. Milton's anti-Trinitarianism is discussed by C. A. Patrides in *Milton and the Christian Tradition*. See also Barbara Kiefer Lewalski, *Milton's Brief Epic: The Genre, Meaning, and Art of "Paradise Regained"* (Providence, R.I.: Brown University Press, 1966), especially chap. 6.

9. Northrop Frye, *Fearful Symmetry*, pp. 52, 157. And, as agencies of inspiration, both are clearly related to the figure of Sleep in *Il Penseroso*, pl. 5.

10. Roland Mushat Frye, *Milton's Imagery and the Visual Arts: Iconographic Tradition in the Epic Poems*, p. 160.

11. See Jackie DiSalvo, "Blake Encountering Milton: Politics and the Family in *Paradise Lost* and *The Four Zoas*," in *Milton and the Line of Vision*, ed. Joseph Anthony Wittreich, Jr., pp. 148–54.

12. Roland Mushat Frye, *Milton's Imagery and the Visual Arts*, p. 65.

13. Desirée Hirst, *Hidden Riches: Traditional Symbolism from the Renaissance to Blake* (London: Eyre and Spottiswoode, 1964), p. 145.

14. Patrides, *Milton and the Christian Tradition*, p. 25; A. S. P. Woodhouse, *The Heavenly Muse: A Preface to Milton*, ed. Hugh MacCallum, pp. 165, 230; Lewalski, *Milton's Brief Epic*, pp. 138–59.

15. Albert S. Roe, *Blake's Illustrations to the Divine Comedy*, p. 14.

16. DiSalvo, "Blake Encountering Milton," p. 165. See also Florence Sandler, "The Iconoclastic Enterprise: Blake's Critique of 'Milton's Religion,'" *Blake Studies* 5 (1972), especially pp. 28–33.

17. Desmond Hamlet, *One Greater Man: Justice and Damnation in "Paradise Lost,"* p. 35.

18. In his later reading Blake absolves the Son of guilt by association, as is particularly evidenced by the two depictions of the Son judging Adam and Eve. In these designs Blake portrays, not an angry, chastizing Son, but a mild figure who seems almost to be blessing Adam and Eve. Clearly, Blake wishes to call attention to the Son less as dispenser of the Father's justice than as "Forgiver of Sin."

19. Northrop Frye, *Fearful Symmetry*, p. 219.

20. See, for instance, the letter to Thomas Butts (11 September 1801) in which Blake remarks that "my Principal labour at this time is Engraving Plates for Cowper's Life, a Work of Magnitude, which Mr. Hayley is now Labouring with all his matchless industry, & which will be a most valuable acquisition to Literature" (K, p. 52), and that to his brother James (30 January 1802) in which he specifically mentions the designs he contemplates creating for "Cowper's Milton, the same that Fuseli's Milton Gallery was painted for" (K, p. 65). These designs, which never did find their way into the Cowper Milton, may well have included the early sets of Milton watercolors we have been considering.

21. I refer to plate 49A in David V. Erdman, annot., *The Illuminated Blake*, p. 265. This is plate 44 in Copies A and B, 45 in Copy C, and 49 in Copy D; it is the penultimate plate in all copies. Because Erdman does not number all the full-page illustrations in *The Poetry and Prose of William Blake*, this plate is identified in that text as plate 42 (E, pp. 142–43).

22. Roland Grimes, *The Divine Imagination: William Blake's Major Prophetic Visions* (Metuchen, N.J.: Scarecrow Press, 1972), p. 110.

23. See Leslie Brisman, *Milton's Poetry of Choice and Its Romantic Heirs*, p. 194; and Jean Hagstrum, "Christ's Body," in *William Blake: Essays in Honour of Sir Geoffrey Keynes*, ed. Morton D. Paley and Michael Phillips, pp. 129–56.

24. Marcia R. Pointon, *Milton and English Art*, p. 147. The point was first made by S. Foster Damon in *William Blake: His Philosophy and Symbols*, p. 213.

25. P. B. Shelley, *The Complete Poetical Works of Percy Bysshe Shelley*, ed. Thomas Hutchinson (1943; rpt. London: Oxford University Press, 1961), p. 205.

26. Beer, *Blake's Humanism*, p. 29.

27. On "voluntary obedience," see Woodhouse, *The Heavenly Muse*, p. 235. On "the free man's mind," see Northrop Frye, *The Return of Eden: Five Essays on Milton's Epics*, p. 111.

28. Woodhouse, *The Heavenly Muse*, p. 192. Blake not only recognizes the pattern in Milton's earlier poems but, as we have seen, uses it repeatedly in his illustrations.

29. James Holly Hanford, *John Milton: Poet and Humanist*, p. 246.

30. Henry Crabb Robinson, *Diary, Reminiscences, and Correspondence of Henry Crabb Robinson*, ed. Thomas Sadler, 2 vols. (Boston: Houghton Mifflin and Co., 1898), 2:29; Anne Kosetlanetz Mellor, *Blake's Human Form Divine*, p. 203.

31. Leland Ryken, *The Apocalyptic Vision in "Paradise Lost"* (Ithaca, N.Y., and London: Cornell University Press, 1970), p. 63. See Beer, *Blake's Humanism*, p. 142; and Northrop Frye, *Fearful Symmetry*, p. 319.

32. See Hanford, *John Milton*, p. 244.

33. Henri Peyre, *The Failures of Criticism*, emended ed. (Ithaca, N.Y.: Cornell University Press, 1967), p. 235.

34. Wittreich gets at this same point in *Angel of Apocalypse* when he suggests that the Devil who speaks on plates 5 and 6 is limited in perspective and deficient in vision: he "advances his critique from the perspective of history rather than eternity" (p. 212). Blake's larger, timeless, and visionary perspective allows him to see the distortions of the views the Devil enunciates. As Wittreich cautions, following Milton's advice in *An Apology for Smectymnuus*, we must avoid confusing the poet's voice with that of one of his personae. Wittreich is rather too cautious though, I think, about the Devil's remarks. Intemperate as they are, those comments bear much of the weight of Blake's criticism. That Blake later came to regard *Paradise Lost* in a different light should not distract us from the critical perceptions embodied in the stinging comments he puts into the Devil's mouth here.

35. Joseph Anthony Wittreich, Jr., "The 'Satanism' of Blake and Shelley Reconsidered," *Studies in Philology* 65 (1968): 819–20.

36. Ryken, *Apocalyptic Vision*, pp. 60–61.

37. See DiSalvo, "Blake Encountering Milton," p. 150, for instance.

38. See Patrides *Milton and the Christian Tradition;* and also Irene Samuel, "The Regaining of Paradise," in *The Prison and the Pinnacle*, ed. Balachandra Rajan (Toronto and Buffalo, N.Y.: University of Toronto Press, 1973). Though Milton is not altogether reluctant to depart from the Bible and its traditional readings, his departures are, as Samuel notes, never toward greater mystery, but rather toward "greater rationality, greater availability as a guide in living" (p. 116). See also J. M. Evans, *Paradise Lost and the Genesis Tradition* (London: Oxford University Press, 1968).

39. Blackstone, *English Blake*, p. 137.

40. Northrop Frye, "The Road of Excess," *The Stubborn Structure: Essays on Criticism and Society* (Ithaca and New York: Cornell University Press, 1970), p. 124.

Chapter 4

1. C. H. Collins Baker, "Some Illustrators of Milton's *Paradise Lost*," *Library*, 5th ser., 3 (1948): 1–21, 101–19; Marcia R. Pointon, *Milton and English Art;* Roland Frye, *Milton's Imagery and the Visual Arts: Iconographic Tradition in the Epic Poem*.

2. See Helen Gardner, "Milton's First Illustrator," *Essays and Studies*, 9 (1956): 35; and Suzanne Boorsch, "The 1688 *Paradise Lost* and Dr. Aldrich," *Metropolitan Museum Journal* 6 (1972): 133–50. Boorsch has demonstrated that the designs to books 1, 2, and 12, previously attributed to Medina, are almost certainly the work of Henry Aldrich. In addition, Boorsch contends that Aldrich may well have exerted considerable influence on the final form of Medina's illustration to book 7.

3. In his use of the iconography of biblical illustration, Medina was ironically drawing upon some of the same visual sources upon which Milton had likely drawn as well, as Roland Frye's study suggests.

I use the term *synoptic* in this manner hereafter. Designs that concentrate on a single scene rather than on a synoptic combination of scenes I call *episodic* designs. An intermediate type of design, discussed below, is best designated *mixed*.

David Bland attributes this synoptic procedure as in the Sistine to the sixteenth-century Italian artist Giolito of Venice, who illustrated *Orlando Furioso* by combining several episodes within each picture (*A History of Book Illustration: The Illuminated Manuscript and the Pub-*

lished Book [Berkeley and Los Angeles: University of California Press, 1969], p. 140).

J. B. Trapp, "The Iconography of the Fall of Man," in *Approaches to "Paradise Lost": The York Tercentenary Lectures*, ed. C. A. Patrides, p. 227.

4. Lens's design was replaced in the seventh edition (1705) and thereafter by another synoptic design, *Adam and Eve Sleep in Their Bower*, drawn by "J. Gweree."

5. On Raphael, see Boorsch, The 1688 *Paradise Lost*," p. 149; Mantegna: reproduced in ibid., p. 135.

6. Aldrich's design derives both from Raphael's painting and from an engraving by Nicholas Chapron based upon that painting (P, pl. 31).

See Merritt Y. Hughes, "Some Illustrators of Milton: The Expulsion from Paradise," *Journal of English and Germanic Philology* 60 (1961): 670–79; rpt. in *Milton: Modern Essays in Criticism*, ed. Arthur E. Barker (London, Oxford, and New York: Oxford University Press, 1965), p. 363; and Gardner, "Milton's First Illustrator," pp. 34–35.

7. Pointon, *Milton and English Art*, pp. 4–5; Gardner, "Milton's First Illustrator," p. 37. See also Roland Frye's comments on the iconography of Satan in *Milton's Imagery and the Visual Arts*.

8. Pointon, *Milton and English Art*, pp. 31–33. Pointon reproduces for comparison two instances of the similarity of designs to the Bible and those to *Paradise Lost*.

9. The whole matter of the landscape garden and the concern with landscape in general is discussed by John Dixon Hunt in *The Figure in the Landscape: Poetry, Painting, and Gardening during the Eighteenth Century* (Baltimore, Md., and London: Johns Hopkins University Press, 1976) and Ronald Paulson in *Emblem and Expression: Meaning in English Art of the Eighteenth Century* (Cambridge, Mass.: Har-

vard University Press, 1975). Though neither deals particularly with Milton's landscape and its metamorphosis in various illustrations, both studies suggest a rationale for the attention to natural scenery that typifies many illustrations—Stothard's, Westall's, or Burney's later in the century, for example.

10. This serpent is a magnified version of that which appears in the Expulsion illustration of an Oxford Bible of 1682, reproduced in Pointon (P, pl. 30). The introduction of the serpent in Cheron's design emphasizes the degree of his indebtedness to Genesis illustration, for Aldrich's Expulsion scene includes no serpent.

11. Pointon says that the dog is howling, "a foretaste of the savage greed that overtakes the whole of nature as one of the first results of the Fall" (*Milton and English Art*, p. 25).

12. Ibid., p. 45.

13. Hogarth's painting was completed in 1764; *Laokoön* was published in 1766.

14. So great was Blake's admiration for Barry, in fact, that he even planned a poem called *Barry*, "of which the only surviving fragment is a violent attack on Reynolds" (Anthony Blunt, *The Art of William Blake*, p. 11 n). Blake also mentions Barry in his annotations to Reynolds's *Discourses*, speaking indignantly there about the lack of public regard for the artist's talents, a point itself rich with autobiographical overtones, (Annot. Reynolds; E, pp. 625–31).

Several other sets of illustrations, lesser known and of generally slighter value in the tradition of *Paradise Lost* illustration, appeared in the period: twelve designs (Italian edition, 1740; material copied or adapted from traditional Genesis illustration), two designs by John Hamilton Mortimer (Bell's *Poets of Great Britain*, 1776–82), three incidental designs by Dodd (a toy edition of the poem, 1781), twelve stipple designs by Frederick Schall (Paris edition,

1792); see C. H. Collins Baker, *Catalogue of William Blake's Drawings and Paintings in the Huntington Library*, pp. 16–18.

Other later editions are detailed by Baker, pp. 20–21, 101–5. The illustrations include a varying number of designs by Thomas Kirk and others published in different formats by C. Cooke in 1795–96 and 1805, twelve designs by Richard Corbould and Henry Singleton issued in 1796, three by J. C. Weinrauch (Vienna edition, 1803), twelve poor designs and woodcut tailpieces issued in a "humble edition" in 1804, three by J. Thurston and Henry Howard in 1805, two by Fuseli and one by Westall in Park's *Works of British Poets* in 1805–1808, a frontispiece by Fuseli in 1806, and another design by Thurston in 1806. The most important of these are discussed below.

15. Edmund Burke, *A Philosophical Enquiry into the Origin of Our Ideas of the Sublime and Beautiful* (London: R. and J. Dodsley, 1757); Pointon, *Milton and English Art*, pp. 110, 111.

16. Pointon, *Milton and English Art*, p. 100. Blake's drawing is reproduced in G. E. Bentley, Jr., *William Blake: Tiriel* (Oxford: Oxford University Press, Clarendon Press, 1967), pl. 2.

17. Ibid., p. 109. Strikingly apropos to the present study in its survey of the Shakespeare Gallery drawings and paintings by many of the same artists we are considering is Winifred H. Friedman's *Boydell's Shakespeare Gallery*.

Fuseli's interest in Satan as epitome of the physiognomical heroic type is explored by Peter Tomory in *The Life and Art of Henry Fuseli* (New York and Washington, D.C.: Praeger Publishers, 1972), especially pp. 162–64.

18. Tomory, *Fuseli*, p. 101. Tomory quotes Reynolds's point, made in a letter to the *Idler* (20 October

1759), that "poetical ornaments destroy that air of truth and plainness which ought to characterize History; but the very being of Poetry consists in departing from this plain narration, and adopting every ornament that will warm the imagination."

19. See Joseph Anthony Wittreich, Jr., *Angel of Apocalypse: Blake's Idea of Milton*, pp. 175–86.

20. See, for instance, Jean Hagstrum, "Romney and Blake: Gifts of Grace and Terror," in *Blake in His Time*, ed. Robert N. Essick and Donald Pearce (Bloomington: Indiana University Press, 1978), pp. 201–12; Pointon, *Milton and English Art*, pp. 130–31.

21. Pointon, *Milton and English Art*, p. 125.

22. Pointon credits him with at least twenty-three designs, published in editions of 1792–93, 1818, and 1826 (ibid., p. 75).

See Gert Schiff, *Johann Heinrich Füsslis Milton-Gallerie*. Schiff examines the Milton Gallery in terms of both the Milton-Fuseli relationship and, apropos of the present study, the relationship of Fuseli to the artistic and intellectual milieu of his time. Pointon, *Milton and English Art*, pp. 77–84, also explores the Milton drawings of John Flaxman in relation to Stothard. These works, in the form of sketches and finished designs, may have been known to Blake, who became well acquainted with Flaxman and did some engraving for him. Blake seems to have borrowed little from Flaxman, but the seeming dissimilarity of the two artists' styles may in fact prove more properly a similarity, as Robert Rosenblum suggests in the final chapter of *Transformations in Late Eighteenth Century Art* (Princeton, N.J.: Princeton University Press, 1967). Some of Flaxman's contorted group figures may be particularly pertinent to a definition of visual influence. So too are the strangely winged figures which seem closely related to some of the

curious winged figures Blake employed in his illuminations to his own poems. See, for instance, the attendant child in *Infant Joy* from *Songs of Innocence* and Flaxman's illustration to Milton's "Elegy to His Tutor, Thomas Young."

23. This gradual return to a critical focus less on preconceived intellectual and doctrinal notions than on the primary material of Milton's own words, the touchstone of which was Thomas Warton's 1785 edition of the minor poems, is outlined by Ants Oras in *Milton's Editors and Commentators from Patrick Hume to Henry John Todd (1695–1801): A Study in Critical Views and Methods* (1931; rpt. London: Oxford University Press, 1969).

24. Morse Peckham, "Blake, Milton, and Edward Burney," *Princeton University Library Chronicle* 11 (1949–50): 113; Peckham notes that Hayley was a subscriber to the Richters' edition.

25. Pointon, *Milton and English Art*, pp. 62–63, 90–99. Friedman suggests that Westall's style owed much to that of John Mortimer, from whom he inherited "a salutary vigor and breadth of style, especially in those compositions in which he limits the number of his figures" (*Boydell's Shakespeare Gallery*, p. 190).

26. This is a good example of the manner in which the illustrator must adjust his conception of the text, or at least of the scene he plans to depict, to the limitations of the medium in which he is working. What works at folio size may fail miserably at duodecimo. We should bear this in mind when we evaluate designs like Medina's and Hayman's, which were frequently reduced in republication. This reduction, coupled with the deterioration of a plate, may totally destroy what began as an effective and aesthetically pleasing illustration.

27. Peckham, "Blake, Milton, and Edward Burney," p. 113.

28. John Milton, *The Poetical*

Works of John Milton, from the Text of Dr. Newton: With a Critical Essay, by J. Aikin, M.D., 4 vols. (London: H. Baldwin and Son, 1801). See also Rigaud's *Satan in the Bower of Adam and Eve* (1805) and *Sin and Death* (1807).

29. Anders Nygren, *Agape and Eros* (New York: Harper and Row, 1967), p. 67.

30. Pointon, *Milton and English Art*, p. 96.

31. Eric Newton, *The Romantic Rebellion* (New York: St. Martin's Press, 1963), p. 28.

32. For a discussion of the applicability of the same point to Milton's prose, see Joseph Anthony Wittreich, Jr., "'The Crown of Eloquence': The Figure of the Orator in Milton's Prose Works," in *Achievements of the Left Hand: Essays on the Prose of John Milton*, ed. Michael Lieb and John T. Shawcross (Amherst: University of Massachusetts Press, 1974), p. 32.

Chapter 5

1. The matter was first explored by Morse Peckham in "Blake, Milton and Edward Burney," *Princeton University Library Quarterly* 11 (1949–50): 107–26. See also his "Blake's Illustrations to *Paradise Lost*," *Blake Newsletter* 3 (1969): 57; and "A 'Minute Particular' Particularized: Blake's Second Set of Illustrations to *Paradise Lost*," *Blake Newsletter* 6 (1972): 44–46. The latter essay particularly explores the history of the Boston set and its "missing" designs, providing convincing stylistic evidence for admitting to this set the three additional designs Butlin suggests. See also Martin Butlin's essay, "Cataloguing William Blake," in *Blake in His Time*, ed. Robert N. Essick and Donald Pearce (Bloomington: Indiana University Press, 1978), pp. 77–90.

2. Martin Butlin has suggested

that the "extra" Huntington *Satan, Sin, and Death* may have been done as a separate work at some time before 1806, by which time Butlin says Blake seems to have given up signing his paintings with his monogram signature; see "Cataloguing William Blake," p. 82; and *William Blake*, p. 113.

3. Marcia R. Pointon, *Milton and English Art*, p. 143. Pointon does note, however, that while the episodes Blake chooses to illustrate are familiar, his concept and treatment of them are "usually entirely novel" (p. 143).

4. Enter into the forms: Northrop Frye, *The Return of Eden: Five Essays on Milton's Epics*, p. 91. Soften, harmonize: Jean Hagstrum, *William Blake, Poet and Painter: An Introduction to the Illuminated Verse* (Chicago and London: University of Chicago Press, 1964), p. 126. See also Pamela Dunbar, *William Blake's Illustrations to the Poetry of Milton*, p. 38, where the claim is repeated.

Blake's correction here is akin to Blake's method later in his Dante designs, where his pictures fall into three basic groups: (1) literal illustrations of the text, (2) metaphoric illustrations, in which episodes in Dante are paralleled with incidents or themes from Blake's own mythology, and (3) corrective illustrations, in which Blake corrects deficiencies of vision on Dante's part. On the Dante series, see Albert S. Roe, *Blake's Illustrations to the Divine Comedy*, p. 35.

5. W. J. T. Mitchell, *Blake's Composite Art: A Study of the Illuminated Poetry*, p. 18; and Peckham, "Blake, Milton, and Burney," p. 121.

6. Pointon, *Milton and English Art*, p. 138.

7. The timelessness of the moment of visionary, prophetic insight is also remarked by Angus Fletcher in *The Prophetic Moment: An Essay on Spenser* (Chicago and London: University of Chicago Press, 1971).

Fletcher notes that "the prophetic moment appears to last forever. And yet being only a moment, it must also be infinitesimal" (p. 51).

Leslie Brisman, *Milton's Poetry of Choice and Its Romantic Heirs*, p. 195.

8. The designs to *L'Allegro* and *Il Penseroso*, to which Blake attached textual quotations and descriptive prose statements, appear to be the only exception to this pattern.

9. See also Blake's illustrations to the Book of Job, in which he employs this same technique (pls. 5, 6, 16) (*Blake's "Job": William Blake's Illustrations of the Book of Job*, ed. S. Foster Damon [1966; rpt. New York: E. P. Dutton and Co., 1969]). Blake may have derived the idea of Satan with reptile scales from Tintoretto's painting, *Michael and the Dragon*. Significantly, Tintoretto also provides Satan with the sort of claw-nails Blake gives Nebuchadnezzar in his well-known color prints of 1795 (B, pls. 393, 406, 407). Dunbar blurs Blake's clear point here when she says he wears a "cod-piece of scales" (*Blake's Illustrations*, p. 46).

10. Hand gestures are an important part of Blake's visual language. As he says himself, "I entreat then that the Spectator will attend to the Hands & Feet to the Lineaments of the Countenances [.] they are all descriptive of Character & not a line is drawn without intention & that most discriminate & particular" (E, p. 550). Blake's use of hand and bodily gestures is discussed by Janet Warner in "Blake's Use of Gesture," in *Blake's Visionary Forms Dramatic*, ed. David V. Erdman and John E. Grant; and by E. J. Rose in "Blake's Hand: Symbol and Design in *Jerusalem*," *Texas Studies in Literature and Language* 6 (1964): 48–49.

11. The first is very likely the "experiment Picture" Blake describes in his 1809 Descriptive Catalogue (E, pp. 537–39). In both Blake expands the scene vertically so that the re-

clining figure is beneath Satan. He also adds a number of new figures and intensifies the flames of hell. But the scene depicted remains essentially that of HH 1 *except* for the decided change in what Satan is doing that his altered gestures indicate. Very likely these pictures mark an intermediate stage between *Fire* (*The Gates of Paradise*) and *Paradise Lost* HH 1.

12. *The Gates of Paradise* was originally published as *For Children* in 1793. George Wingfield Digby, *Symbol and Image in William Blake*, p. 26.

13. See Mitchell, *Blake's Composite Art*, p. 57, where the point is applied to *Satan Smiting Job with Boils*.

Northrop Frye has noted that Milton's Satan is Orc, "the power of human desire which gradually and inevitably declines into passive acceptance of impersonal law and external reason" (*Fearful Symmetry: A Study of William Blake*, p. 219). Frye suggests that for Blake to correct Milton's error in *Paradise Lost* he will have to settle upon a more satisfactory hero than Orc. But Frye falls victim here to the dangerous practice of trying too hard to explain Blake's Milton illustrations in terms of his own mythology, and his explanation might almost deceive the novice into concluding somehow that Blake's work preceded Milton's. Blake's own mythology is *involved* in the *Paradise Lost* designs, as Dunbar's study labors very hard to demonstrate, but that involvement should not distract us from the fact that Blake's primary focus in the designs is on Milton's poem as he reads it.

14. Northrop Frye, *The Return of Eden*, p. 23. A. S. P. Woodhouse likewise notes that "Hell is the antithesis of the heavenly order," suggesting this same parodic relationship (*The Heavenly Muse: A Preface to Milton*, p. 194).

15. See S. Foster Damon, *William*

Blake: His Philosophy and Symbols, pp. 225–29; and *A Blake Dictionary: The Ideas and Symbols of William Blake,* p. 237.

16. Their dimensions average about about 51 cm x 39 cm, with slight variations owing to trimming; the HH set's dimensions average about half this size, or approximately 27 cm x 21 cm.

17. David Bindman, *Blake as an Artist,* p. 192.

18. Indeed, Butlin quotes Linnell's note that Blake "began copies from his Drawings from Miltons P. L.," which suggests, as do details of the subjects, that Blake was working with the Butts pictures, and on the same scale (*William Blake,* p. 116).

19. Both the portcullis and the key seen in *Satan, Sin, and Death* are reminiscent of details from the engraving of Hogarth's *Beggar's Opera* (pl. 3) upon which Blake had earlier worked; see A. G. B. Russell, *The Engravings of William Blake* (London, 1912), pl. 30; and Dunbar, *Blake's Illustrations,* pp. 51–52.

20. Roland Mushat Frye, *Milton's Imagery and the Visual Arts: Iconographic Tradition in the Epic Poems,* p. 117.

21. See also Dunbar, *Blake's Illustrations,* pp. 49–51.

22. Reproduced in William Blake, *Pencil Drawings by William Blake,* ed. Geoffrey Keynes ([London]: Nonesuch Press, 1927), pl. 17.

23. See Warner, "Blake's Use of Gesture," p. 177.

24. J. G. Davies, *The Theology of William Blake,* p. 116.

25. On this point, note Woodhouse's comment that "the doctrine of the atonement held by Milton and formulated here [in book 3] strikes something of a chill by its hard legality, but the defect, if there is one, is in religious sensibility, not in epic propriety, and anyway this impression is certainly mitigated by the terms of the Son's offer of himself as sacrifice and its simple motivation in love" (*The Heavenly Muse,* p. 230).

26. In view of the more obviously phallic significance of Satan's alter ego the Serpent, little attention has been paid the spear he carries here and in *Satan, Sin, and Death.* Yet the connections, particularly with the physical sexuality associated with secular figures like Cupid, are striking. Especially in this design, Satan's grip on his spear is remarkably reminiscent of the way in which Cupid's arrows are fondled by female figures, as, for instance, in Bronzino's enigmatic allegory *Venus Disarming Cupid,* in which the visual suggestion of autoeroticism is clear. Satan's infatuation with his alter ego the Serpent, which Blake develops explicitly in designs like *Satan Watching Adam and Eve,* has clear iconographical and intellectual ties with both autoeroticism and narcissism.

27. It is important to note here that though she remarks on "the beneficence and central importance of Christ" in Blake's designs (*Blake's Illustrations,* p. 42), Dunbar falls into the same eighteenth-century error to which Blake objected in saying that Blake gives his "undivided attention to the poem's crucial dramatic moments: Satan rousing his fellow devils from the floor of hell and confronting Sin and Death at the gates of hell, the expulsion of the rebel angels from heaven and of man from Paradise, the birth of Eve, and the fall of man" (p. 36). While the Son's offer may not be good *theatre,* it is clearly the most important act in all of man's experience, and Blake knew it and stressed it throughout his designs.

28. See Roland Frye, *Milton's Imagery and the Visual Arts,* pp. 281–85.

29. Damon, *A Blake Dictionary,* p. 355.

30. On perverse influence of Satan, see Barbara Kiefer Lewalski, "Innocence and Experience in Milton's Eden," in *New Essays on "Paradise Lost,"* ed. Thomas Kranidas (Berke- ley, Los Angeles, and London: University of California Press, 1969), p. 116.

I quote from the title page of *Songs of Innocence and of Experience.* Since the drama of *Paradise Lost* is played out on a psychological-imaginative stage, where it is symbolically regarded by Blake, the state of innocence and experience obviously figure in Blake's interpretation of the epic. The occasional visual cross-references between the *Paradise Lost* designs and the illuminations for the *Songs* provide interesting and enlightening perspectives that shed light in both directions and deserve fuller consideration than they have so far received from students of Blake's work.

31. In *The Art of William Blake,* Anthony Blunt reproduces Fuseli's *Lazar House* (pl. 27b), another possible source for Blake. For a variation, *The Fertilization of the Nile,* see pl. 21b. Blunt claims that figure is based upon a depiction of Jupiter Pluvius (pl. 25c). The figure in its variant forms is discussed by Warner, "Blake's Use of Gesture," pp. 182–87.

32. See Pointon, *Milton and English Art,* p. 148. Blake later employed a variation on the position of Adam and Eve in *Jerusalem,* plate 28, where it is given a more immediately sexual connotation in both the original and the revised versions of the plate (*IB,* pls. 307, 399).

33. This is the same procedure of structural inversion Blake employs in designs 2 and 5 of his *Nativity Ode* illustrations (B, pls. 661, 662; 667, 668); see Chapter 2.

34. We may assume the sketch is for this painting, done in 1806, because even if Blake *was* resketching the scene for HH 5, he would not likely have resketched Adam and Eve, whose positions he scarcely alters there.

35. Blake customarily associates stars with reason and the rational

sciences, or the narrow, empirical conception of the universe. In this light they form an appropriate backdrop for the Satan who parodies the Urizenic Father. In fact, in the 1822 version of this design (B, pl. 657), some of the stars appear on Satan's body. See Damon, *A Blake Dictionary*, pp. 385–86; and Digby, *Symbol and Image*, pp. 25–26.

36. Keynes attributes a sketch of this scene to Blake (*Pencil Drawings of William Blake*, pl. 35), but Robert Essick notes that the drawing is by Burney, not Blake ("A Finding List of Reproductions of Blake's Art," *Blake Newsletter* 5 [1971]: 90).

37. Roland Frye, *Milton's Imagery and the Visual Arts*, p. 179. This latter pointing gesture, a common iconographical device for reminding viewers (and characters within the picture) of heaven, also figures in Rigaud's design to book 8.

38. Damon, *A Blake Dictionary*, p. 189. In *Milton*, as Damon notes, Satan's attempt to drive Palamabron's plow results in the maddening of the *horses* and the disruption of Palamabron's work.

39. On this matter of the tree-cross, which occurs as a visual symbol from the twelfth century onwards, see also Gertrud Schiller, *Iconography of Christian Art*, trans. Janet Seligman, 2 vols. (Greenwich, Conn.: New York Graphic Society, 1972), 2:135–36.

40. John Milton, *Milton's Paradise Lost: A New Edition*, 2 vols. (London: T. Bensley and J. Du Roveray, 1802), vol. 1, Facing p. 263. Interestingly, Rigaud's 1801 design for book 6 disregards the episode entirely, showing instead Abdiel leaving the rebel band.

41. An early sketch (B, pl. 429) depicts Hyperion and a hovering spirit. Though she makes no mention of these pictures, Dunbar suggests that Blake's concept of the Son (whom she simply calls Christ) "must also owe something to the

classical sun-god Apollo—archer, prophet, and creative artist" (*Blake's Illustrations*, p. 65).

42. *William Blake's Water-colours Illustrating the Poems of Thomas Gray* (Chicago: J. Philip O'Hara, 1972), p. 54.

43. In *William Blake the Artist* (New York: E. P. Dutton and Co., 1971), p. 72, Ruthven Todd dates the drawing at about 1809–10. Butlin dates it around 1800 and titles it *Christ Trampling down Satan* (B, p. 372, pl. 613).

44. Roland Frye, *Milton's Imagery and the Visual Arts*, pp. 157–58.

45. Of additional interest here are the various depictions of Jesus in the illustrations to Young's *Night Thoughts* and Blair's *Grave*, all of which predate the *Paradise Lost* designs. The resurrected Jesus of those designs has affinities with the naked Milton of *Milton*, plate 16, Albion in *Jerusalem* (especially plate 76), and the Christ of *Christ Trampling upon Urizen*. The fullest discussion of this matter is Jean Hagstrum's study, "Christ's Body," in *William Blake: Essays in Honour of Sir Geoffrey Keynes*, p. 196.

46. John Beer, *Blake's Humanism*, p. 196.

47. Blunt, *The Art of William Blake*, pp. 74–75. Blunt also errs in naming the central figure neither the Son nor Christ, but, rather, the undifferentiating "God," which tends to include as well the Father and the Holy Spirit, whom Blake separates.

48. Woodhouse, *The Heavenly Muse*, p. 188.

49. Baker mistakenly identifies him as the Father (*Catalogue of William Blake's Drawings and Paintings in the Huntington Library*, p. 21). This is incorrect, of course, for it is the Son, acting as the Father's agent, who accomplishes the actual creation.

50. Previous illustrators also generally avoided depicting the Son actually shaping Eve, choosing instead to show either Eve rising from the sleeping Adam with a God figure in the background (see Fuseli's designs)

or Adam seeing Eve for the first time (see Burney's design).

51. See Damon, *A Blake Dictionary*, pp. 285–86. Blake had experimented with the visual motif of Eve's separation from Adam's side much earlier. We see a female figure rising from a male's side in *All Religions Are One*, plate 5 (*IB*, p. 25); and *Jerusalem*, plate 31 (*IB*, p. 310) provides a subsequent example. Blake's conception of Eve's creation as he finally realized it in the *Paradise Lost* design is surely more successful than either of these related renditions of her separation from Adam's side. Compare, for instance, *The Angel of the Divine Presence Bringing Eve to Adam* (B, pl. 512; about 1803), which shows the more conventionally established scene of the Father figure bringing Eve to the awakening Adam. In this picture, incidentally, the awakening Adam rests on a large leaflike bed resembling that in *The Creation of Eve*.

52. Albert "C. Labriola, "The Aesthetics of Self-Diminution: Christian Iconography and *Paradise Lost*," *Milton Studies* 7 (1975): 272.

53. See especially Damon on this point: *William Blake: His Philosophy and Symbols*, pp. 84, 145, 212–13. The mental dimension of the Fall is discussed also by Bernard Blackstone in *English Blake*, p. 136; Northrop Frye in *Fearful Symmetry*, p. 319; Beer in *Blake's Humanism*, pp. 19–20; and Roe in *Blake's Illustrations to the Divine Comedy*, pp. 12–16.

54. In a rejected sketch (B, pl. 825) Eve stands upright with the Serpent coiled about her body. In *Drawings of William Blake: 92 Pencil Studies* (New York: Dover Publications, 1970), pl. 44, Geoffrey Keynes suggests that since the fruit is not visible, Eve may be kissing the Serpent, an interesting suggestion when we recall that in *Satan Watching Adam and Eve* she was kissing Adam even as Satan was apparently kissing the Serpent.

Such repetition is the very device by which Blake links both the youthful poet of *L'Allegro*, pl. 6 (fig. 9) and Eve in *Eve Tempted by the Serpent* (B, pl. 402) with the figure of Mirth in *L'Allegro*, pl. 1. The reclining poet's posture is exactly that of the upright Mirth. This point is discussed in greater detail in Stephen C. Behrendt, "Bright Pilgrimage: William Blake's Designs for *L'Allegro* and *Il Penseroso*," *Milton Studies* 8 (1975): 123–47.

55. This is a significant change from a first version (B, pl. 384) in which Satan's gaze is more horizontal.

56. Anne Kostelanetz Mellor, *Blake's Human Form Divine*, p. 203. Adam does, of course, subsequently turn his back literally upon Eve when he blames her for his own sin. In order to redeem himself, he must first redeem her by accepting his own responsibility for his actions and hers as Milton does for Ololon in *Milton*. Thus, when he does so, he moves away from his posture of accuser and toward that of forgiver or redeemer. This matter of responsibility is explored by Stella P. Revard in "Eve and the Doctrine of Responsibility in *Paradise Lost*," *PMLA* 88 (1973): 69–78.

57. See also Northrop Frye, *Fearful Symmetry*, p. 352.

58. As such, we might expect the tree to assume some visible resemblance to an oak, Blake's standard symbol for error. It does not, however; the leaves are nondescript in both designs—perhaps left vague, like the fruit, to avoid solving a necessarily ambiguous problem—with the exception of two leaves in the second design. The first, at almost exact top center, *may* be an oak; the second, slightly lower and to the left, may be a holly. Why Blake variously detailed these two leaves remains a mystery.

59. The figure of Christ is nearly the same as that Blake used in his designs to Blair's *Grave*, published in 1808. Here, however, Christ's *right* foot, not his left, is forward. The difference likely is meant to alert us to the particular spiritual significance of Christ's action in *The Fall of Man*.

60. Satan and Michael are related to their appearance in Blake's separate painting, *Michael and Satan* (around 1805) and to their predecessors in Michelangelo's representations of the Fall and Expulsion. My suspicion is that these animal figures are related both to the animals of Eden, now turned bloodthirsty (the tiger and lion appear to be attacking the horse and ox, and the left eagle has grasped the sheep's head), and to the emblematic representations of the evangelists whose accounts provide the history of Christ's redemptive ministry on earth. The figures may also prefigure the horsemen of the Apocalypse which appear in conjunction with the Expulsion in Blake's final *Paradise Lost* design.

61. The relationship of his left hand to Satan's right could scarcely be merely a coincidental allusion to Michelangelo's *Creation of Adam*, nor should the image-and-likeness relationship of God and man be forgotten when we view this demonic travesty. The beardless figure's visual similarity to the outstretched figure in *A Poison Tree* (*Songs of Experience*) provides a useful allusion to the psychological nature and implications of the Fall as Blake perceived it.

62. Cheron depicts incidents that also figure in Medina's synoptic design for this book. Medina concentrates, however, on emphasizing the general chaos of the fallen world, with the two most prominent tableaux being two departing angels (upper center) and Adam and Eve covering their ears (lower center).

63. Reproduced in Peckham, "Blake, Milton, and Edward Burney," pl. Y11.

64. See Joseph Anthony Wittreich, Jr., "William Blake: Illustrator-Interpreter of *Paradise Regained*," in *Calm of Mind: Tercentenary Essays on "Paradise Regained" and "Samson Agonistes" in Honor of John S. Diekhoff*, ed. Joseph Anthony Wittreich, Jr., p. 113.

65. Reproduced in Roger Easson and Robert N. Essick, eds., *William Blake: Book Illustrator: A Bibliography and Catalogue of the Commercial Engravings* (Normal, Ill.: American Blake Foundation, 1972), vol. 1, pt. 4, pl. 6.

66. Butlin, *William Blake*, p. 115.

67. J. B. Trapp, "The Iconography of the Fall of Man," in *Approaches to "Paradise Lost": The York Tercentenary Lectures*, ed. C. A. Patrides, p. 224.

68. Mellor discusses this painting and *Christ in the Carpenter's Shop* (B, pl. 558), in which the young Jesus holds a compass, in *Blake's Human Form Divine*, pp. 247–49. In a related painting (B, pl. 495) Joseph stands at the head of the cross holding the compass.

69. His garb here and in *The Expulsion* recalls that of the figures in the angel-sphere in *Nativity Ode*, pl. 2 who are so identified in Milton's text.

70. James Holly Hanford, *John Milton: Poet and Humanist*, p. 257.

71. On the prophecy, see also Northrop Frye, *The Return of Eden*, pp. 118–19. Frye notes appropriately that from this biblical reference "is derived the conventional symbol of Christ as a dragon-killer" (p. 119). Hagstrum, "Christ's Body," p. 140.

72. See Janet Warner's comments on the significance of the cruciform gesture as emblem of creativity in "Blake's Use of Gesture," pp. 177–88; see also Davies, *The Theology of William Blake*, pp. 110–25.

73. See also *Queen Katherine's Dream* (B, pl. 589), another painting from this later period employing the same technique of radiant light to indicate dream-vision.

74. The painting is probably based upon the Young design of the risen Christ inscribed *The Christian Triumph*, reproduced in Easson and Essick, eds., *William Blake: Book Illustrator*, vol. 1, pt. 4, pl. 31.

75. See Digby, *Symbol and Image in William Blake*, pp. 22–24.

76. This is, of course, very near Jung's anima image, the perfect counterpart or spiritual soulmate that has always held a particular attraction for the Romantic artist.

77. Shelley echoes this perception at the conclusion of "The Sensitive Plant," when he asserts,

For love, and beauty, and delight,
There is no death nor change:
      their might
Exeeds our organs, which endure
No light, being themselves obscure.

78. Damon, *William Blake: His Philosophy and Symbols*, p. 151.

79. Two figures in the sketch itself are considerably worked up: those of Satan and one of his crew. Blake may have considered these as figure studies for use elsewhere. See, for instance, *Paradise Regained*, pl. 5, *Satan in Council* (B, pl. 688), where Satan's wings are very similar to those he possesses in this sketch.

80. See Merrit Y. Hughes, "Some Illustrators of Milton: The Expulsion from Paradise," *Journal of English and Germanic Philology* 60 (1961): 364, and Wittreich's comments on Hughes's conclusions regarding Blake's Expulsion in "William Blake: Illustrator-Interpreter of *Paradise Regained*," p. 102; and *Angel of Apocalypse: Blake's Idea of Milton*, pp. 95–97.

Lot's Escape is reproduced in Easson and Essick, eds., *William Blake: Book Illustrator*, vol. 2, pt. 10, pl. 2. In the background of this design we see the jagged lightning that reappears in *The Temptation and Fall of Eve* (pls. 16, 17). Dunbar also discusses this picture (*Blake's Illustrations*, pp. 87–88).

81. Wittreich, *Angel of Apocalypse*, p. 95; Butlin, *William Blake*, pp. 113–14.

82. Wittreich, *Angel of Apocalypse*, p. 96. The point was made originally by Kester Svendsen in "John Martin and the Expulsion Scene of *Paradise Lost*," *Studies in English Literature 1700–1900* 1 (1960): 70. Svendsen, however, fails to consider the alterations Blake made in the second version of his design.

83. George Ferguson, *Signs and Symbols in Christian Art* (1954; rpt. London, Oxford, and New York: Oxford University Press, 1961), p. 38.

84. A. G. B. Russell, *Blake Centenary Exhibition* (London: Burlington Fine Arts Club, 1927), p. 18.

85. Butlin associates these two portraits with *The Virgin and Child in Egypt* (B, pl. 962) and the half-length frontal *Christ Blessing* (B, pl. 892), all of which belonged to Butts and presumably date from 1810 (*William Blake*, pp. 110–11).

86. Probably we should also recall Blake's right-left symbolism: while Adam's right hand hails us and directs our attention, his left is occupied with the Serpent. Perhaps *this* is Adam's error.

87. Blake's engraving is reproduced in Easson and Essick, eds., *William Blake: Book Illustrator*, vol. 1, pt. 6, pl. 1.

88. Adam and Eve have many visual predecessors in Blake's work, to be sure, and an interesting study of their evolution remains to be made. The figures of Los and Enitharmon are obviously involved here as is the intriguing family group on the first plate of the "Preludium" to *America* (*IB*, p. 139), whose female figure draws upon the Eve of traditional Judgment or Expulsion illustrations. Another related couple appears in scanty vine leaves in the *Night Thoughts* illustrations; see Easson and Essick, eds., *William Blake: Book Illustrator*, vol. 1, pt. 4, pl. 33.

89. Fuseli's picture is reproduced in Gert Schiff, *Johann Heinrich Füsslis Milton-Galerie*, pl. 37.

90. Reproduced in Easson and Essick, eds., *William Blake: Book Illustrator*, vol. 2, pt. 36, pl. 1.

91. See also Warner, "Blake's Use of Gesture" and "Blake and the Language of Art: From Copy to Vision," *Colby Library Quarterly* 13 (1977): 99–114.

92. See Roe, *Blake's Illustrations to the Divine Comedy*, p. 12.

93. On *Tiriel* see Stephen C. Behrendt, " 'The Worst Disease': Blake's *Tiriel*," *Colby Library Quarterly* 15 (September 1979): 1975–87. On desire, see also Northrop Frye, *The Return of Eden*, p. 69.

94. See Wittreich, *Angel of Apocalypse*, p. 97.

À Mme architecte du gouvernement français le 27 août 1824.

T. Crofton Croker — Author of Researches in the South of Ireland.

B R. Haydon

William Blake one who is very much delighted with
being in good Company

January 16
1826

Born 28 Novr 1757 in London
& has died several times since

The above was written & the drawing annexed by the desire of Mr Leigh how far it is an
Autograph is a question I do not think an Artist can write an Autograph especially one
who has Studied in the Florentine & Roman Schools as such a one will Consider what
he is doing but an Autograph as I understand it is Writ helter skelter like a boy upon
a rope or a Man who walks without Considering whether he shall run against a Porter a
House or a Horse or a Man & I am apt to believe that what is done without meaning is very
Different from that which a Man does with his Thought & Mind & ought not to be called by
the same Name.
   I consider the Autograph of Mr Cumberland which very justly stands first in the Book
& that Beautiful Specimen of Writing by Mr Comfield & my own; as standing the same Predicament they are in some measure Works of Art & not of Nature or Chance

Heaven born the Soul a Heavenward course must hold
For what delights the Sense is False & Weak
Beyond the Visible World she soars to Seek
Ideal Form, the Universal Mould

Michael Angelo. Sonnet as Translated by Mr Wordsworth

Selected Bibliography

Figure 56. Blake's autograph in William Upcott's album. 1826. 7.5 cm by 20.5 cm. *The New York Public Library (Berg Collection)*

Baker, C. H. Collins. *Catalogue of William Blake's Drawings and Paintings in the Huntington Library.* Revised and edited by Robert Wark. San Marino, Calif.: Henry E. Huntington Library, 1963.

———. "Some Illustrators of Milton's *Paradise Lost.*" *Library,* 5th ser., 3 (1948): 1–21, 101–19.

Beer, John. *Blake's Humanism.* Manchester and New York: University of Manchester Press, 1968.

Behrendt, Stephen C. "Blake's Illustrations to Milton's *Nativity Ode.*" *Philological Quarterly* 55 (1976): 65–95.

———. "Bright Pilgrimage: William Blake's Designs for *L'Allegro* and *Il Penseroso.*" *Milton Studies* 8 (1975): 123–47.

———. "*Comus* and *Paradise Regained*: Blake's View of Trial in the Wilderness." *Milton and the Romantics* 3 (1977): 8–13.

———. "The Mental Contest: Blake's *Comus* Designs." *Blake Studies* 8 (1978): 65–68.

———. "The Polished Artifact: Some Observations on Imitative Criticism." *Genre* 10 (1977): 47–62.

Bindman, David. *Blake as an Artist.* Oxford and New York: Phaidon / Dutton, 1977.

Blackstone, Bernard. *English Blake.* Cambridge: Cambridge University Press, 1949.

Bloom, Harold. *Blake's Apocalypse: A Study of Poetic Argument.* Ithaca, N.Y.: Cornell University Press, 1969.

Blunt, Anthony. *The Art of William Blake.* New York and London: Columbia University Press, 1959.

Brisman, Leslie. *Milton's Poetry of Choice and Its Romantic Heirs.* Ithaca, N.Y., and London: Cornell University Press, 1973.

Butlin, Martin. *William Blake.* London: Tate Gallery, 1978.

———. *The Paintings and Drawings of William Blake.* 2 vols. London and New Haven, Conn.: Yale University Press, 1981.

Damon, S. Foster. *A Blake Dictionary: The Ideas and Symbols of William Blake.* 1965. Reprint. New York: E. P. Dutton and Co., 1971.

———. *William Blake: His Philosophy and Symbols.* 1924. Reprint. Glouster, Mass.: Peter Smith, 1958.

Davies, J. G. *The Theology of William Blake.* Oxford: Oxford University Press, Clarendon Press, 1948.

Digby, George Wingfield. *Symbol and Image in William Blake.* Oxford: Oxford University Press, Clarendon Press, 1957.

DiSalvo, Jackie. "Blake Encountering Milton: Politics and the Family in *Paradise Lost* and *The Four Zoas.*" In *Milton and the Line of Vision,* edited by Joseph Anthony Wittreich, Jr. Madison and London: University of Wisconsin Press, 1975.

Dunbar, Pamela. *William Blake's Illustrations to the Poetry of Milton.* Oxford: Oxford University Press, Clarendon Press, 1980.

Figgis, Darrell. *The Paintings of William Blake.* London: Ernest Benn, 1925.

Franson, John Karl. "Christ on the Pinnacle: Interpretive Illustrations of the Crisis in *Paradise Regained*." *Milton Quarterly* 10 (1976): 48–53.

Friedman, Winifred H. *Boydell's Shakespeare Gallery*. New York and London: Garland Publishing, 1976.

Frye, Northrop. *Fearful Symmetry: A Study of William Blake*. 1947. Reprint. Princeton, N.J.: Princeton University Press, 1969.

———. *The Return of Eden: Five Essays on Milton's Epics*. Toronto: University of Toronto Press, 1965.

Frye, Roland Mushat. *Milton's Imagery and the Visual Arts: Iconographic Tradition in the Epic Poems*. Princeton, N.J.: Princeton University Press, 1978.

Grant, John E. "Blake's Designs for *L'Allegro* and *Il Penseroso*." *Blake Newsletter* 4 (1971), 117–34; 5 (1971–72): 190–202.

———. "Blake's Title Pages for *Songs of Innocence and of Experience* and Other Visions of the Expulsion from Eden." In *Examining the Sister Arts: Essays on English Art and Literature 1700–1850*, edited by Richard Wendorf. Minneapolis: University of Minnesota Press, 1982.

———. "The Female Awakening at the End of Blake's *Milton*: A Picture Story, with Questions." In *Milton Reconsidered: Essays in Honor of Arthur R. Barker*, edited by John Karl Franson. Salzburg Studies in English Literature, vol. 49. Salzburg: University of Salzburg Press, 1976.

Hagstrum, Jean. "Christ's Body." In *William Blake: Essays in Honour of Sir Geoffrey Keynes*, edited by Morton D. Paley and Michael Phillips. Oxford: Oxford University Press, Clarendon Press, 1973.

———. *William Blake, Poet and Painter: An Introduction to the Illuminated Verse*. Chicago and London: University of Chicago Press, 1964.

Halsband, Robert. *"The Rape of the Lock" and Its Illustrations, 1714–1896*. Oxford: Oxford University Press, Clarendon Press, 1980.

Hamlet, Desmond. *One Greater Man: Justice and Damnation in "Paradise Lost."* Lewisburg, Pa.: Bucknell University Press, 1976.

Hanford, James Holly. *John Milton: Poet and Humanist*. Cleveland, Ohio, and London: Press of Case Western Reserve University, 1966.

Hughes, Merritt Y. "Some Illustrators of Milton: The Expulsion from Paradise." *Journal of English and Germanic Philology* 60 (1961): 670–79.

Mellor, Anne Kostelanetz. *Blake's Human Form Divine*. Berkeley, Los Angeles, and London: University of California Press, 1974.

Mitchell, W. J. T. *Blake's Composite Art: A Study of the Illuminated Poetry*. Princeton, N.J.: Princeton University Press, 1978.

Patrides, C. A. *Milton and the Christian Tradition*. Oxford: Oxford University Press, Clarendon Press, 1966.

Peckham, Morse. "Blake, Milton, and Edward Burney." *Princeton University Library Chronicle* 11 (1949–50), 107–26.

Pointon, Marcia R. *Milton and English Art*. Toronto: University of Toronto Press, 1970.

Roe, Albert S. *Blake's Illustrations to the Divine Comedy*. Princeton, N.J.: Princeton University Press, 1953.

Rose, Edward J. "Blake's Illustrations for *Paradise Lost, L'Allegro,* and *Il Penseroso*: A Thematic Reading." *Hartford Studies in Literature* 2 (1970): 40–67.

Sandler, Florence. "The Iconoclastic Enterprise: Blake's Critique of 'Milton's Religion.'" *Blake Studies* 5 (1972), 13–57.

Schiff, Gert. *Johann Heinrich Füsslis Milton-Gallerie*. Zurich and Stuttgart: Fretz and Wasmuth Verlag, 1963.

Svendsen, Kester. "John Martin and the Expulsion Scene in *Paradise Lost*." *Studies in English Literature 1500–1900* 1 (1960), 63–73.

Tayler, Irene. *Blake's Illustrations to the Poems of Gray*. Princeton, N.J.: Princeton University Press, 1970.

———. "Say First! What mov'd Blake? Blake's *Comus* Designs and *Milton*." In *Blake's Sublime Allegory: Essays on "The Four Zoas," "Milton," and "Jerusalem,"* edited by Stuart Curran and Joseph Anthony Wittreich, Jr. Madison and London: University of Wisconsin Press, 1973.

Trapp, J. B. "The Iconography of the Fall of Man." In *Approaches to "Paradise Lost": The York Tercentenary Lectures*, edited by C. A. Patrides. Toronto: University of Toronto Press, 1968.

Warner, Janet. "Blake and the Language of Art: From Copy to Vision." *Colby Library Quarterly* 13 (1977): 99–114.

———. "Blake's Use of Gesture." In *Blake's Visionary Forms Dramatic*, edited by David V. Erdman and John E. Grant. Princeton, N.J.: Princeton University Press, 1970.

Wittreich, Joseph Anthony, Jr. *Angel of Apocalypse: Blake's Idea of Milton*. Madison and London: University of Wisconsin Press, 1975.

———. "'Divine Countenance': Blake's Portrait and Portrayals of Milton." *Huntington Library Quarterly* 11 (1974): 125–60.

———. *The Romantics on Milton: Formal Essays and Critical Asides*. Cleveland, Ohio, and London: Press of Case Western Reserve University, 1970.

———. *Visionary Poetics: Milton's Tradition and His Legacy*. San Marino, Calif.: Henry E. Huntington Library, 1979.

———. "William Blake: Illustrator-Interpreter of *Paradise Regained*." In *Calm of Mind: Tercentenary*

Essays on "Paradise Regained" and "Samson Agonistes" in Honor of John S. Diekhoff, edited by Joseph Anthony Wittreich, Jr. Cleveland, Ohio, and London: Press of Case Western Reserve University, 1971.

Woodhouse, A. S. P. *The Heavenly Muse: A Preface to Milton*, edited by Hugh MacCallum. Toronto and Buffalo, N.Y.: University of Toronto Press, 1972.

Index